"There's something here for everyone ... Great insight into how the mind affects military outcomes."
SOLDIER

"Murray approaches his subject with both passion and frustration. The result is ... a rousing book with an urgent message: Western armies must wake up to the utility of exploiting psychology in warfare."
LUCY FISHER, *TLS*

"A thought-provoking argument for the importance of psychology on the battlefield."
MILITARY HISTORY MONTHLY

"An eloquent and well-argued case for the importance of battlefield psychology."
MARK PACK

"Leo Murray's War Games *is a seriously good piece of work. Focusing on the close tactical level where battle contact takes place, it shows what is going through soldiers' minds and why, and how to exploit it to win. It shows what we have forgotten and need to remember. And it sets it out very clearly, pulling no punches.*

I have 'been there and done that' as a soldier and I have studied soldiers at war for most of my adult life, and I cannot fault this book. Anyone with even the slightest interest in war should read it. Everyone directly or indirectly involved in making decisions connected to war must read it. Why? Because it tells it like it is, and it tells it very well."
DR CHARLES KIRKE, LECTURER IN MILITARY ANTHROPOLOGY AND HUMAN FACTORS, CRANFIELD UNIVERSITY DEFENCE ACADEMY

"Leo Murray has achieved the seemingly impossible: taken an arcane, complex but vitally important subject, stripped it down and explained it so that the layman can understand it.

This book could save lives: those of our soldiers, next time we ask them to fight; and those of our enemies, if they're lucky. Just as importantly, this book could help commanders win battles faster and at less cost. Unfortunately, it also explains why we're not likely to give our soldiers and commanders that chance. Unless, that is, some of those commanders read it and do something about it.

Everyone involved in the sharp end of war should read this book."
DR JIM STORR, DEFENCE ANALYST AND
AUTHOR OF *THE HUMAN FACE OF WAR*

Leo Murray is a military analyst and former soldier who has spent half his lifetime studying the psychology of armed combat. He has interviewed hundreds of war veterans, young and old, and worked with some shady collections of staff officers and war geeks. With a few exceptions, he has only ever been shot at by accident or under carefully controlled laboratory conditions.

THE PSYCHOLOGY OF COMBAT

WAR GAMES

LEO MURRAY

Biteback Publishing

This edition published in Great Britain in 2018 by
Biteback Publishing Ltd
Westminster Tower
3 Albert Embankment
London SE1 7SP
Previously published in Great Britain under the title *Brains & Bullets*
Copyright © Leo Murray 2013, 2018

ISBN 978-1-78590-351-9

10 9 8 7 6 5 4 3 2 1

A CIP catalogue record for this book is available from the British Library.

Set in Chronicle and Knockout

Printed and bound in Great Britain by
CPI Group (UK) Ltd, Croydon CR0 4YY

MIX
Paper from
responsible sources
FSC® C020471

CONTENTS

PREFACE TO THE PAPERBACK EDITION

When *War Games* was first published, British and American soldiers were still mired in the fight for Afghanistan; trying to build a country with explosives, without even the basic skills needed to win the fight. The Afghan war followed decades of our troops being managed as 'capability delivery platforms', while enemy soldiers were targets for 'kinetic effects'. Humans had been obscured by buzzwords.

The failure to see combat soldiers as human precluded the use of the tactics that are essential for making enemy soldiers surrender. And it is only when enough soldiers surrender that they, their comrades and leaders really accept defeat and start negotiating peace. As the armed branches of neoconservatives and neoliberals are keen to point out, every insurgent killed simply inspires two more. Yet we kept on killing. Somehow, the techniques that ordinary soldiers had used to make Nazis surrender weren't tried on Afghan farmhands. So even with a kill ratio of twenty-to-one, we still lost.

As the war dragged on, it became increasingly difficult to motivate Western combat soldiers even for brief periods. While publicly praising our brave boys and girls, leaders slyly bemoaned their collapse in morale – the platforms weren't delivering the capability like they were supposed to. When soldiers refused to go outside the wire without air cover or a credible explanation of what the war was for, the war fizzled out. Leaders got bored and brought most of the troops home.

Lessons were learned by the bad guys. Having been forced to make the most of their meagre resources, rebel bandits had developed small units of suitably trained and motivated soldiers. These were used to eject larger government forces from key corners of Iraq and Afghanistan. They moved quickly and stealthily, tricking the defenders into thinking they were outflanked and outgunned. Their lessons spread to Syria, Egypt, Nigeria and beyond. It often takes years before these pockets of misery are cleared by foreign-backed armies – armies that succeed only when they outnumber the enemy thirty-to-one. Yet the core of the enemy force slips away from the rubble to set up shop elsewhere. Their use of tactical psychology has fuelled a remarkably efficient business model.

Lessons were learned by the good-ish guys too. Having realised soldiers are not automata, Western and Eastern governments are now investing in real killing machines: war robots with lightning-fast reflexes, unhindered by fear, fatigue, pity or common sense. Yet autonomous war machines will need to kill a lot of people to counter the rage they will generate. Every enemy killed breeds two more, but every enemy killed by a robot will breed a dozen. It's like defence planners have taken the *Terminator* films as their blueprint for excellence. They haven't spotted all the humans fighting back or the earth reduced to wasteland.

War Games is intended to show that we can win by accepting human frailty rather than hiding from it.

Leo Murray
January 2018

PROLOGUE

On the edge of an Afghan poppy field, a young soldier gets his first taste of battle. He crouches, waist deep, in the rancid sludge and water of an irrigation ditch as bullets fly over his head. He has been on the move since dawn, looking for trouble but secretly hoping not to find it. Already near exhaustion, buoyed only by emergency reserves of adrenalin, he tries to wade through the mire while keeping his head low enough to avoid the fatal shot.

The intense heat adds dehydration to stress and fatigue, making spots and sparks dance before his eyes. Thirst, fear and the surprising, desperate joy of battle rush up from his belly, making it difficult to see or think straight. His friends are shouting but he cannot hear their words over the noise of battle and his own laboured breathing.

When he risks a quick look over the lip of the ditch, he can see no enemy and has only the vaguest notion of where they might be. A mental programming older than humanity works outside his conscious control to force a rapid cycle of scanning and fixation, widening and narrowing his perception of events. Time seems to slow down then speed up again, creating moments of absolute clarity and minutes of desperate confusion. Almost randomly, his attention latches onto places that could hide the enemy: a bush, a wall, a line of trees. Critical information is blocked or ignored as his brain forces blinkers onto his senses.

When he tries to return fire, his heart is running so hot that he cannot hold his assault rifle steady. Like millions of soldiers before him, he breaks cover for a second to spray a burst of fire towards a bush that might have some enemy behind it. Despite battle inoculation and a basic form of brainwashing, this burst is biased by a primal, almost imperceptible, aversion to killing and by a powerful urge to hold onto the protection of the ditch. His will to fight is twisted at the last moment so his point of aim is just a fraction off and his stream of bullets flies harmlessly into the distance.

This young soldier was brought to the war by unemployment, nationalism and machismo, but these now-distant forces cannot compete with immediate threats to his life. Like most soldiers, he would soon stop fighting were it not for the intense social pressure from the men in the ditch with him. His friends and leaders provide encouragement, unspoken threats and the example of their actions to keep him in the firing line. But if his comrades stop fighting, whether killed, wounded or pinned down by fire, fear and common sense, he will stop fighting too. Like all battles, large or small, this fight will be decided more by the psychology of close combat than by a simple body count.

Our soldier is Taliban, at least that is what most of his enemies call him. In fact his link with extremism is tenuous. Like any soldier, he will freeze, flee, fuss or fight depending on the tactics used against him.

Sadly, after decades fixated by the lethality of weapons, Western armies have forgotten that their enemies are people. So, like thousands of almost identical small battles in Afghanistan, this fight will almost certainly end one of two ways. Either our young soldier will disappear home then fight again tomorrow, or a lucky shot, most likely from an aircraft, will end his life and create another martyr. It is usually far more efficient to capture an enemy, but to do this requires an understanding of combat that looks beyond killing power. *War Games* shows how lethality and psychology work together to decide the outcome of wars when soldiers meet in close combat.

ONE

BATTLE MORALE

SERGEANT DAWSON, FALKLAND ISLANDS, 1982

I hear three loud cracks as a quick burst of fire passes over our heads. A few blokes drop into cover and this spreads through the platoon like a Mexican wave. We're all on our bellies and the attack on Wireless Ridge has stalled. Here we are, the hardest, brilliant-est bunch of airborne bastards there ever was and a few wafty rounds of 7.62mm have us screwing our belt buckles into the peat.

It's been another filthy sleepless night in a month of being dicked around something chronic. There's flares going up and tracer rounds arcing off in the distance and the sounds of a firefight away to our left but it's all gone quiet in our bit of the war. We're all wet, we're all cold and there's been a massive sense-of-humour failure because once again we're the ones leading the advance on an Argentine position of unknown size and strength.

But now we're all laid flat and can see nothing but the turds and rocks in front of our faces. All the drills for reaction to effective enemy fire are out the window. And let me tell you this is definitely not effective fire. I'm not fully sure the Argentines even know we're here.

There's a pause of a few seconds while we all look around embarrassed-like and try to work out whose idea it was to flop down. There's just a dribble of fire coming our way, so a couple of the corporals start dishing out bollockings and one or two lads return fire in roughly the right direction. I jump up hoping that no one's noticed how I joined in the lying-down competition. I start to run round kicking arses, I pick people up by their webbing, point them at the enemy and bawl at them until they start to lay down fire. If we can just get enough people acting in a warry fashion we might just be able to un-stall this attack. I swear that the half of them go back to their bellies once I'm out of sight.

Now it's a few minutes since we first went to ground, though I'm sure you'll know that time's a bit funny when you're in contact, but out of thirty blokes that should be firing, there are maybe a half-dozen doing anything useful. The rest are awful keen on clearing weapon stoppages or changing magazines or just looking at sheep shit. Some blokes are genuinely looking for targets or fire positions or trying to work out what's going on, but most have decided to hand in their notice and they've withdrawn their labour, at least for the time being. It's only the last dregs of regimental pride and a few angry men with moustaches that stop some of them running back to the start line or back to San Carlos Bay.

There's a heap more of this woeful fannying about, but slowly-slowly we get to a point where you might say we're winning the firefight. Mind you, most of this is down to the impressive amount of shit the gunners and the navy have been dropping on the objective. It's a good ten minutes, I checked my watch this time, before we're all happy that the dribble of incoming isn't worth worrying about and then we all start moving again.

We're mostly OK after this little embarrassment and things run pretty sweet. The attack, what there is of it, goes in well enough, but the opposition know the score and bugger off before we get to them. Unlike our boys, the Argentines aren't just thinking about getting a new job, they've told Galtieri to shove his Malvinas up his arse and have legged it back to Port Stanley. And none of us blame 'em neither. Despite what the nutters, Walts and Rat Pit Heroes might tell you later, we're all glad that the Argies have bugged out.

In the end the battalion took out maybe seventy Argentines for the loss of about a dozen of ours killed and wounded. That's bloody good going if you look at the ground and think of it as a defended position. Our route in was a forward-sloping rocky bog with mines all over it, no cover and 'look at me, I'm a killing area' written on it in big red letters. But all of their casualties and half of ours are down to our artillery support; the close-quarter battle we were all revved up for and shitting ourselves about just didn't happen.

Come daylight, the ground shows us what little fire they managed to put our way. One well-sited machine gun with a few good blokes behind it and you'd have had a beaten zone full of dead Toms no matter how much wriggling we'd done.

Sure, our lot aren't anything like the Argentines: we're all picked men with professional pride and we all like a scrap. There's not a man among us who didn't earn his place in the fight and we'd all have been kicking ourselves if we'd been left at home. But the guilty secret is that we've got more in common with those conscript ranch boys than we'd like to admit. Let's face it, fire came our way and it was ostrich time. For a short while there all our macho bullshit was thrown in the gutter.

Maybe the lads thought we'd already done more than our share before we got to Wireless Ridge. Maybe we knew the war was over and weren't keen on getting killed or having our nuts shot off. But truth is, even when we'd all had our blood up in our first battle back at Goose Green, a lot of the team weren't really in the game. Don't get me wrong, the rest were good lads but come the day they were just subs that could've stayed sat on the bench.

You see, fighting's just a whole lot harder than you think it's going to be. This is the bit of truth that is at the heart of it: no matter what fight you're talking about, there's a whole bunch of Joe Crows only half doing what they're paid to do, and it's the same on both sides.

The winning side, and this is important so make sure you write this down, the winning side is the one that makes more of the other side's blokes stop fighting.

Sergeant Dawson was interviewed on the Falkland Islands a few days after the battle for Wireless Ridge. His interview was recorded, filed and forgotten. Ten years later a large dusty box full of research papers was dumped onto my desk. In a corner of the box was a batch of cassette tapes and on one of the tapes was Dawson's interview.

'Are you the new bloke who's doing the research on battle stress?' asked the man with the dusty box.

'I think so...'

'Well, we're chucking stuff out and the colonel says this is yours if you want it. If you don't want it then it's going on the skip with the rest.' He left the box and my office before I could give him an answer.

Scrawled on the side of the box were the words: 'human factors – war/stress/etc. – 1988 – unclassified – bin?' It was my second day as a military psychologist and that box was my introduction to what was then called 'battle morale'.

Getting the battle morale job really made my head swell. Despite being the new boy, I was the only psychologist in the department who had been a soldier. So, in my mind at least, it was clear that my bosses had given me the project because they had spotted my scientific and military genius. Rather than setting me to work on some tedious questionnaire about soldiers' pay or making me design the buttons for a missile launcher, I had been given the real juicy stuff: brains, balls, bullets and bayonets. This was the Holy Grail of military psychology.

It took a few days for me to realise the truth. Four other people in my department had been offered the battle morale project and turned it down. I only ended up with the work because I was too junior and too gullible to get out of it. The clues were in the dusty box. It held the tattered remains of an earlier project that had died when the research team could not find a hard number for the 'human factor' in war. They had listed hundreds of things that might be expected to influence battle morale: everything from leadership and fear to sleep loss and whether men's boots fit properly. Then they had drawn a huge wiring diagram with blobs and arrows that linked all these things together. But they had failed to work out how any of these factors changed the bottom-line measure of combat effectiveness. Clearly, things like leadership made men better at fighting, while fear or bad boots made them worse. But how much better and how much worse? It seemed that no one had the answers.

That abandoned project was itself based on previous attempts to uncover the truth about morale or fighting spirit or cohesion, or whichever label was in use at the time. It was worrying how no one could even agree on what name to give this important but slippery subject. Each project had started when morale came back into military fashion for a while. Then each project was abandoned after a year or so, when priorities changed or when it was found that there was no quick answer to the battle morale problem. The study of battle morale was dropped and everyone went back to looking at something simpler: usually things like that pay questionnaire or the missile launcher.

There were only two things in the box that proved to be of any real use. One was Dawson's interview tape. The other was a paper on battle morale, written by Brigadier Nigel Balchin at the end of the Second World War. For a time, Balchin was mildly famous for his novel *The Small Back Room*, but during the war he was scientific adviser to the Army Council. It was in this capacity that he described how the psychology behind battle morale shaped war for front-line soldiers, and how it was the real key to military victory. His paper pointed to a mass of research and practical experience. It also bemoaned the fact that this had never been translated into anything of practical value.

Balchin summed up the debate about battle morale as being divided into two parts: 'The stage of woolly abstractions in which people talk solemnly of "leadership" or "discipline" or "group spirit" without ever defining the meaning of these phrases in practice; and the all-too-concrete stage, in which the whole subject suddenly degenerates into discussions about supplies of beer.'

The contents of the box made it clear that there had been little change in the decades since Balchin wrote his paper. Over the next few months, I interviewed staff officers and scientists, and worked my way through archives. I gradually came to realise that everybody thought they understood battle morale but no one really had any hard facts about it. There were some fragments of truth hidden in memoirs and reports, but these were lonely lumps of flotsam that bobbed about in a sea of opinions and guesswork.

Like all those analysts and staff officers who examined battle morale before me, I was swamped. I strapped together a few of those flotsam facts, but I never really made any headway. When my military boss changed jobs, his replacement had no interest in this suddenly unfashionable hobby-horse, and the project died. I had added a few thousand words to the mass of reports but, in the end, I was just another war geek who had failed to answer the big question. I was no closer to understanding battle morale than I had been when I opened the dusty box.

The battle morale project died before I realised that Brigadier Balchin and Sergeant Dawson were both saying the same thing. Their language was very different but they were both saying that, sometimes, even the best soldiers will stop fighting. The key to winning wars, they said, is to make 'more of the other side's blokes stop fighting'.

This is not something that comes from bombing cities, dropping propaganda leaflets or launching steamroller attacks by tanks and artillery. These all play their part, but wars are finally decided by small groups of men making other small groups of men surrender or run away.

Convincing small groups of enemy soldiers to withdraw is good, but getting them to surrender in battle is far more efficient. It ends a fight quickly, means you lose fewer of your own men and tells the next lot of enemy that it is OK to surrender. It starts a snowball rolling and wins wars from the bottom up.

*   *   *

I shamefully abandoned the battle morale project, but it refused to let me go. It served as an introduction to the elusive collection of soldiers and scientists who eventually unlocked the secrets of what makes men stop fighting.

To mark the end of the battle morale project, I was sent on a 'jolly' to present my findings at a conference in Vienna. The audience included an Austrian General, who cornered me the instant I stepped down from the podium. He then spent the next four hours telling me where I had gone wrong and how I could put things right.

The General was very persuasive. My time in the army had been dominated by the whims of much lower life forms than an actual general. I was almost overwhelmed by the way he very nearly fit a powerful stereotype. Some deep coding, programmed into me by a childhood full of Airfix models and *Warlord* comics, told me that, with a darker uniform and maybe a monocle, Austrian General could be the Nazi villain from a war film.

But in the end, it was Austrian General's insight that won me over. He had been trained by German and Austrian veterans of the Second World War and, as I found out much later, he had tasted war himself when the Reich was smashed by the Red Army. He knew more about battle morale than any of the experts I had interviewed and he would not accept my bleating excuses about project funding or research priorities. And he kept on hounding me. He even followed me to the toilet, where I found it very difficult to concentrate with a senior officer in the next booth describing the emotional impact of machine-gun fire.

The General made me promise to get in touch with a group he called the Sennelager Club, a loose collection of soldiers, mostly American and British but with a healthy smattering of members from a half-dozen Allied and almost-Allied nations. The club was first formed during a massive NATO training exercise in the 1970s.

Over a boozy end-of-exercise celebration in an officers' mess in Sennelager, this motley collection of grumpy idealists took turns to rail against the most farcical side effects of the Cold War. By the end of the evening, they had set themselves on a quest to understand war and improve tactics.

The Sennelager Club was born in reaction to the way military thought had been stifled by the threat of nuclear holocaust. Atomic weapons were seen to have caused such a shift in the way wars would be fought that Western armies had allowed themselves to forget history. Things like battle morale had come to be seen as irrelevant because the next war would be won by torching half the world.

This started a trend for wearing blinkers, a habit which was exaggerated by the activities of vested interest groups. Air forces, armoured corps or Vietnam-deniers would argue from their uniquely narrow perspectives and cherry-pick evidence to bolster their bias. Weapon and gadget manufacturers aligned with these biases to ensure decisions that generated a healthy profit. The desk officers who controlled research were usually aligned to one or two vested interest groups, so rather than a tool for answering important questions, research came to be an activity for heating up an endless competition between sexy weapon systems. Thousands of lives and billions of dollars came to be staked on wishful and woolly thinking.

The Sennelager Club tried to inject some reality into this dysfunctional system. To do this they winkled out obscure facts on diverse matters from radio signal propagation to exercise nutrition. But the club maintained a focus on the big questions: how command works, what makes a weapon or tactic effective and what shapes battle morale. In their time, the club members claimed to have derailed a gaggle of flawed 'silver bullet' decisions which had wilfully ignored the laws of physics, psychology or common sense.

Being an impressionable youth, I imagined the Sennelager Club to be a kind of secret society, working for the greater good but doing so in a vaguely sinister and exciting way. The reality was both disappointment and comfort. The club was closer to a pre-internet Facebook group than a khaki mafia. The club had no political power because membership seemed to fizzle out on promotion or re-posting; a soldier might gravitate towards the club when he became a NATO liaison officer or worked for a research branch but, two years later, he would disappear back to commanding a unit or stacking blankets. The club was only able to shoot down biased decisions by passing facts into the chain of command and hoping for the best.

At any one time, the core members of the club would be a dozen middle-ranking officers. This core group reached out to young soldiers, combat veterans and half-civilian researchers like me. The club came to form the hub for a network of fighters and boffins who strove to understand battle morale. They took me along for the ride.

Whether I was working on a project about parachute training or officer selection, a member of the club always found a way to trick me into looking at an aspect of battle morale. Whenever I reached a dead end, they introduced me to some Old Boy or weird academic who would get me back on track. It was through the Sennelager Club that I was able to track down Sergeant Dawson and flesh out some of the details from his interview tape.

*   *   *

By the time I met Dawson he had been out of the army for many years. Dissatisfied with the routine of peacetime soldiering, he left the regiment that had been his home since seventeen. He found a new home with a wonderful woman who could cope with his odd habits. Now pushing sixty, Dawson is a doting grandfather and shows few obvious signs of his military past. Most of the time he walks and talks like any civilian, but he still has the wiry strength of a paratrooper and shaking his hand is like squeezing a sharpened shovel. Time has not dimmed his memories of fighting in the Falklands War.

Back in 1982, Dawson was a member of 2 Para, an elite battalion where each man was the product of a gruelling selection and training regime. The traditions and ethos of the battalion helped create a tightly knit, aggressive and dependable unit that could, within reason, go anywhere and do anything.

Two weeks before Wireless Ridge, 2 Para won a stunning victory against a much larger enemy force at the Battle of Goose Green. They instantly became the stars of the Falklands War. Armchair generals still gush about Goose Green, but it was a vicious and costly battle for the battalion. They had men killed by friendly fire and men killed while accepting a false offer of surrender. Their commanding officer was killed while being point man for the whole of the British army.

At Goose Green, sixteen men from 2 Para men were killed in one day. This is more than the whole British army loses in the hardest month in Afghanistan. When US forces had 100,000 men in that broken country, they rarely suffered more than half as many fatalities in one day of ground fighting.

In addition to their dead, sixty men from 2 Para were wounded at Goose Green. The battalion broke the 10 per cent casualty rule:

the point where most experts agree that a unit should be withdrawn from combat to rest and reorganise, at least for a few weeks. A battalion can cope with much heavier casualties over a longer period, but losing a tenth of its men in one day usually makes it unfit for offensive operations.

Yet, instead of getting an easy time between Goose Green and Wireless Ridge, the men of 2 Para were, as Dawson says, 'dicked around something chronic'. They were shoved around the islands like chess pieces, given 'on the bus, off the bus' orders and spent long nights marching over rocks and bogs or lying out in the open without food, sleep or shelter. Every few days they were shot at by enemies or friends.

Even the official history noted that Wireless Ridge 'would pose special problems of motivation' for 2 Para. So when the time came to attack the ridge, their new commanding officer made sure the battalion had plenty of artillery fire support.

On the receiving end of this fire was a composite unit based on elements of the Argentine 7th Infantry Regiment. The unit included a mix of conscripts and professional soldiers, but it was far from being an elite force like 2 Para. The 7th Regiment's men had also been dicked around before the battle: they were cold, wet, underfed and ignored by most of their officers. They knew the war was going against them and they knew something very unpleasant was heading their way.

Then, in the twelve hours before the ground assault was launched, they were hammered by 2 Para's fire support. Artillery and naval gunfire pounded the ridge. Later, as British mortars, machine guns and light tanks joined the fight, Argentine casualties shot up towards 20 per cent.

Armchair generals, and even a few professional analysts,

have suggested that Argentine soldiers were a walkover in the Falklands. Anyone who thinks this of the men of the 7th Regiment needs to check on the numbers. Even the most motivated unit would have difficulty holding out against such a storm of fire. At Wireless Ridge, one or two men stayed and fought, a few hid or surrendered but the vast majority were forced to withdraw.

The same thing can be seen in all but the most perverse battles. The men who run, hide or surrender outnumber the dead five, ten or twenty times over. Even in battles where units are said to be wiped out, most of the body count comes from men killed while trying to avoid fighting. When the details of a battle are examined, it becomes clear that both sides have problems getting their men to fight, but in the end, the winners somehow manage to make more of the enemy stop fighting.

This quick look at the battle for Wireless Ridge suggests how training and experience set the psychological backdrop for a battle. There are also hints of intangible qualities that make some units fight harder than others. Finally, there is a broad idea of the way firepower, fear and casualties can shape battle morale once the fighting has started. But, like most war stories, it says very little about the desperate details that define the battle for small groups of men advancing over open ground or clinging to a pile of rocks swept by fire.

Dawson's account goes a little deeper and mentions some of these elusive details but it raises many awkward questions. What was that Mexican wave that made Dawson's platoon go to ground? How exactly did that arse-kicking from corporals and sergeants get people back into the fight? Why did the Argentine defenders choose to leave cover and then withdraw under such intense fire? Finally, given their heavy casualties, why did the men of the 7th Regiment not surrender? Everybody has an idea why these things happened, but the ideas are usually just collections of stock phrases.

Fighting spirit, firepower, battle morale and all the other lazy clichés cannot answer these questions because they are just abstract labels applied to fighting by those at a safe distance. The critical problem with abstraction is that it is no use to a combat soldier; he cannot whistle up some extra firepower or some more fighting spirit to help him win the battle.

*   *   *

It is incredibly difficult to measure something as vague as battle morale. Astute veterans like Sergeant Dawson or Austrian General have developed an understanding of how it works, but they speak a different language to the peacetime commanders and defence accountants who make the big decisions. This is not the fault of either party. Defence departments have to make decisions based on evidence, and the battle morale evidence has been particularly slippery.

But the language barrier has helped to drive a wedge between what Churchill called slaughter and manoeuvre. Attrition, the politically correct word for slaughter, focuses on wearing down until the enemy lacks the physical strength to resist. In contrast, manoeuvre aims to make the enemy surrender or retreat by moving to a position of advantage. The advocates of these two extremes have been arguing for years but, in practice, most accept that fighting involves a mix of the two.

Despite this, most wars are usually dominated by attrition because a body count is much easier to understand than something fluffy and elusive like the psychology of manoeuvre.

Killing can be quantified and used to support big decisions about training or weapon design. A weapon salesman has a distinct advantage because he can say, 'this bomb will kill anyone within fifty metres', or, 'this missile will hit the target 90 per cent of the time'. Nobody has been able to say how many of the enemy would surrender when surrounded, or how many would flee from a sudden attack. So, while military think-tanks make a lot of noise about manoeuvre, the idea never really sinks in with defence departments.

The weight of numbers has created an imbalance in defence. It is like a football team that trains so hard for the penalty shootout that players cannot dribble or pass the ball. Or like a hospital so blinkered by waiting-list targets that the staff forget about patient care. The compounded focus on the wrong target (killing) has made Western armies very bad at winning.

A combat soldier has a similar problem when he gets his first taste of war. He knows the range and rate of fire for all his unit's weapons, but he usually has to guess the psychological impact of any tactic he might use. His limited training in battle morale has centred on the leadership tricks he will need to keep his own men fighting. In most cases, the only training related to enemy battle morale has been an abstract discussion about willpower or a few hazy lectures on surprise. The actual effect that tactics might have on how hard the enemy fights has had a mention; but only in the very loosest terms.

The lack of hard facts about battle morale means that soldiers are taught that 'While set within a manoeuvre framework, the infantry battle is essentially one of attrition.' The infantry battle certainly involves a lot of killing but, if it is all about attrition, then small units would never capture hundreds of prisoners. If it is essentially attrition, then the fight for Wireless Ridge would only have ended when one side had been wiped out.

The mix of attrition and manoeuvre can be seen in the small-unit tactics of fire-and-movement. At the lowest level, a corporal commanding a fire-team of four men will break his team down into two pairs, with one pair firing to cover the movement of the other. With alternating steps of firing and moving, the fire-team will advance until they are close enough to assault; this usually involves throwing hand grenades then rushing directly onto the enemy position for an intimate exchange of violence.

The basics of fire-and-movement are echoed right up the chain of command, with sections (composed of two or three fire-teams), platoons (three or four sections), companies (usually three platoons) and battalions (three or four companies), also taking turns to fire and move. The sergeants and lieutenants who command platoons can bring in some extra firepower and the majors and colonels running companies and battalions can have all kinds of weapons on call. But the basic trick remains the same: no one moves unless somebody else is keeping the enemy busy by shooting at them.

Each step of firing and moving combines physical and psychological effects. Fire can kill or injure but most of it only serves to suppress: it pins the enemy down and discourages him from returning fire. Likewise, movement puts the attackers in a better position for killing but it also makes the enemy more likely to surrender or withdraw.

In the final assault, a commander can opt for a frontal or flanking move onto the enemy position. Flanking attacks have a profound psychological effect, and get a whole chapter later in the book, but for now they need a little explanation to help outline the dilemma of balancing attrition and manoeuvre.

Few defensive positions are equally strong in all directions; if the main threat is expected to come from the north, then it makes sense to have most of your men and weapons arranged to face north. If the attacking soldier can work out which way the defence faces, he can try to outflank it by approaching from another direction to strike from the side or rear.

Every soldier has some idea that flanking has a psychological impact on the enemy. He has seen glimpses of this in pub fights, war films and history books, but his training has over-emphasised the physical aspect. Flanking usually involves more effort than a frontal assault because men have to run or crawl further to get into position. There is also a need to balance risks: for example, the unit might have to split up, so part of it can keep the enemy looking to the front, but this makes the two half-units more vulnerable. Field training exercises have shown a soldier how much longer it will take to move his team round to a flank and how tired they will get while they move. Exercises have also helped the soldier to work out the chances of his team getting strung out or engaged by a second enemy position.

But repeated experience of attacking with blank-firing weapons has hidden the psychological impact on the enemy. Whenever the soldier has attacked from the side or rear in training, the 'enemy' have simply turned to face him and fought just as hard as they would against a frontal attack. He might get a small physical bonus, but the number of enemy soldiers who fight back is barely changed. This is at odds with real war, where, when outflanked, most of the enemy usually try to surrender or run away.

So, while a soldier can put a rough number on all the physical costs involved in a flanking attack, he can only guess at the psychological benefits. This imbalance means that when a man finds himself in a real battle, his decisions can rest almost entirely on the physical aspect of flanking. Deep down, he might suspect that the main effects will be psychological, but this belief is not something he will stake his life on.

The same problem applies to any tactical trick that might have a psychological effect on the enemy. The soldier does not know how many rounds to fire to keep the enemy pinned down, how much of a bonus he will get from mixing two types of fire or how much his chances of winning will increase if he threatens the enemy from two directions.

One of the main aims of the Sennelager Club was to find out how all these things really worked. They wanted to fill the gap between attrition and manoeuvre by looking beyond all the vague labels.

*   *   *

Before delving into the details, we need to start with a few basic facts that stand up to scrutiny. In a real war, units are roughly six times less effective in a real battle than on a training exercise. Almost all of the difference is down to soldiers not fighting as hard in a real war as they do in a pretend one. There are a few secondary factors, but most of the outcome is down to a half-conscious decision to avoid fighting. In a real battle, men are much more likely to stop fighting when bullets pass near them, when their mates stop fighting, when their mates are killed or injured and when they get very close to the enemy.

But when a battle like Wireless Ridge is fought on a training exercise using tactical engagement simulation (basically a big game of laser quest but with real guns firing blanks and safe lasers), men are not pinned down by 'a few wafty rounds of 7.62mm'. The attacking soldiers continue marching into enemy fire until they take 10 or 20 per cent casualties. Only at this point will they go to ground and try to find a better way to attack.

The attackers suffer these heavy casualties on a training exercise because the defenders are almost completely unfazed by incoming fire. The rounds fired in training include none of the rushed and aimless bursts of spray-and-pray seen in real battles; almost all fire is deliberately aimed shots. The defenders are not even worried when the enemy get close enough for a bayonet fight; they simply keep on firing everything they have until they all 'die' or run out of ammunition.

The same reality gap can be seen in most of the computer simulations that defence departments use to help make decisions. To have any chance of winning a battle like Wireless Ridge in a training exercise or computer simulation, 2 Para would need twice as many men and guns as they had in the real fight.

This difference between real and pretend war might seem obvious but, once we understand the overall effect, we can look at why it varies. On a good day, a unit can be 90 per cent effective and fight nearly as hard in a real war as it does on an exercise. On a bad day, that same unit will have trouble being 5 per cent effective. Most of this difference is determined by the way each side exploits tactical psychology.

*   *   *

Tactical psychology is a new way of understanding combat. It is not, like battle morale, a vague label that includes everything from national culture to the quality of boots. It is a sharp focus on what soldiers do once they are in contact with the enemy. Instead of looking at the things governments and generals might be able to control, or worrying about the million tiny problems that no one can control, tactical psychology focuses on what a front-line soldier can do to win a battle.

The emphasis means that tactical psychology is not about making our own men fight more but making the other side fight less. It is all about using tricks like suppressive fire, flanking attacks and fast attacks. It is sometimes about simply telling the enemy they have the chance to surrender.

Like many aspects of war, tactical psychology combines art and science. The art is the practical application: all those dirty and not-so-dirty tricks that get the job done. The science blends psychology, history and field experiments to put a number on how each trick works. The numbers can help armies and soldiers mix attrition and manoeuvre more effectively. They can help civilians to gain insight into the reality of war.

This book is the first to pull together the major features of tactical psychology to show what really matters at the sharp end of a battle. It is an unashamed attempt to make a 'popular science' description that people can understand without their heads catching fire or shutting down through sheer boredom. *War Games* describes the secret heart of war that armies have forgotten; it uncovers one of the key reasons for the unfolding disaster in Afghanistan.

TWO

WHO FIGHTS?

BRIGADIER MARSHALL, MAKIN ISLAND, 1943

The enemy, crazed with saké, began a series of banzai charges at dusk, and the pressure thereafter was almost unremitting until dawn came. The frontal gun positions were all directly assaulted with sword and bayonet. Most of the killing took place at less than a ten-yard interval. Half of the American guns were knocked out and approximately half of the occupants of the forward foxholes were either killed or wounded. Every position was ringed with enemy dead.

When morning brought the assurance that the defensive position had weathered the storm and the enemy had been beaten back by superior fire, it seemed certain to those of us who were close enough to it to appraise the action that all concerned must have acted with utmost boldness. For it was clear that the whole battalion was alive to the danger and that despite its greatly superior numbers, it had succeeded by none too wide a margin. We began the investigation to determine how many of our men had fought with their weapons. It was an exhaustive search, man by man and gun crew by gun crew, each man being asked exactly what he had done.

Yet making all allowances for the dead, we could identify only thirty-six men as having fired at the enemy with all weapons. The majority were heavy-weapons men. The really active firers were usually in small groups working together. There were some men in the positions directly under attack who did not fire at all or attempt to use a weapon even when the position was being overrun. The majority of the active firers used several weapons; if the machine gun went out, they picked up a rifle; when they ran out of rifle ammunition, they used grenades. But there were other witnesses who testified that they had seen clear targets and still did not fire.

It is true that these were green troops who were having their first taste of combat. Likewise, it is to be observed that the nature of perimeter defence, as it was then used in the Pacific, limited the freedom of fire of troops inside the perimeter.

But thereafter the trail of this same question was followed through many companies with varying degrees of battle experience, in the Pacific and in Europe. The proportions varied little from situation to situation. In an average experienced infantry company in an average stern day's action, the number engaging with any and all weapons was approximately 15 per cent of total strength. In the most aggressive infantry companies, under the most intense local pressure, the figure rarely rose above 25 per cent of total strength from the opening to the close of action.

Now maybe I should clarify the matter still further. I do not mean to say that throughout an engagement, the average company maintained fire with an average of 15 per cent of its weapons. If that were it, there would be no problem, for such a rate of fire would necessarily mean great volume during the height of an assault.

The thing is simply this: that out of an average 100 men along the line of fire during the period of an encounter, only fifteen men on the average would take any part with the weapons. This was true whether the action was spread over a day, or two days, or three. The prolonging of the engagement did not add appreciably to the numbers.

Moreover, the man did not have to maintain fire to be counted among the active firers. If he had so much as fired a rifle once or twice, though not aiming it at anything in particular, or lobbed a grenade roughly in the direction of the enemy, he was scored on the positive side.

This account from Brigadier S. L. A. Marshall's *Men Against Fire* is one of the few in this book that is not based on direct combat experience. Rather than learning through fighting himself, Marshall came to understand the psychology of war by interviewing hundreds of soldiers soon after they returned from battle.

Soldier, journalist, analyst and historian, Marshall was a complex and colourful character. He did a lot of good for Western armies and over the years he provided profound insights into training, tactics, weapons and the weight that soldiers carry into battle. He developed a new way of thinking about combat and he was able to make others think this way too. His journalistic side generated some *Boy's Own*-style war porn, but this only served to make his message more forceful.

When *Men Against Fire* was published in 1947, it came as a revelation to people who had not been in combat. Despite the initial fuss caused by his book, very few people questioned Marshall's methods and most armies soon came to accept the fire ratios as gospel. That 15 to 25 per cent still overshadows the art and science of tactical psychology.

The central message was a variation on an old chestnut: 'There are two kinds of people in this world: those who fight and those who don't.' Marshall's fire ratios seemed to provide fairly solid evidence that something like four out of five people are not natural fighters. The trick for military analysts was to spot the difference.

I had been told about Marshall's fire ratios long before I got the battle morale job but it was a month into the project before I saw a copy of the book. I was interviewing a colonel from the Royal Armoured Corps about the design of a new light tank when I happened to mention the battle morale project. The conversation immediately switched to one of those rambling chats about fighting spirit, gore and bayonets. It turned out that the colonel was obsessed with the genetics of fighting. What he really wanted was not some new armoured vehicle but a way to find and recruit men who were naturally good at fighting. He wanted nothing to do with the 'wishy-washy pinko nonsense about culture and society' which many professional analysts were keen on. He wanted to find a gene that made super-soldiers.

The Tank Colonel pressed a copy of *Men Against Fire* into my hands and said: 'Read this. This man's a genius. If you can work out what makes the difference between the men that fight and the men that don't, you'll get two ticks and a gold star.'

We spent the rest of the morning swapping ideas and drawing on scraps of paper. The light tank was forgotten as we generated elaborate plans for working out 'what makes men tick' and how to turn Marshall's work into something useful for a modern army. When we parted, we were almost of one mind regarding fire ratios. I had reservations about the simplicity of the genetic answer but we both agreed that it needed to be understood. Over the years the Tank Colonel, now retired, has given me regular updates on the genetics of fighting.

Sadly, the light tank turned out to be a white elephant; too heavy, too complicated and too full of clever ideas, it is still on the drawing board after twenty years of development. The genetics of fighting, and the 'pinko' version with society and training included, have also proved to be a bit trickier than expected. At the heart of the problem was Marshall's fire ratio theory.

Over the years it has become apparent that Marshall's scientific-sounding fire ratios were not the result of laborious study. In fact, they turned out to be a bit of a guess. He had the best of intentions: in many battles there really were too few soldiers firing at the enemy, but the fire ratio problem was far from being universal. Other pressures were at work, and these made it very difficult to spot any stable characteristics that could be separating soldiers who fight from soldiers who run or hide. To understand this, we need to trace the origin of Marshall's figures.

* * *

Marshall was not the first to propose a limit on the number of men doing all the fighting. The idea had been bubbling along for millennia, but Marshall was inspired by a report written by Lionel Wigram. Wigram was a British army officer who started as a theorist and instructor before developing his understanding through direct experience of combat.

Wigram was instrumental in the development of Second World War battle drills. The standard battle drill was similar to the fire-and-movement example we looked at in the last chapter, with half a unit giving suppressive fire while the other half move to assault the enemy. The drills were based on storm tactics used by both sides at the end of the First World War but, because so much had been forgotten between the wars, many of the details came from a purely theoretical understanding of combat.

Wigram was not entirely happy with the theory, so he left his classroom and went to the war in Sicily, to see whether the drills he taught were being used in action. When he got there, he took part in dozens of small battles, from section to battalion level, and this experience made him realise that the battle drills were not working. Rather than using fire-and-movement, Wigram found that battles were won by what he called 'guts and movement'. He described the typical platoon attack like this:

Enemy machine guns open fire, the whole platoon lie down except the platoon commander and three or four gutful men. Five or six men start making tracks for home, meanwhile the gutful men under the platoon commander dash straight in to the enemy position without any covering fire and always succeed in taking the position. In some instances some positions are taken by as few as two men, and every battalion commander will confirm that it is always the same group of nine or ten who are there first, and on whom the battle depends.

In 1943 Wigram included this observation in a report to his bosses, who then passed it up the chain of command. Unfortunately for Wigram, he was bright, wealthy and Jewish. These qualities did not sit well with a small clique of old-school British staff officers, who portrayed Wigram as a wide-boy who was telling General Montgomery how to do his job. Wigram had a very uncomfortable meeting with Monty (the classic interview without coffee) and was demoted from lieutenant colonel to major. A few months later he was killed in action leading an Italian guerrilla unit behind the German lines.

Despite the effort to quash Wigram's report, many soldiers

were keen to make use of his observations, and they sent copies to friends in all corners of the Allied war effort. By the time a copy reached Marshall, the report had a simple percentage added to show how many men were in that most combative or 'gutful' group. This figure rang a loud bell with Marshall because it matched the impression he got from talking to the survivors of Saké Night. From that point on, all of Marshall's post-combat interviews seemed to confirm that he and Wigram had discovered some kind of universal truth about the psychology of war: that there was a force of human nature preventing most men from killing.

That bell ringing for Marshall had echoes down through decades of research. By the late 1990s, analysts had managed to find something close to 20 per cent doing most of the fighting in infantry combat, in tank battles and even in submarine war. Even Warsaw Pact analysts found a similar magic number after they had seen Marshall's work.

No one knew that Marshall was basically copying what Wigram had said. The close correlation between their numbers was seen as confirmation that there was something stable, and probably genetic, deciding who fought. Yet there was still something fishy about the way Marshall's and Wigram's numbers matched up so neatly. It was strange how the same figure should apply to American novices defending in Pacific jungles and to British veterans attacking up the mountains of Sicily. It took many years for anyone to spot the obvious physical and psychological differences between firing, 'once or twice, though not aiming it at anything in particular', and charging at a machine-gun nest.

When analysts and staff officers eventually looked into the nitty-gritty of battles, they found an enormous variation in fire ratios. The average certainly looked to be about 20 per cent but sometimes nearly every man in a unit would fire. Sometimes no one would fire.

This was spotted only after the general agreement between Marshall and Wigram had been compounded by years of effort and some complicated statistics. New analysts like me were inheriting work started by our line managers and we found it very difficult to voice our concerns. Most decided that the variation was just noise in the data: something irrelevant like the crackle on a badly tuned radio. We all kept on thinking that fire ratios were set. They might not be set in stone but they were at least in some very thick porridge.

So for nearly forty years, the small niche of defence research that bothered to look at battle morale was looking at one big question: 'who fights?' Our effort was directed to understanding a soldier's baseline level of combat motivation, the elusive quality that a soldier takes into battle to make him fight more, or less, than the man next to him. Researchers were asked whether, as Marshall suggested, there were two types of soldier or, as Wigram indicated, three types of soldier. (The US Department of Defense was slightly annoyed when the answer came back as, 'Probably sixteen, but that depends on which theory is trendy this week.')

Irrespective of the number of types, if armies could understand the difference between 'heroes and zeroes' or 'hawks, doves and chickens', they could train men to be heroic, or recruit those who were naturally hawkish. As a consequence, instead of looking at the differences between battles, researchers were kept busy looking at the differences between people.

If we overlook the distasteful way that people many miles from combat have described soldiers with lazy labels like 'heroes and zeroes' (veterans generally dislike both these words), it is clear that personal characteristics do influence the outcome of a battle. These characteristics can be enduring and profound. As Wigram pointed out and many others have confirmed, there is a tendency for good fighters to stay good fighters and be battle-winning assets.

Unfortunately, the main result of the 'who fights?' question was that research became trapped in an argument about whether nature or nurture was responsible for some men fighting more than others. The role of society and upbringing were of interest for a while, and warrior cultures are still a hot topic for two of the Sennelager Club hangers-on. But military analysts soon learned to stay away from this quagmire, and the argument boiled down to whether genes or training had the main effect on baseline motivation.

The Tank Colonel was not the only man to be a fan of the super-soldier ideal. In the US and UK there was formal research to assess whether different ethnic or social groups had a greater proportion of hawks, doves or chickens. Could the same gene that made someone Caucasian or wealthy also make them a better fighter? As you might suspect, studies funded by American and British military officers tended to find that middle-class white men were particularly good at fighting.

Despite the many biases behind it, there is some sound analysis to support the genetic idea. If we strip away all the pseudo-science jargon, these men tend to be slightly larger, more outgoing, more intelligent and richer than the average man. It was argued that most of these things were determined by genetics. Yet there are plenty of men who appear to be natural fighters but do not fit this mould. Small men, quiet men, poor men and some men who appear to be psychotic have often been seen to be very effective combat soldiers too.

Meanwhile, Wigram's three-way split of men who fight, lie down or make tracks for home had parallels in mainstream psychology, with things like extraversion and aggression sometimes used to put people in three separate boxes. There have been some grand claims, based on dubious statistics, but the more balanced work on baseline motivation indicates a relative modest difference. Using a three-way split for a cadre of men with broadly similar training, the hawks are about 50 per cent more likely to fight than the doves and twice as likely to fight as the chickens. Even so, this is clearly big news: it suggests that there is potential maybe to double combat effectiveness if a way could be found to recruit only hawks.

There is also some evidence from civilian research to support the idea of a warrior gene. This is a controversial idea in academic circles but the big problems for the military are all technical. The primary technical hurdle is pinning down a gene for a collection of behaviours that no one fully understands.

No one is sure whether the key factor in baseline motivation is pure aggression, the willingness to fight to help your friends (aggressive altruism) or a whole mix of things. A genetic anomaly might make a man more likely to beat his wife, or more prone to road rage. It cannot fully explain why he will stalk a Tiger tank armed only with a 'spring-loaded turnip thrower' (the PIAT anti-tank weapon). Genetics cannot explain why many men will risk their lives to rescue wounded friends yet shy away from firing their rifles at the enemy. Armies need both types of men and policy-makers worry that any supposed good-at-fighting gene might turn out to be just a gene for being trigger happy.

There are many personal characteristics that have a greater effect than a simple predisposition towards fighting. Even on training exercises, there are 'top guns' who are much better at pretend fighting than everyone else. These men are not more heroic or hawkish than their friends, they just happen to be better at a range of skills that are useful in simulated combat. In general, these skills are directly translated to live combat, with most of the men who fight well in realistic training also being the most effective in battle.

While everyone accepts that some men are natural fighters, the most profound results have come from nurture, in the form of realistic training. Despite his suggestion that fire ratios were set in porridge, Marshall helped to encourage training where, rather than lying down to shoot at bulls-eye targets, men fire from awkward positions at targets that look and move like real people. He also encouraged the development of tactics which made more use of area fire and suppressive fire: shooting at things rather than people. On the basis of Marshall's recommendations, commanders were taught to make every effort to encourage their men to fire; often shooting for shooting's sake.

This combination appears to have caused a considerable increase in the number of men who fire their weapons in combat. In Korea, Marshall said the fire ratio was above 50 per cent; in Vietnam and the Falklands it was seen to be closer to 90 per cent. By 2009, the fire ratio for US, Canadian and British troops in Afghanistan looked to be touching 100 per cent. Almost every man is firing his weapon at some point during the fight.

Training cannot take all of the credit for this. At the same time as being drilled to be shooting machines, soldiers now go to war with far more automatic weapons and carry much more ammunition. The precise weighting for how much training or improved weapons have altered fire ratios is still uncertain, but training accounts for a much larger share. If fighting is judged solely on the number of men shooting, it seems that training beats genetics hands down. It would seem that genetics might allow units to be twice as effective but that training has helped to make them maybe four times as effective.

*   *   *

Yet the increased fire ratios that come from better weapons and training have not increased the number of men who will assault a defensive position. In those Vietnam and Falkland battles, with fire ratios near 90 per cent, battalion objectives were still being captured by a handful of men, while everyone else appeared to be hanging back. In Afghanistan today, an assault usually comes down to a few men who, at first glance, look to be more gutful than the rest.

Although the number of men pushing home an assault is still very similar to the figures proposed by Wigram and Marshall, a careful dig into combat reports and psychological tests shows that this is not due to a profound difference between two or three personality types. The real difference between firing and assaulting will be examined later, but first we have to escape from the shortcomings of the heroes-and-zeroes theories.

Whether focused on training or genetics, the act of lumping soldiers into big categories is more to do with the way analysts think about the world than the way soldiers fight. A clear separation into two or three types of soldier gives an illusion of stability: it suggests that, no matter what happens in a battle, the outcome has almost been decided before the shooting starts.

The stability illusion sprang from the assessments by Wigram and Marshall being very rough first attempts at putting a number on how many men fight. Their figures were unavoidably biased because they came from narrow samples of combat.

In his assessment of Second World War fire ratios, Marshall's journalistic tendencies attracted him to desperate victories against heavy odds. He never paid much attention to easy victories because they did not make good stories. He never got a good look at defeats either, because most of the witnesses were captured or killed. The few soldiers who escaped intact had been too busy running or hiding to give reliable accounts.

Wigram's observations suffer from a similar unintended bias. When machine guns suddenly fill the air with lead, very few men will rush to attack the enemy. Yet all the attacks Wigram took part in were successful, so, just like Marshall, he only got a good look at desperate victories.

One of the main reasons why Marshall recorded a higher fire ratio in Korea was that more of the battles involved men in strong defensive positions firing at easy targets. So, compared to his Second World War sample, Marshall interviewed far fewer men who had been in confused close combat and far more who had been at 'turkey shoots'. Compared to his earlier observations, the training and weapons had changed a little but the tactical situation had changed a lot.

It turns out that the 'noise in the data' for fire ratios was actually the main effect. When different tactical situations are compared, a platoon sometimes has half of its men being gutful, half lying down not firing and no one making tracks for home. On another day, all the men in that same platoon will fight or all of them will run away. When one or two shots come from a tree line, everyone in the platoon will return fire; when they swap places with the men in the tree line and have thousands of bullets heading their way, they will all make tracks for home. These men have not had their personalities changed overnight. They have not suddenly remembered or forgotten their training. It is the tactical situation that has changed.

Decades of wondering whether baseline motivation was determined more by nature or nurture have not yielded a reliable answer because they interact in a complex mesh of causes and effects. Training probably has the greater effect but a precise number can never be defined and, even if it could, it would have little practical value to men in combat.

In any event, changes to training, recruitment and weapons have probably pushed baseline combat motivation to its practical limit. There is no benefit to be had from making our own soldiers fire more than they already do. In fact, many of the problems in recent wars have been due to our men doing too much firing. The real trick, the heart of combat, is to do those things that make the enemy fight less.

*   *   *

The answer to the question 'who fights?' is 'pretty much everybody'. If the conditions are right then almost any man will fight, but change those conditions and almost everybody will stop fighting.

Marshall got some of the details wrong and, yes, he made up some of his numbers, but he did understand the realities of combat. When almost everyone else was looking at tanks, planes and nuclear bombs, he was looking at people. His greatest legacy is not the fire ratio theory but a single line in *Men Against Fire*. He said that the nub of battle, and therefore the outcome of war, was a simple question that a soldier asked himself when he was under fire: 'Will the possible effect on the enemy of my active participation be worth the possible adverse effect on me?'

This 'is it worth it?' calculation is an almost unconscious, quick and dirty comparison of the costs and rewards of fighting. It lies at the heart of Sergeant Dawson's 'bit of truth' that winning is about making the other side fight less. The 'is it worth it?' calculation underpins all tactical psychology, but it is shaped by some very basic human characteristics.

Twelve years after I left the Tank Colonel's office, we met up at one of the rare Sennelager Club meetings. Over the years we had traded emails and phone calls but we had stopped being of one mind about fire ratios and combat effectiveness. He was still obsessed with finding the genetic key and had spent the intervening years sifting through regimental histories to examine the differences between units recruited from French and British colonies.

He could say with reasonable certainty what the average combat effectiveness would be for a particular African or Indian unit but he had never found a genetic explanation for it. He also refused to accept that the enormous day-to-day difference in any unit's effectiveness was anything more than noise in the data.

As expected, the Tank Colonel started the evening by repeating the mantra that some ethnic groups produce more heroes than others. But by the time we left the meeting, I had seen his faith in heroes-and-zeroes crushed by a young American analyst who had used the Tank Colonel's own historical data to show how artillery beats heroism every time.

THREE

FEAR AND FIREPOWER

LIEUTENANT J†NGER, FRANCE, 1917

You cower in a heap alone in a hole and feel yourself the victim of a pitiless thirst for destruction. With horror you feel that all your intelligence, your capacities, your body and spiritual characteristics, have become utterly meaningless and absurd. While you think it, the lump of metal that will crush you to a shapeless nothing may have started on its course. Your discomfort is concentrated in your ear that tries to distinguish amid the uproar the swirl of your own death rushing near. It is dark, too; and you must find in yourself alone all the strength for holding out. You can't get up and with a blasé laugh light a cigarette in the wondering sight of your companions. Nor can you be encouraged by the sight of your friend clipping a monocle to his eye to observe a hit on the traverse close beside you. You know that not even a cock will crow when you are hit.

Well, why don't you jump up and rush into the night till you collapse in safety behind a bush like an exhausted animal? Why do you hang on there all the time, you and your braves? There are no superior officers to see you.

Yet someone watches you. Unknown perhaps to yourself, there is someone within you who keeps you to your post by the power of two mighty spells: Duty and Honour. You know that this is your place in the battle, and that a whole people relies on you to do your job. You feel, 'If I leave my post, I am a coward in my own eyes, a wretch who will ever after blush at every word of praise.' You clench your teeth and stay.

This account from Ernst Jünger's *Storm of Steel* reflects the simplest reason for soldiers not fighting: the fear of injury and death from impersonal munitions.

At some point during the First World War, artillery addicts realised that the most profound effect of bombardment was psychological. They then switched their mathematical minds to calculating how much ammunition was needed to stop German soldiers from fighting; not to stop them fighting for ever, but for long enough to let Allied infantry cross no man's land without being shot to pieces. Much thought was given to whether it was fear that stopped people fighting. After nearly a century of trying new tricks and collecting data from battles, it transpires that the answer is wrapped up in Marshall's 'is it worth it?' calculation.

The best way into this is through that young American analyst's re-examination of the Tank Colonel's heroes-and-zeroes work. A clean-cut, Midwest lad, Young American was earnest, bookish and gangly. With a good job as an engineer for one of the big defence contractors, he was also an artillery reservist who had allowed the study of war to take over his life. Halfway through a PhD in operational research, he was presenting his initial findings to the Sennelager Club and their hangers-on at an artillery conference in London.

Very nervous to begin with, he was clearly overawed by the

swanky hotel and the gaggle of senior officers in the room. His unease was heightened by the presence of the Tank Colonel, whose life's work he was about to trash. But his nerves abated as he got into the comfort zone of numbers and battles.

He began by showing us the wide variations in the Tank Colonel's data. This came in the form of a very spiky graph, with unit effectiveness swinging wildly around the average. By the end of the slideshow, there was a lot less spikiness in the graph and, to the Tank Colonel's horror, it was clear that artillery casualties had far more impact than genetics.

The main effect was not the number of men killed but the way these casualties reduced the effectiveness of those who survived the bombardment. With 5 per cent casualties to artillery, a unit's effectiveness was usually halved; with 10 per cent casualties, effectiveness often disappeared altogether. The Young American suggested that fear was the key to all this. 'Fear of artillery,' he said, 'does not just separate the heroes from the zeroes. The correct application of fire turns all men into zeroes.'

The Young American explained the gaps in his data and in his understanding. There were still some spikes in the graph that he could not explain, but his main worry was that he was unsure how fear actually worked. While he was convinced that fear was the thing that was switching a bombardment's survivors from hero to zero, the mechanism behind this had proved too difficult for him to fathom.

*   *   *

Fear has proved difficult for psychologists to fathom too. It can be measured, after a fashion, through physiological arousal in the form of increased heart rate, sweating and hormone levels. Fear can also be measured, in a vague kind of way, by asking people how scared something makes them feel. Unfortunately, it can be very difficult to link how much people sweat with how scared they say they are. It is even more difficult to link measures of fear to what happens in combat.

People interpret arousal and events inconsistently, so a man might see the same situation as exciting one day but frightening the next. Fear is rarely linked to the reality of the threat. There are many examples of men putting dive bombers or suicide bombers at the top of their fear list, despite having lost no close comrades to these weapons. Meanwhile, the mortars or mines that have killed half of their friends can be quite a long way down the list. Very often, people fear the noisiest or least understood threat.

It has also proved very difficult to link fear with how men respond to a threat. A man awarded the Silver Star for fighting through a cave complex admits that he was scared witless. Meanwhile, the men who followed him but did not fight, say they were only mildly anxious. These men might not be telling the whole truth, but sometimes a man will stand and fight when he is terrified then run from a fight when he is much less scared. There is a problem unpicking cause and effect, but there are enough accounts of the most frightened man doing the most fighting to make the link between fear and effectiveness very uncertain.

The result is that all the hard facts we have about fear point only to it degrading the details of fighting when people actually choose to fight. Tests show that fear will make a man's shooting less accurate but no one can say how much fear will stop him shooting altogether. Other tests show that fear can make a man run a bit faster but no one can be certain how much fear will make him run towards a fight, or how much will make him run away.

Fear clearly plays a part in the 'is it worth it?' calculation, but it has been difficult to see the full strength of its effect. In most cases, weak knees, a racing heart and all the other measurable effects of fear have been seen to be only fudge factors. This 'fear wobble' accounts for just 10 per cent of the total degradation in modern combat.

Fear works in mysterious ways but, luckily, it works alongside the brain's more-or-less rational thought process, the thing that people usually call common sense. When combined, fear and common sense help a soldier to work out whether to fight or not.

*   *   *

This chapter's opening passage was written between the world wars, when Germany was rushing towards Nazism. This might be why Jünger overplays duty and country as the main reasons for enduring bombardment. A more balanced view comes from post-combat interviews and prisoner debriefs. These tend to emphasise the role of common sense, most notably the fact that any 'rush into the night' would be almost suicidal in a barrage as powerful and widespread as those that Jünger endured.

By 1917, a soldier caught in a barrage was nearly ten times more likely to survive when lying down than standing up and almost three hundred times more likely to survive if he was in a trench with a sturdy roof. In the late-war concrete bunkers, a man was perhaps 1,000 times safer than he would be running around on the surface.

A typical barrage would cover many square kilometres, so Jünger would have had to run a long way to reach a place of safety. Therefore, despite his fear, he did the common-sense thing and stayed put. It can be very difficult to think straight under fire, but most men retain an element of rational thought in even the heaviest bombardment. This usually tells them to sit tight and wait for the storm to pass.

Common sense is the main reason why the psychological effect of bombardment is usually so short-lived. One military psychologist, another Sennelager Club hanger-on, abandoned the political correctness of her trade and put it this way: 'If it doesn't make them mental or retarded, the survivors of a barrage are generally pretty keen to hit back at the bad guys.' This is exactly what happened with Jünger's regiment. Their common sense forced them out of cover to man their weapons and cut down waves of attacking infantry.

Similar massacres occur whenever artillery is used without a proper understanding of its physical or psychological limits. To see these limits, we need to cut through some of the exaggerated reports about the power of bombs and shells.

* * *

The best data on bombardment effects comes from Second World War field experiments. In some of these experiments, the fathers of Sennelager Club members were dropping artillery shells on each other just to test what the 'morale effect' would be. They uncovered some surprising facts. In north-west Europe in 1944, Allied bombardment by air and artillery was found to have very little physical effect on men in prepared positions. It was usually very hard to hit the enemy, let alone kill him, especially by dropping bombs from aircraft.

Tactical use of heavy and medium bombers, like the British

Lancaster and American Mitchell, was particularly disappointing given the propaganda spread by airpower advocates. As an example, during one of the attacks to break out of the Normandy beachhead, the Allied air forces attempted to drop over 1,600 bombs on the village of Secqueville. Fewer than 100 landed anywhere close to the target. Similar results were achieved whenever the larger bombers were used to hit anything smaller than a city.

Aircraft specifically designed for close support to ground troops performed only a little better. Bombing range trials found that, in near-perfect conditions, the average Typhoon pilot was lucky to get a rocket salvo within 150 metres of a target's centre. Accuracy dropped even further in real combat. A ten-metre gun emplacement needed 100 rockets to score a single hit. A 500-metre viaduct needed eighty-two bombs from close support aircraft to get one hit.

The gap between propaganda and reality came to a head in a Normandy battle dubbed 'the day of the Typhoon', where hundreds of sorties were flown to try to blunt an attack by a panzer division. Eighty-nine tank kills were claimed but a careful count after the battle found that, at best, only ten tanks had been destroyed by aircraft. The air bombardment clearly had some kind of psychological effect though: the division withdrew in disarray, abandoning as many undamaged tanks as were destroyed by bombs and rockets.

Artillery was also surprisingly bad at destroying people and equipment. For the Canadian assault on Boulogne, nearly 6,000 shells fell within 150 metres of a German anti-aircraft battery. But this storm of fire destroyed only two of the eight guns and the remainder were able to continue firing for most of the battle.

Later in the war, during one of the early British attacks into Germany, 14,000 shells were fired onto carefully selected point targets. Only 5 per cent fell within fifty metres of the thing they were supposed to hit. The whole barrage, including speculative fire at likely enemy positions, fired nearly half a million shells to inflict only sixty casualties. This was typical of the physical effects that were achieved throughout the war unless a trained observer could talk to the guns and adjust fire onto particularly vulnerable targets.

Like aerial bombardment, the main effect from artillery fire was the way it appeared to reduce the enemy's willingness to fight. Over the years, words like suppression, neutralisation and artillery shock have been used to describe the psychological effect of bombardment. In practice, these labels overlap, so for our purposes 'suppression' is a good enough word to describe all the ways that fire stops people from fighting.

Second World War suppression research found that one or two shells falling every minute within 200 metres of the enemy kept men 'firmly in their trenches'. Six rounds per minute stopped anybody from returning fire during the barrage. But to induce a complete collapse of resistance appeared to require a massive amount of fire.

In 1945, this kind of battering was suffered by 150 soldiers defending the German village of Bauchem. In the first ten minutes their defensive area was hit with forty-nine tonnes of artillery shells. After this, they took a steady battering from forty-four tonnes of mortar bombs and eighteen tonnes of shells from tanks and anti-aircraft guns. Then, in the final half-hour, they were hit with another seventy-three tonnes of artillery before being attacked by the 5th Battalion of the Dorset Regiment.

More than a tonne of ordnance per defender caused only twenty-five casualties (17 per cent, about the same as that suffered by the Argentines on Wireless Ridge) yet the Dorsets said they met not the slightest resistance. British troops described many

Bauchem defenders as 'absolutely yellow-coloured', physically shaken and 'overwhelmed with a sense of helplessness'. The lucky men who found shelter in cellars during the barrage were not so shaken but they still offered no resistance.

The Bauchem fire plan was seen as overkill, with 10 per cent casualties judged to be sufficient to tip a unit into complete collapse. Other attacks in the Bauchem operation used far fewer rounds to get a very similar result. In these attacks, a bombardment causing only 3 per cent casualties made for an 'easy victory'.

The first big conclusion here is that, in these attacks and in scores of other 'easy victories', physical destruction claimed between 3 and 20 per cent of the defenders' effectiveness. Something psychological appears to have accounted for most of the rest.

* * *

For a while, just after victory in 1945, there was a concerted effort to work out what was going on. Was fear or common sense having the biggest impact? What type of munitions had the greatest effect? How long did suppression last after a barrage lifted?

Figures from hundreds of battles and from experimental trials on firing ranges were used to calculate the amount of fire needed to suppress the enemy. Eventually, armies were given paper charts and tables to help them work out how many shells would be needed to suppress different targets.

Suppression charts give different figures for the weight and duration of fire needed to stop the enemy fighting during a bombardment and for the critical hangover period after the fire has lifted. With the right barrage, the attacking force should be able to move freely while shells are falling on the enemy and then assault while the defenders are still shaking off their suppression hangover.

The charts are said to have worked reasonably well on the rare occasions when they have been used, but they have never separated psychological and physical effects. Perhaps one in twenty men were labelled 'suppressed' because they had been killed, wounded or buried under rubble. The charts also fail to mention how much of the psychological suppression is due to fear and how much is common sense. Luckily for us, people like the Young American have unpicked the historical analysis and firing range experiments that were used to create suppression charts.

Historical analysis is an arcane branch of military research which involves the application of statistical techniques to numerical data extracted from historical sources. The findings for artillery suppression are often clouded by time but careful assessment has produced some very realistic data. The main problem is that historical sources often give an overall weight of fire but no detail on the size and type of bombs or shells fired.

These details can be very important. Blasts from high-explosive shells, or flying metal splinters from fragmentation or 'shrapnel' have a different physical and psychological effect to being surrounded by intensely hot shards of white phosphorus. It is also widely believed that many small explosions have a greater psychological effect than fewer big ones. Historical analysis has not been able to provide much detail about these effects.

Peacetime experiments on firing ranges have attempted to fill this gap by putting soldiers in bunkers and dropping different types of barrage around them. The soldiers are then asked to fill in questionnaires to estimate whether they would be willing to leave a bunker two, five or ten minutes after the barrage stops. This approach can give plenty of detail about the number, type and size of explosions, but the men ticking the boxes are generally pretty sure that they will not be hurt, so there is a big realism gap.

Firing range experiments generally show only the common-sense side of suppression, while historical analysis shows common sense, fear and destruction all rolled into one. Considerable effort has been used to unpick problems with this data, for example checking when box tickers are lying to themselves or saying what they think researchers want to hear. The output includes handy charts which show how fear, common sense and destruction combine to cause an overall suppressive effect.

A typical example would be that, after a barrage where 5 per cent of defenders had been killed or injured, 10 per cent will not fight because they are frightened and nearly a quarter will not fight because it is simple common sense to stay in cover. When fear and common sense are added together, they appear to have close to seven times the effect of physical destruction.

*   *   *

Suppression charts give the impression that simply multiplying the number of rounds by the duration of fire will provide a fairly predictable result. Some variation is accepted: for example, a short, sharp, whirlwind barrage is known to have a more intense suppression hangover than a longer, more sedate fire plan. Apart from this, most of the human details are overlooked.

One of these details concerns the way soldiers under fire are, in effect, being taught to sit tight. Civilian psychology has spent a lot of effort looking at how to train animals and people through a system of conditioning, using rewards to promote the desired behaviour. Artillery suppression applies the same principles. Sitting tight is the desired behaviour and not being blown up by each explosion is the reward. If a bombardment lasts long enough, the desired behaviour should become so ingrained that people stay in cover long after the fire stops.

Conditioning was discovered by a Russian, and Russians have always been very keen to include it in their artillery doctrine. For many years, Soviet forces believed that even an impregnable fortification could not prevent its occupants from becoming completely ineffective if it was pounded with enough shells. But when this type of conditioning was attempted by Egyptian forces attacking Israeli fortifications during the Yom Kippur/October War of 1973, they had only partial success.

What happened was that the soldiers who had nothing to do but sit tight were forced into a kind of feedback loop and stayed sitting still after the barrage lifted. In contrast, those who had the chance to do something useful during the barrage, even if they were only carrying ammunition, continued to do something useful after the fire lifted. Many of them fought back despite very unfavourable odds.

In any barrage there are some people, usually those separated from their comrades, who enter a catatonic state like some of those yellow-coloured men in Bauchem. But most people reach a fearful peak and then get used to the bombardment, almost as if conditioning and fear run out of steam. They stay scared but they adapt, control their fear, start to think rationally and can then do something useful if they get the chance.

This appears to work like those phobia therapies which force people into close proximity with the object of their irrational fear for an extended period. With a long enough exposure to the threat, most people pass through their terror until their bodies effectively get bored with making a fuss. Once this happens, the fear subsides, common sense takes over and they are able to assess the situation in a more rational manner.

There are many exceptions to the simple view of artillery suppression as a predictable, visceral response to a given weight of fire. The most profound exceptions come from the intervention of common sense. To understand this, we need to have another look at the Argentine soldiers on Wireless Ridge and compare them to the men who suffered bombardment in earlier wars.

Far fewer rounds were fired at the Argentines on Wireless Ridge than at the German force battered into submission at Bauchem. But the Argentines suffered similar casualties because, instead of cellars or bunkers, their only protection came from very shallow shell-scrape trenches or from low-walled sangars made from loose rock and peat. The incoming fire was also far more accurate because guns and radios had improved since the Second World War, making it much easier to hit the target.

But the accuracy of the Wireless Ridge barrage made it very narrow. The defenders could sometimes see the edge of the barrage just 100 metres away. There were some long periods with very little incoming fire. These gaps were not intentional but they meant that a rush into the night was a much more sensible idea than waiting around to get killed. Those men from the 7th Regiment saw the chance to withdraw and they took it.

A similar effect was reported in Desert Storm and there are hints of it in some Afghanistan operations but, once again, the effect was recorded most accurately in the Second World War. The best example comes from a British attack on a strong German company position near Castel del Rio in Italy. The attackers initially launched a traditional 'bite-and-hold' attack, with a heavy bombardment followed by a ground assault. This attack failed, so the British unit withdrew and carefully set up their artillery for a steady and accurate barrage. They then fired one round every three minutes for seven hours.

When the British infantry attacked for the second time, they met no opposition. All but two men from the defending company had ignored their orders and withdrawn. This attack cleared the position with 140 artillery rounds and without the infantry having to fire a shot. The average bite-and-hold alternative required 4,000 artillery rounds to have a similar effect. Clearly, fear would have had an effect in this case (one of the captured defenders said the intermittent fire had nearly driven him mad) but the main factor was the gaps in the second barrage. The first barrage did not allow them the means, motive or opportunity to withdraw; it had not had the power to batter them into passivity either, so they stayed and fought. The second barrage, like the one hitting Wireless Ridge forty years later, allowed them to apply their common sense, weigh up the odds and withdraw.

*   *   *

These exceptions to the rule of suppression charts suggest a mechanism to get an improved psychological effect, with less killing and without wasting expensive ammunition. But, like any aspect of tactical psychology, the ability to understand suppression has been limited by the problems of getting good data, which is always subject to the fickle fashions of defence research.

When the Young American gave his talk to the Sennelager Club, the invasion of Iraq had already made artillery suppression passé. His work could not compete with the charms of smart bombs and precision missiles. A few months after his presentation, the funding for his PhD was withdrawn. He returned to engineering and his suppression work became another lump of tactical psychology flotsam. He mailed all his papers to the Tank Colonel and now they sit gathering dust in an old Wiltshire farmhouse.

Suppression charts have also gathered dust. They are rarely mentioned by modern armies because precision weapons have reinforced the focus on killing. When every bomb costs more than a new Porsche, it seems wasteful to think they might not be killing somebody. But there are still some suppression facts hiding in corners, where they are hoarded by grumpy old soldiers and war geeks who worry that one day we might be forced to fight another big war with cheap dumb weapons.

When the facts of artillery suppression are brought together, they show that it is more effective to exploit common sense than fear or destruction. In general, if a barrage causes 10 per cent casualties, the defenders will be overwhelmed by almost any ground assault. If a barrage causes as few as 2 or 3 per cent casualties but also offers an escape option, it is likely that the defending force will withdraw. Lacking a withdrawal option but with a short gap between suppression and assault, 2 or 3 per cent casualties will cause most survivors to surrender.

However, if the survivors have not been overwhelmed, have seen no option to withdraw and, critically, if there is a longer delay between barrage and assault, it is very likely that they will put up a stiff resistance. When this happens, the gap between barrage and assault usually has to be filled by suppression from the weapons carried by infantry soldiers.

FOUR

BULLETS AND COMMON SENSE

CORPORAL MURPHY, PROBABLY SOMEWHERE IN TENNESSEE, 1863

There was a roar of shouting from the trees and all at once there was a shower of lead pouring at us across the glade. Volleys of a sort at first but soon blending into one thick windblown sideways rainstorm of metal. Me and the boys around me took what cover we could and soon forgot about trying to shoot back. Smoke and noise and metal. Sods of black earth and stones and bits of tree bark and leaves leaping about. And not the space to poke up your cap without it being torn away and your head with it.

Then the shooting eases off a touch and we hear more shouts going up and down their line.

Old Ham says 'That would be them be coming for us now Finn,' and right enough the fire stops and there's another roar as they rile themselves up to rush us. Well, let me tell you, old Murphy might not be the best corporal in this fine army but he was its best sprinter on that day. Up we jumped and were away like coursing hares. The hounds were on our heels but not for long, I'd say. We had no rifles and no packs and all the Rebs had none of was shoes. So by the time we got back down the mountain there was no sign of the chase.

All along the creek there's men and boys panting or laughing or sitting with the shakes, all taking in a drink from the stream and blessing their luck. For a while it's like a civilised Sunday. But pretty soon the Captain starts reminding us there's a war on so we make ourselves into something that looks a mite like a company of soldiers and we troop off looking for bed and board.

There are some important differences between suppression by small-arms fire and what we have already seen for artillery. There is the same mix of destruction, fear and common sense but the physical circumstances make for different reactions. Strictly speaking, to be classed as 'small arms', a weapon must be something one soldier would normally carry (anything from a pistol to a light machine gun) but for our purposes we have had to stretch this to include heavier machine guns. Small-arms fire is usually 'direct' because the projectile travels in fairly straight line from firer to target. In contrast, fire from artillery or mortars is usually called 'indirect' because projectiles are lobbed in a pronounced arc at targets the firer cannot see.

The physical circumstances of an engagement make all the difference. Imagine (or remember) being an infantry soldier under artillery or mortar fire. The fire comes from over the hill so you cannot shoot the people who are dropping things on you. Then the shell fragments, flame and blast come from above and all sides, so the ideal protection is a sturdy bunker or some other kind of enclosed space, such as a snug trench with a roof on it. The common-sense response to artillery fire is to get into that hole, stay there until the fire stops and then, after it has stopped, wait a while, just to be on the safe side.

In contrast, small-arms fire usually comes from one or two directions and runs parallel to the ground. Many of the benefits of hard cover melt away when a battle shifts from a barrage of indirect fire to a small-arms firefight. Bunkers do give good protection from small arms, but they limit your mobility and make it more difficult to spot and engage any enemy infantry who might be sneaking up on you. Now those lovely thick walls of your bunker will only serve to reflect violence back at you if someone sneaky posts a grenade through the window. At this point it is much healthier to find cover that does not constrain your ability to fight back; open trenches or folds in the ground provide a much better chance of survival.

These basic physical differences alter the common-sense weighting for staying still, moving about and firing. Fear also changes as the fight shifts. As the two sides compete to win the firefight there is some comfort from returning fire at an enemy who is now tangible and killable. Now the soldier is able to do something other than sit tight, the 'fear wobble' starts to kick in but it is still that half-conscious 'is it worth it?' calculation that has the biggest effect. It would be useful to know whether this calculation is influenced more by the size, number or proximity of enemy bullets.

Round for round, smaller bullets have less suppressive effect than larger bullets, so the standard NATO 5.56mm rounds from most assault rifles will have less effect than the heavier 7.62mm round of sniper rifle or the monster 12.7mm (.50 calibre) round of a heavy machine gun. While all of these bullets can kill, a .50

calibre bullet will hit with close to ten times the force of 5.56mm and this is reflected in their suppressive effect.

Despite the weight advantage of larger calibres, it is generally accepted that more rounds have a greater suppressive effect than more weight: so while a 7.62mm weapon wins round for round, 5.56mm should win pound for pound. This is one of the reasons the US first switched from 7.62mm to 5.56mm in the 1960s and why the rest of NATO followed suit over the next few decades. Yet there is still no reliable way to work out how many 5.56mm rounds are equal to one 7.62mm or one .50 calibre round.

It is just as difficult to determine how close rounds have to come to a soldier for them to have a suppressive effect, but this appears to depend on the sound of a near miss. Most bullets travel faster than sound so a man under fire hears the crack of the bullet passing close to him, and then hears the thump of the round being fired. Some research suggests that hearing the crack makes all the difference, with a louder crack making more suppression and no audible crack causing almost no suppression.

* * *

Historical analysis of small-arms suppression is less clear cut than for indirect fire because it is much harder to count rifle bullets than artillery shells. Armies have tended to rely on the results of firing-range experiments to generate some rules of thumb for small-arms suppression. One rule of thumb states that a soldier will become suppressed if a bullet passes within one metre of him every second, and stay suppressed if one bullet passes within one metre every three seconds.

This 'one-metre rule' assumes that a very objective version of common sense is being applied. A soldier would have to be very highly motivated to break cover with rounds passing so close and so often. The two or three seconds needed to pop his head up and take an aimed shot would involve close to a one-in-ten chance of being hit: a far higher risk than that facing Corporal Murphy.

The one-metre rule does not fit with what has been seen in real small-arms firefights. For example, Second World War field studies suggested that one round passing within three metres every six seconds would appreciably degrade return fire from a whole fire-team, and two rounds every three seconds would prevent any return fire at all. Put simply, the one-metre rule requires about twelve times the volume of fire than is suggested by experience of real combat.

*   *   *

Recent combat reports seem to support the Second World War version of small-arms suppression, but it would appear that NATO soldiers are firing incredible amounts of ammunition 'just to be on the safe side'. In Afghanistan, most patrol contacts have run something like this example from a Canadian company commander in Kandahar:

A patrol is engaged by four insurgents from cover at 200 metres. The insurgents each fire a few aimed shots then a burst of twenty rounds in the hope of hitting a man while he is upright and in the open.

Every man in the patrol instantly fires off a burst towards a likely firing point and then takes cover. More rounds are fired while the patrol leader tries to work out where the enemy is. The outgoing rounds make this difficult.

The patrol leader eventually manages to stop all outgoing fire but by chance, some of these rounds have passed close to the enemy. The insurgents have taken cover then moved, unseen, to another firing point. With only a rough idea of where the insurgents were, and no idea where they are now, the patrol leader directs heavy fire at one or two likely firing points.

While the patrol continues to fire at the wrong firing point, the insurgents fire another volley. The process then repeats itself until one side takes a casualty or runs low on ammunition and withdraws.

It can be incredibly difficult to find the enemy in modern close combat, especially in the Afghan green zones, where men often fight in high crops bordered by tree-lined irrigation ditches and walled compounds. This has increased the reliance on speculative suppressive fire because it is so hard to spot clear targets. In an effort to win the firefight, there has been a tendency for patrols to shoot at everything: likely firing points, unlikely firing points, even things that are almost certainly not firing points.

Through no fault of their own, some units have erred on the side of caution and fired enormous amounts of ammunition in the general direction of the enemy. This usually has little immediate benefit. A patrol of ten men can fire off 3,000 rounds without the engagement having a positive outcome. In some cases this has caused civilian casualties and, by doing so, has strengthened the insurgency. This kind of response has its roots in peacetime training which wrongly emphasises a need to lay down a lot of fire in order to suppress. This is partly a hangover from Marshall's fire ratio theory and partly the result of misleading assessments like the one-metre rule.

A few units have managed to buck the trend and limited their use of fire to make sure that they can work out where the enemy are.

After the initial reaction to fire, these units often fire only at targets that are confirmed by the enemy's fire or movement, sometimes with the help of a direct radio link to airborne surveillance. Once the enemy are located, a heavy surge of fire is used to get the insurgents' heads down. But this is followed by a steady rate of as little as thirty rounds a minute: a figure much closer to Second World War experience than Marshall or the one-metre rule would suggest.

Sometimes speculative fire is unavoidable but, overall, these patrols fire about one quarter of the rounds that the less canny units use. They also tend to win more engagements. The three keys are said to be having the patience and resolve to let the enemy give away his position, not mistaking firing for suppressing, and not seeing suppression as an end in itself.

Perhaps the most telling aspect of this development is that it did not come from formal training based on the lessons of previous wars. Like most of tactical psychology, soldiers had to learn these tricks through bitter experience.

The limitations of small-arms suppression research reflect the confusion of close combat and the small amount of effort directed to understanding it. Over the years, I have come across perhaps a hundred soldiers and analysts who, while less obsessive than the Tank Colonel, have given serious consideration to understanding the 'who fights?' question. I have also met over forty artillery experts who, like Young American, had a genuine interest in indirect fire suppression. But in all that time I have met only six soldier-boffins who have really paid much attention to small-arms suppression.

It seems that the gap in collective understanding increases as we get closer to the sharp end of battle. This trend continues in the next chapter, where we look at aversion to killing.

FIVE

AVERSION TO KILLING

PROVOST SKOBELEV, RUSSIA, 1860S

Elsewhere in the war, your Particular Friend *continues with his oddities; to this end he is running the magazine, indeed the whole* District, *like he was one of your damned Austrians. His most distasteful effort to adhere to his Benefactor's whimsy is an investigation into the efficacy of Field Tribunal firing parties; into which he has ensnared all of the spare Young Gentlemen in the garrison along with every company and criminal to pass through its sphere.*

I have copies of the accounting document from this investigation; for your entertainment, one of these copies accompanies this letter. You will see from the document that Elements of his Command, and said passing companies, have been compelled to conduct sixty-one executions this season and each, whether military or criminal, has had the Sentence imposed by musket ball. To compound this travesty, *and in accordance with his Benefactor's Direction, thirty-four of the executions have, as per custom and warrant, been overseen by the Young Gentlemen or Regimental Officers of The Garrison, yet the remainder have been left to the supervision of whichever* common soldier *led the firing party on the morning of execution. These simple souls, often lacking even the meanest corporal to herd them, were given cursory instruction and then abandoned to complete their gruesome task ungoverned. Executions of both varieties were observed in secret from enfilade by a certain Adjutant of Your Acquaintance or, on a very few occasions, by one of his aides, who on all occasions ensured compliance with The Benefactor's Instructions.*

Further to these Instructions a selection of firing parties was also directed to fire on mannequin targets in circumstances which were, in every other aspect, identical to the executions performed. Much smoke was blown after dinners about the way that this expedient and the use of varied firing parties, from districts and regiments other than those of the Condemned, upheld the principles of natural philosophy. Similar self-congratulation was attached to the way each execution was performed before a freshly constructed pinewood butt to allow accurate accounting of hits and misses. Gentlefolk and even Nobility were prevented from viewing the executions after their enthusiasm was found to cause a disturbance to the proceedings.

The Outcome of his investigation is being trumpeted by Particular Friend as a Wonder *of the* Modern Age *and he is linking it with any and all Moral, Religious or Philosophical doctrines one could mention. Yet the accounting reflects truths, if truths they are, that any Educated Gentleman could have arrived at in a skirmish with the French or following a long hot bath. These apparent truths, as detailed in the accounting document and so meanly purchased, are: that firstly, the common soldier has above twice the accuracy when discharging his piece at a mannequin as he has when discharging at a condemned man; that secondly, the incidence of a misfired charge is considerably increased when attempting to discharge his piece at a condemned man rather than a mannequin; that thirdly, unless*

watched over and directed by a Gentleman or Officer of social stand-
ing, the chance of the common soldier hitting a man is more than
halved yet again, and there is again a further small increase in the
likelihood of a misfired charge.

Your Particular Friend is already composing letters and reports
proposing an increase in the number of Regimental Officers and,
without any hint of shame, changes to the conduct of executions.

Hidden in the middle of an enormous ranting letter about imagined slights and the latest fashions, this account comes from a
distant time and place, where officers were gentlemen amateurs
and soldiers were little better than slaves. But this flimsy piece
of gossip might represent the clearest hard facts we have on a
soldier's aversion to killing.

This aversion is often seen as the twin of fear and there has
been a long academic debate about the idea that men might dislike
projecting violence. Many men enjoy killing, at least at a distance
or when their blood is up, and even those with the lowest baseline
motivation accept that they are being paid to kill people. But for
over 90 per cent of soldiers, the closer they get to killing, the less
they like it.

Aversion to killing and fondness for killing are shaped by a
complex mess of forces. These include biological drives that are
shaped by experience, societies, tribes and leaders. Sometimes
empathy and morality halt a trigger finger; sometimes a soldier's
professional pride and boyish enthusiasm meet at the edge of
psychopathy to increase his so-called killer instinct.

Then there is an enduring assumption of reciprocity which
runs along the lines of: 'if I don't try to kill them, they won't try
to kill me'. Very often, once men get close to their enemy, they

find they have more in common with the bad guys than they do with their own commanders. Small battles, even whole wars, can develop a 'live and let live' character. At other times they spiral into barbarity.

All of these features collide with the common-sense balance of rewards and costs. They shift the 'is it worth it?' calculation away from personal physical cost (I could get shot) to the emotional cost of taking life (he'll be dead and I'll be screwed up about it). But armies are much happier for soldiers to talk about fear than the emotional cost of killing. Confronting fear is sold as a manly way to increase combat effectiveness; the moral debate surrounding aversion is messy and tactically irrelevant. For long periods, the whole aversion debate was delegated to a few army chaplains and university peace studies departments.

Fortunately, the only concerns in this book are how much the combat effectiveness of a soldier is degraded by aversion to killing, and how aversion fits in with fear and common sense. The basic facts can be distilled from some of the classics of military research.

*   *   *

Skobelev's letter mirrors studies of field firing that are far more reliable than Russian court gossip. Armies and historians have often looked at how many rounds were fired for each enemy soldier hit or killed. In many cases, this research into hit rates and kill rates has stretched back to examine battles and firing range tests involving muskets almost identical to those used by Russian execution parties.

The British military historian (and part-time brigadier) Richard Holmes had a hand in this research, and he would have been an ideal candidate for the Sennelager Club, were it not for his high rank and profile. I was present when Holmes gave a talk at one of the club's hidden-in-plain-sight meetings, in this instance during a symposium on infantry weapons. He opened with a description of an eighteenth-century Prussian study into the accuracy of musket fire.

In contrast to the unrealistic tests used by gunsmiths, where a weapon is given to a picked man or even clamped into a bench vice to keep it steady, this study used a group of ordinary soldiers firing in conditions much closer to those of a real musket battle. The men were arrayed in two tightly packed ranks, with the front rank kneeling, the rear rank standing and both ranks firing when ordered; they fired at a target which was roughly the size and shape of an infantry company. The firers therefore suffered many of the problems of combat shooting in the musket era; they were jostled by men next to them, flinched when weapons fired and had difficulty seeing through clouds of gunpowder smoke. At a range of 200 metres, 25 per cent of their shots hit the target; at seventy metres, 60 per cent hit.

Holmes combined this Prussian study with a collection of similar weapon tests to estimate an achievable hit rate of around 50 per cent for the average musket firefight. Yet he found that, at the Battle of Maida, 1806, where men fired muskets at ranges of between thirty and 100 metres, the hit rate was only just over 10 per cent. A series of similar musket battles have since been examined to show the hit rate in musket combat was typically between 10 and 20 per cent of what could be expected when firing at non-human targets.

This assessment has been extended to breech-loading rifles, where Holmes and others found a similar level of degradation. At

400 metres, a trained shot using the French Chassepot rifle would hit a man-sized target with two shots out of five. Yet, during the Battle of Wissembourg, 1870, firing at similar ranges against large clumps of men, the hit rate dropped to less than 1 per cent.

Later, at the First Battle of Ypres, 1914, the Grenadier Guards, firing bolt-action Lee-Enfield rifles, should have scored a hit rate considerably higher than 50 per cent. Yet the Guards, perhaps the best infantry in the world at the time, appeared to achieve a hit rate below 5 per cent. This figure, very close to those of other First World War battles where the enemy offered easy targets, meant that the average guardsman firing rapid aimed shots would still be likely to hit one enemy every thirty seconds. Such firepower devastated attacks by massed infantry formations.

In all of the battles outlined here, soldiers were firing at crowds of men moving in tight groups. Their targets were not crawling or popping up in twos and threes as they do today, but walking or jogging forward in large groups, often moving like agitated marching bands. In each of these battles there was no need to expend ammunition simply to suppress the enemy or to fire at places where the enemy might be hiding; there were more than enough visible people to shoot at. So why were soldiers hitting so few of the enemy? Before answering that question we need to have a quick look at one of the ways firepower changed tactics.

*   *   *

In the century between Maida and First Ypres, infantry firepower increased dramatically, but tactical developments had not been able to keep pace. Musket infantrymen did their firing and moving in a 'close order' formation, with two, three or four ranks standing as near to each other as is possible without overly hampering each man's ability to operate his weapon. They needed to use close order to mass their firepower, to allow their commanders to control the battle and to present a hedge of bayonets to ward off enemy cavalry. They were able to get away with offering such a large target because enemy fire, like their own, was so ineffective.

Armies had, for the most part, been fighting in close order for millennia. The bolt-action rifle, with considerable help from artillery and machine guns, changed everything. By 1914, standing close together had become a very unhealthy pastime. With a bolt-action rifle able to fire ten times faster and five times further than a musket, there was no longer a need to stand close together to mass fire. The hedge of bayonets was no longer required because firepower had rendered the cavalry threat almost irrelevant.

Gradually, units began to fight dispersed, in some form of open order formation. Rather than rubbing shoulders, men started to stand three, four or five metres apart, and to hide behind things or lie down once bullets started flying. Loss of control became a problem, with officers no longer able to see and direct all of their men, but this was eventually accepted to be a small price to pay for survival. Yet for that whole period where men were firing at large groups of people, they were surprisingly bad at hitting them. Why?

Armies have largely ignored the embarrassing facts related to aversion, but some morally minded analysts have taken great interest, often misreading some of the basic facts to over-inflate the aversion effect. The 'ignore aversion' and 'pro-aversion' camps have never had a real argument because the ignorers never bothered to state their case. So our assessment needs to start by looking at the pro-aversion interpretation.

A common morally minded assessment holds that almost all of the degradation between the firing range and the battlefield was due to aversion to killing. It was argued that in the days when soldiers fought in close order, in full view of their comrades and leaders, they could not simply avoid firing like Marshall's Saké Night soldiers. They had to be more creative to avoid killing. They appear to have used a variety of tricks to do so.

In the most famous and most contentious example, 24,000 loaded but unfired weapons were found lying on the field after the Battle of Gettysburg, 1863. Eighteen thousand weapons carried two or more loads in the barrel, and many carried over a dozen unfired rounds. It would appear that soldiers were loading and reloading their weapons, cramming powder and shot down the barrels but only pretending to fire. Yet eyewitness reports indicate that most men fired but fired high, low or wide. The pro-aversion argument holds that these non-firers and wide firers must have overcome their fear and, with the boss watching over them, the balance of common sense promoted firing; or at least pretending to fire. So, by a process of elimination, it was suggested that almost all the degradation must be due to aversion.

By comparing firing range and combat, some assessments have proposed that aversion to killing reduces combat effectiveness by as much as 80 per cent. This would pretty much account for all of the combat degradation we see when comparing exercises with real battles. Any remainder could be easily accounted for by the 10 per cent fear wobble, leaving no room for common sense to have any effect.

A few researchers have used creative accounting to posit an even larger aversion effect. For example, ammunition expenditure for a whole campaign has been used to suggest that between

500 and 3,000 rounds were needed to kill a man in the musket era. These dubious figures fail to account for major events, such as ammunition stores exploding or being captured, and the mass of minor incidents, like soldiers being killed or captured along with their ammunition. Unfortunately, despite some wishful thinking, aversion to killing cannot account for anything like this level of degradation.

The biggest flaw in the pro-aversion argument comes from the way it often confuses hit rates with kill rates. Firing-range tests give hit rates, because they count holes in targets; most war records only give kill rates, because they count the dead instead of the number of holes. In any battle, there are many men who are hit but not killed and many others who are killed but hit several times. Yet some sources brush over this fact.

Musket battles highlight another limitation of the pro-aversion argument. Friction is a musket-era concept developed by Carl von Clausewitz to describe the aggregate effect of all those unpredictable errors and minor disasters that distinguish real war from war on paper. For a musket soldier, this aggregate can be broken into its constituent parts. In hand with psychological effects like aversion come physical and physiological frictions; the jostling, flinching and smoke of that Prussian accuracy study will grind down a soldier's performance, but so will dozens of extra factors like fatigue, cold or damp gunpowder. The stack of little frictions made it particularly difficult to shoot straight when standing or kneeling in a crowd full of small explosions.

Weapon characteristics greatly increased the effect of the fear wobble for musket battles. The matchlock musket, used in the Thirty Years' War and English Civil War, was nearly as dangerous for the firer as the target. Heavy and cumbersome, it needed an

elaborate drill to load and fire. The weapon fired when a glowing taper was thrust into an open pan of gunpowder close to the
firer's face. Many soldiers chose to fire with their eyes closed. All
around the firer were other men with glowing tapers and bags full
of gunpowder: a health and safety nightmare that increased the
level of anxiety considerably.

Later musket designs were far less risky to the firer and his
comrades but still required the soldier to engage in a convoluted procedure that was almost certain to unravel under
pressure. Sometimes men forgot one of the more fiddly steps in
the process. Sometimes they accidentally shot their friends.

Napoleon launched one of the earliest examples of military
operational research to find out why thousands of his soldiers
suffered minor injuries from being shot at very close range.
There was concern that soldiers were shooting themselves in the
hand or the arm in an attempt to avoid combat, but the investigation found that nearly all cases were due to men in the rear
ranks accidentally shooting their comrades in the front ranks.
It has since been estimated that it would take only six hours of
combat shooting in close order for half a Napoleonic unit to be
killed or injured by its own fire. This may be an exaggeration
but it is clear that combat frictions combined to make the fear
wobble have a much greater effect than the 10 per cent seen
in modern war. This appears to have had as much of an effect
as aversion.

Yet, when the frictions and biased calculations have been
stripped away, there is still a large drop in kill rates that can only
be explained by people not being keen on killing each other. This
is reflected in the way that weapon improvements have influenced
kill rates.

If the effectiveness of fire was only down to weapon characteristics, every technological advance would be matched with an
increase in the kill rate. But there is a variety of Parkinson's Law
in operation here. Rather than work expanding to fill the time
available, expectations rise to meet weapon improvements. Each
improvement in ease of use or engagement range is countered by
soldiers firing more quickly at more distant targets; the gun gets
better so the man fires at harder targets. Meanwhile, as we have
already seen, weapon improvements also encourage the enemy to
make better use of camouflage, cover and dispersal. People adapt.
Sometimes it takes an initial bloodbath or two but, when weapons
improve, soldiers improve their tactics too.

When kill rates are compared across history, it is clear that a
musket was actually more likely to hit a crowd of redcoats at thirty
metres than an assault rifle is to hit a camouflaged man crawling
at 100 metres. That is most of the reason why battles in Korea,
Vietnam and the Falkland Islands give us kill rates far lower than
those from musket wars.

There are some very tenuous kill rate figures that need to be
treated with caution: for the Vietnam War, claims swing from
3,000 to 50,000 rounds per kill. More recently, US forces were
reported to have fired a quarter of a million rounds for each insurgent killed in Afghanistan. These loose figures hide ammunition
spent in training and weapon testing, rounds lost or stolen, and
rounds given to allies or thrown out due to faults. But the number
of rounds fired to kill a man is still enormous.

The highest kill rate reported for a unit in Afghanistan is far
lower than the average for a musket battle. This unit fired nearly
400,000 small-arms rounds in anger and killed about 200 insurgents. Compared to later Afghan engagements, more of the dead

were untrained men who tried attacking over open ground. Even so, most of the insurgent deaths were from shelling and bombing, or from the 30mm chain gun on the Apache attack helicopter.

It is always tricky finding honest figures for recent wars, but a junior staff officer used his spare time in Kabul to calculate the current kill rate. He found that, by using only firing in contact and subtracting a reasonable amount for speculative fire, the average is still near to 3,000 rounds per kill.

*   *   *

If we looked only at kill rates, it might appear that soldiers with muskets were maybe twenty times better at killing than men with modern weapons. Modern counter-pressures, like range and dispersal, play a part and there are a few pressures peculiar to current wars, but there is still a big chunk of aversion involved.

Like the musket men who fired with their eyes closed, many modern soldiers are obeying the letter but not the spirit of the law. As one Helmand veteran put it: 'We're not firing *at* them, we're firing *towards* them. There's a difference.'

The modern classic is spray-and-pray, where a weapon is fired on full automatic, around cover and without observation. Then there is hose-and-pose, where men take turns to pop out of cover and fire whole belts of ammunition in the general direction of the enemy. The soldier then nips back into cover to get a pat on the back from his buddies. Drug-addled Senegalese irregulars are not the only men tempted by this kind of show; the internet is full of videos of professional soldiers whooping and cheering when a man breaks cover to fire a missile or machine gun without much attempt at aiming the weapon. These represent the modern tip of an iceberg of firing but not quite fighting.

Information technology has let us see more common and subtle variations. I helped an Australian team who found that about half of soldiers are failing to fire all the way around or all the way over a piece of cover. Helmet camera and surveillance videos show how these men look like they are shooting to kill but are frequently aligned ten or twenty degrees off the bearing to the target. They are still exposing themselves to fire, so it is not so much fear of being hit or even a common-sense assessment of personal survival that is to blame; but they are firing towards the enemy rather than at them. The obvious explanation for this is that these slight but significant deviations also result from aversion to killing. But are any of these assessments valid?

The surprising conclusion to the aversion argument came from a group of war college students who, almost by accident, measured the mismatch between potential and actual lethality. Their study started life as an accounting exercise in cost-benefit analysis. It was also based on the 'ignore aversion' assumption that the physical characteristics of a firefight would directly translate to the number of casualties, with easier targets leading to a predictable increase in kill rates. The findings undermined this assumption.

The group examined a collection of battles where, like First Ypres, the attacking force employed tactics unsuited to the weapons used by the defenders. These 'human wave' battles were then compared with others where tactics and weapons were more evenly balanced. So, in effect, this compared firefights where frictions, fear and common sense stayed the same but the enemy were easier or harder to kill. The actual increase in the kill rate was much more modest than the physical characteristics of the battle dictated.

In the end both the pro-aversion and ignore aversion camps were proved wrong. Soldiers are not killing machines and they are not angels in uniform, but there is a glass ceiling to killing. When all the statistics have been picked apart and the frictions stripped away, the result is a single key number. Soldiers are three times less likely to at shoot a man than they are a target.

SIX

BUT KILLING ANYWAY

CORPORAL RABUKA, AFGHANISTAN, 2007

It doesn't look like it from the video but I'm engaging at 200 metres here. That group along the bund line there are trying to snurgle up behind our platoon house while their mates are blasting away at the front gate. That's a pretty long burst I'm firing because they're close and a good target. I think two go down and the rest bomb-burst.

Corporal Rabuka is talking over a video taken from a static camera that was mounted behind him while he was firing at insurgents from the roof of a building. In the video he is firing a belt-fed 7.62mm General Purpose Machine Gun (GPMG or Gympy). The GPMG is resting on the sangar wall and kicking up dust as it fires. On Rabuka's left is another man who is armed with a 7.62mm L96 sniper rifle.

The 'bund line' at 200 metres is a scrub-lined bank of earth running from right to left. Beyond the bund line are a few mud-brick farm compounds linked by more irrigation ditches and scrubby foliage bordering small grey-brown fields. The ground between the bund line and the camera looks to be a garbage dump littered with scrub and piles of rubble.

Five men can be made out crawling from right to left over the track as it crosses the bund line. As Corporal Rabuka fires, one of the men stops moving and another falls back into the ditch to the right; the others jump up and dash to the left. Other men can now be seen breaking cover along the bund line. A crack of incoming fire can just be made out as the GPMG falls silent.

Now I'm back to short bursts trying to rip them up as they head for cover. You can just make out two of them scooting back toward the compound on the right. One goes down.

That's Yank on my left taking the odd shot with the L96 but he's mainly spotting for me. A few more bursts at the bunch on the left. Missed but it helps them on their way.

Now there's no targets. Hey fuckin' presto they've all dropped into cover, so Yank keeps an eye out while I get a new belt in the Gympy. That cracking is incoming and ... wait for it ... there! The Yank catches a spent round on the lip of his helmet. Look how he sits down like he's got to take an urgent dump – disco legs – ha! I check him out but he's OK and just needs a breather to get the colour back in his cheeks. The soft twat scared me for second there.

I'm back up firing at likely positions. No targets visible, not much incoming. Now I'm using a gash rifle scope to check beyond the bund line and off to the far right.

Fast forward through this bit. The Yank gets back to spotting and we talk a bit. Colours Bry comes to check on us and I fire a few short bursts for no real reason.

Now we're back to it. Another bunch looks to be crawling up the bund line. You can just make out the odd head and arse sticking up.

Maybe it's the first bunch again. I wait while they get to that big bush there. They've got cover from view but no cover from fire.

Yank takes the first shot. They all jump up and try to dash for it again. Burst, burst, burst. Six or seven of 'em. One goes down there see. And another. I think The Yank gets one. Now they're back in the trees. Long burst. Stoppage.

Now it's just Yank firing while I sort the stoppage. No joy. The Gympy's a sturdy weapon but ours have had a lot of hammer. I think the round extractor snapped off or something but I haven't got time to sort that out. Switch to my rifle because they're getting pretty close.

If we could've panned left you'd see a group of them pepper-potting, using fire-and-movement. One's got the RPG and a bunch of rounds in a sack on his back. You can see two lads firing from cover in the foreground, the rest are out of the picture. That's good drills they're using. Three or four rounds then change position. We're both doing aimed shots. The Yank is shouting up some help but Fabio and the boys are on it already. See that one go down? That's Fabio got him.

More incoming, more outgoing. This goes on for a few minutes. I get a stoppage on the rifle. And another. Usual stuff, soon sorted. Back to aimed shots. Not Bisley stuff but you get what I mean. Now that Fabio's free to help out and the attack has pretty much culminated, the fuckers have shot their load and now they've got to clean up the mess.

Now they're pulling sticks. Still pepper-potting you see. Coming back into the picture now as they withdraw. Another down. Might have been me but I'm doing bursts so could've been anybody. Now those last two have gone firm on the bund line. They stay there for a good while so you can fast forward again while we wait for the mortar rounds coming in on them. We might get them, we might not, but we haven't got rounds to waste so that's it for the day.

All told there's probably twenty of them dead or hurt out there and twenty or more maybe laying low waiting for night. The others have turned back into farmers and in half an hour they'll be walking round doing chores as if butter wouldn't melt.

*   *   *

The battle for Corporal Rabuka's platoon house has been taken apart in some detail because, by chance, a field analyst was stuck there for the week. The insurgent plan appeared to be to use the frontal assault to draw defenders towards the main entrance, while the infiltration group moved in from the rear to cause casualties at close range with rocket-propelled grenades, hand grenades or pipe bombs. Rabuka, Yank and their Gympy foiled that part of the plan.

The insurgents may have been trying to break in and overwhelm the defenders but the back wall of the compound was very high and thick, so they would have had a tough job doing that. Either way, they took a lot of casualties. No one in the platoon house was killed or injured that day.

Corporal Rabuka is in here to bring a bit of balance back to the book and to allow a quick stock-take. Previous chapters may have given the impression that hardly anybody fights. Clearly, lots of people do fight, but the aim of tactical psychology is to make the enemy stop. There is a chance that this focus on not fighting could give the wrong impression.

Like many soldiers, Corporal Rabuka did not revel in killing, he did not brag about it and, unless he was at work, he did not talk about it. But he did do it. He hit maybe eight insurgents and half of them would have been dead by nightfall. Most of the time, most soldiers will fire their weapons when they have something like a valid target. Whether professionals like Rabuka or semi-pros like the men attacking his platoon, many take pride in shooting to kill.

Despite the effects of fear, common sense and aversion, it is best not to get sucked into the trap of thinking that men are overly inclined to not fight. Generations of soldiers and researchers, biased by Marshall's fire ratios, have made this mistake and it is difficult to shake off the idea once it gets into your head.

* * *

The basic motives underpinning a soldier's 'is it worth it?' calculation are still present in Afghanistan but they have been twisted by the peculiarities of the war. There are tactical psychology lessons in Afghanistan, but we must accept that, when compared to that facing the soldiers in most wars, the threat to Corporal Rabuka was quite low.

The platoon had superior firepower and protection when compared to their opposition. They also had more effective weapons and much more body armour and ammunition than soldiers in previous wars.

This trend has accelerated in the last few years, with more ballistic plates being added to body armour and heavier weapons being issued to small units. The amount of armour men wear has increased static protection by an incredible amount. A Falklands veteran wore a helmet but no body armour; in addition to his helmet, a coalition soldier in Afghanistan will often fight wearing sixteen kilos of armour. The insurgents wear none.

The average platoon now carries so many machine guns, grenade launchers and bunker-busters (anti-tank missiles used to shoot people in buildings and trenches) that, at 200 metres, they can project nearly twice the violence of a platoon in the Falklands or Vietnam, and maybe seven times that of a platoon in 1914. In addition, they have indirect fire support undreamt of by their predecessors. Even in small skirmishes, a platoon can usually call up support from fast jets, attack helicopters or artillery, all of which can have exceptional suppressive power and killing power when handled correctly. In contrast, most insurgents have tired old Soviet infantry weapons and ramshackle indirect fire support; in toe-to-toe fights against coalition troops they are consistently overmatched.

This is not to say that the modern Western soldier is somehow softer than his father, grandfather or the insurgents. But this level of firepower and protection shifts a man's perception of rewards and costs, and changes the way he fights.

In an engagement where the odds are in the soldier's favour and the cost of defeat is severe, almost everyone will fire. (One vein of black humour in Corporal Rabuka's platoon centred on how embarrassing it would be to be captured then castrated and beheaded on video. 'Hey Rab, what's your mam going to say when she sees your nuts in your mouth on YouTube?') It might still be tricky getting men to assault a strong enemy position but they will certainly fire plenty of rounds when they have to.

In many ways the current Afghan war is an aberration. Like the Guards at First Ypres, Corporal Rabuka found himself fighting at a point where one side's tactics had not caught up with the other side's weaponry. Despite this, the behaviour of both sides at the platoon house obeyed what we know of the rules for fear, common sense and aversion.

Inside the platoon house, there was little suppression, and common sense helped outweigh aversion to killing and the fear of being hit with the fear of what would happen if the insurgents breached the compound. There were two men who admitted to not pulling their weight but there was nobody rendered insensible by incoming fire. Occasionally and briefly, men were pinned by small-arms fire, but in this fight, fear and common sense turned against aversion to killing.

Outside the platoon house, the insurgents appeared to be following the script proposed by Wigram and Marshall. When they came under fire, most of them took cover and stayed there, many did not appear to be firing and only a few tried to push home the assault. A curious feature, not covered by the basics we have looked at so far, is that just as the insurgents got close enough to use their explosives effectively, their attack stalled and they withdrew.

*   *   *

This chapter is also a place to examine the search for that Holy Grail of tactical psychology. Formal research missed a trick at the end of the Second World War, with the few people examining battle morale sucked into the heroes-and-zeroes debate. Gradually, as memories of the last big war faded, veteran soldiers and experienced researchers were replaced by new blood; formal understanding of tactical psychology dissolved or mutated.

While small groups like the Sennelager Club tried to fill the gap, they had difficulty piecing together the flotsam of facts. The

Sennelager Club mutated too. The original members set themselves on that quest to understand war and improve tactics. In the early years they worked in the background to counter the trend towards complicated weapons and ill-conceived doctrine. Some of them encouraged war geeks like me to look at the things that really mattered. Others, like the Tank Colonel, beavered away in their spare time.

But as the founder members retired or drifted into the military mainstream, the club's priorities changed and the original focus and energy were lost. Newer members lacked the fervour of the founders and the club became too cliquey and too complacent. Somewhere between Desert Storm and the War on Terror, the Sennelager Club turned into a quirky international cocktail party. It helped the careers of its members and hangers-on but it did little of real value.

The Sennelager Club had managed to pin down the basics we have seen in the last few chapters: the 'big three' motives of fear, common sense and aversion to killing. They even helped to put numbers to these effects which will prove useful later. But the club failed to put real meat on these bones. As far as fighting soldiers were concerned, the Sennelager Club was still talking about abstractions and had not shown the way to turn these into action.

For a while, the Sennelager Club became a barrier to understanding. Eventually a new group of soldiers and scientists emerged to find a way around this. The first thing they did was to combine everything they could from the Sennelager Club's archives and to dole out unpaid jobs to people. Other people dealt with history, tactics and weapons; I got the job of pulling together the psychology.

When I started to do this, the numbers did not seem to stack up. The difference between exercises and real war was plain enough, with a unit, on average, fighting at one-sixth of its peacetime effectiveness. But then, by my reckoning, effectiveness should be halved by suppression, two-thirds should be knocked off by aversion to killing and then another 10 per cent removed for the fear wobble. If a further chunk was removed for the frictions of combat, there would be nothing left: a unit would be not one-sixth effective but completely ineffective.

I sulked for a while before ringing round all the Old Boys and the boffins. The soldiers told me to get a grip and the scientists told me my sums were bad. The effects do not all work at the same time and they do not simply subtract from the whole. In a real small-arms firefight, aversion only comes into play at those times when a man is not suppressed by enemy fire. The fear wobble runs in the background but again only comes in when a man is actually moving or firing. I had also failed to account for common sense in exercises. The 'is it worth it?' calculation is very different when a man is not really risking his life, but common sense still has a place; even in an exercise, a soldier still wants to win and he will still try to avoid getting shot.

The Tank Colonel had also been doing some sulking, but now he was bouncing back. He started by giving me some sound advice: 'What you need to do is spend less time with analysts and staff officers. Get out there and talk to real soldiers who have tasted war.' I did as I was told.

Eventually, with a lot of help from friends, combat veterans showed me that, in practice, the 'big three' form a bridge between baseline motivation and action. This does not work through some abstract voodoo; it is shaped by what happens on the ground and in a soldier's head. To understand how the basic forces change the outcome of war, we need to sink a little deeper into the world of brains and bullets.

SEVEN

FREEZING, FLEEING AND FIGHTING

MASTER SERGEANT JOHANSSON, PARACHUTE TRAINING, 1994

Maybe I sound dumb saying this but I never really got the idea of how fighting worked until I was sent parachuting. I've always been a fighter, don't you doubt it, and I'm as good with my fists or a bottle as I am with a rifle. Kuwait backed this up. I'd never been prissy of killing or over-worried about being killed and I never got fazed by pressure under fire. That is until somebody had the fine idea of sending us off with a gang of Brits and making us jump out of airplanes.

After Desert Storm a lot of the guys got out and tried their luck in the real world but I stayed in; after all, my bayonet skills 'did not readily translate to a civilian working environment'. A while after that a few of us got sent on an exchange visit to England to do their parachuting course at Brize Norton near Oxford. Unlike most of the guys I'd never done a military jump and I must admit that I had a few 'issues' before we even left the ground. I had no problem with heights or nothing but those Royal Air Force instructors kept on listing all the things that could break your bones. 'Knowledge Dispels Fear' my fat behind; those sadistic RAF rats just liked to see us 'Yankee Pongoes' squirm.

I should maybe point out that this is on no account similar to a civilian jump where you pop out into empty sky for a bit of a buzz, pull a cord, then touch the ground all graceful and standing-up-like. No way. Dozens of 'blokes' sweating adrenaline and worse are all squeezed into the back of the C130 like tinned anchovies and you're all standing up for what seems like an age holding onto a bit of a strap with 100 pounds of doggy bag tied on your leg. Then the lights change and they're firing guys out of the two side doors at every half-second.

Once you're out, the prop wash shoots you off sideways and you're in a sky full of guys counting and kicking out twists, letting go of containers and trying to work out which way the wind's blowing them. You can collide with other people, get the air stolen from your chute by somebody or have a dozen other crappy things happen between the door and the ground.

If none of these things happen then eight seconds after you leave the plane you hit the ground real hard, specially hard if you're my size, and you roll around on the floor wondering what freakin' day it is. There's a lot to do on the way out and down, not an awful lot of time to do it in and your head's full of what to do if something bad happens.

The course went on for near on a month but the English weather meant we spent a lot of time sitting around. We'd get up in the morning all crappin' ourselves about that day's jumps then be relieved but pissed when we found out we couldn't jump. In the meantime they could think of nothing better to do than tell us again and again about twists and air steals and hooked-up parachutists and all that bad stuff.

After about a week of this, things started to prey on my mind a little. From what I saw, the drop zone at Weston is the biggest flattest bit of field in the whole of England but I slowly got persuaded that I'd land in a tree or a lake or some spiky piece of farm machinery. And, in my head at least, that was only in the unlikely event of me not being battered to death against the side of the plane when my chute stayed tied to the airframe. As time went by I was sleeping less and smoking more.

Then the weather turned and we did a whole load of jumps in a few days. It takes it out of you doing a lot of jumps so we were all a bit frayed by the end of it. I was still worried but I kept the lid on by telling myself it wasn't as if we were being shot at while we jumped, now that would take real balls, and the chances of anything bad were real slim. I wasn't fully convinced by this logic but I kept on saying it anyway.

For some reason I was always jumping out of the starboard side of the plane and I was always either first out the door or right down inside the plane at the back of the stick. This meant that I either got a butt-clenching look at the ground and the wind in the long wait before we jumped or I had that shuffle-step tension builder as the other guys jumped and the door got closer. By the time we got to what they said was the qualifying jump I was stressed but confident. The combination of it being a man-test and a kind of school exam seemed to make it worse but the clincher was down to me being on the port side of the plane for the first time and me being last man out the door.

We got to the 'Green on – GO!' bit OK, but my arms felt all the wrong way around what with being used to the other side of the plane. This and the fear magnet they keep at the back of the stick allowed me to open the gap between me and the man in front and so I got to the door all confused, tried to switch my hands round to starboard style. For some reason I just couldn't stop myself from swapping and un-swapping my grip; and then I just stalled and dug my hooves into the floor of the plane.

For a second or two, I was frozen in a little world of confusion and panic and if it had just been up to me I'd have thrown in the towel there and then. I was starting to back away like a steer from a slaughterhouse ramp. At the same time I was planning all my excuses for *failing the course: something in my eye, problem with my strop, who wants your pansy-ass wings anyway.*

That's when those RAF guys showed how they earn their pay: somehow one or two of them managed to get a hold of me and ju-jitsu me out of that door. Next I know I'm out into the sky two seconds after everyone else and looking like a freakin' starfish. I hit the ground with all my parts intact and it was over.

I'm grateful to those RAF guys, they might be haughty little suckers but they're kind-hearted. If they hadn't thrown me out of that plane the shame would have unmanned me. I'd have turned to those excuses I'd been practicing and turned into one of those rat-faced little men who talks tough and beats on his wife. They saved me from that shame and though we all had a laugh at my expense over a pint or three that night, nothing was said to the folks in charge and I got my wings.

Well, when we got back home I knew something had changed. For the first time I understood all those men that get overwhelmed in a fight. Now I knew what losing was about I just was not happy about facing it again. The first thing I had to do was avoid parachuting so a word with the XO got me out of that and I had a weapons instructor job for a while. But my heart wasn't in infantry work anymore, and pretending would have been wronger than hell so as soon as I got my pension straight I got myself out.

Master Sergeant Johansson is a big cranky bear of man and, in his parachuting days, his 240-odd pounds of mostly muscle must have hit the ground with considerable force. He likes to keep strangers at a distance, with an ingrained aggressive suspicion of civilians, airmen, sailors and anybody from outside a narrow slice of North America. His most often recited 'fact' is that many warrior tribes use the same word for stranger and enemy. But, once someone can prove they are not an oxygen thief, the bear stops being cranky and becomes, not quite cuddly, but certainly far less troublesome.

I worked with Johansson at the British army training centre in Alberta (a gigantic square of prairie rented off the Canadians, allegedly in exchange for second-hand submarines). Johansson was part of a team who were building a new training simulator and I was there to assess whether it worked or not. It took nearly two weeks for him to accept me but I must have done something right eventually, because suddenly he took off his angry mask and started cracking jokes.

One of the things that helped bridge the gap between us was that we both got our jobs by mistake. Johansson's employers thought his war record would make him a good people manager; I got my job because a Sennelager Club member wanted a geek he could trust. A few months later, Johansson hit a colleague 'fairly gently' and had to find another job; I upset my Sennelager Club boss because I did not endorse his preferred answer: 'Yes, I know you're merely presenting the facts; they're just not the facts we want to hear right now, thank you very much.' I got no Christmas card from him that year but we eventually patched things up.

At the end of the Alberta job, a gang of us had a night out in Medicine Hat, the nearest town to the base, which at that time was filled with bars that catered to the needs of ranchers, gas riggers and squaddies. It was in one of these that, with a few beers inside him and a pop-country cowboy singing in the background, Johansson told us his parachuting story.

There has been an argument for over seventy years about whether military parachuting has passed its sell-by date. Since the Second World War, parachuting has only proved effective for small raids and rescue missions, so most armies no longer maintain large jump-ready units. The hidden benefit of military parachuting is that the training gives soldiers a rare taste of the stress and confusion they will experience in battle; it also helps commanders assess which men can cope best under pressure.

The logic is that if a man cannot jump out of a plane when the chance of injury is about 300 to one, he will not jump into a battle where the chance is twenty to one. Likewise, if stress makes a man forget parachuting drills, it will probably make him forget fighting drills. About a quarter of paratrooper recruits are rejected because they cannot perform under stress. But military jumps also give a man a chance to weigh himself up, so about one-in-ten of those who get through the training do something like Johansson, and find a way to avoid jumping in future.

Johansson was convinced that he froze in the back of the C130 due to the same mechanism he had seen crippling other men in combat. He also believed that once this had infected him, it would be certain to reactivate in battle. He took too much pride in his fighting ability to risk that happening. It seems that the special circumstance of being a big man jumping through a small hole in the side of an aircraft made him realise something he had managed to overlook in battle.

*   *   *

Along with muttering about morale or willpower, armies have occasionally been fond of the 'fight or flight' response. The basic idea – that people react to combat in a similar way to animals – is fairly sound, but even animal combat involves more than a simple yes/no response. Biologists and military analysts are now fairly certain that freezing is a more common response than either fighting or fleeing.

But doing nothing can be a complicated business. The first part of freezing is the brain's automatic response to a sudden or threatening event. This has been called a cognitive blink because, for a second or so, the brain focuses only on the threat and stops processing other information. The cognitive blink is a kind of automatic 'stop, look and listen', which has evolved because it has high survival value in natural threat situations. It makes best use of limited brainpower and usually allows people to make a better decision more quickly. But, like a rabbit caught in headlights, it can have fatal consequences in unnatural situations.

Any behaviour has its own gravity: like getting children to bed or kicking drinkers out of a bar, considerable effort is needed to move people from one type of activity to another. It is the same with freezing: once a man is doing nothing, he is that bit more likely to carry on doing nothing. In armed combat, new threatening events can occur in quick succession, so the cognitive blinks can overlap and start to work with the other types of freezing.

Freezing has been linked to studies of prey animals, many of which, like possums, benefit from playing dead because most predators only attack live prey. More simply, keeping still helps prey animals to avoid detection. There are echoes of both these motives in combat accounts but the link can soon be stretched too thin. Our closest animal relatives rarely play possum and most soldiers have been encouraged to see themselves more as predator than prey. So, while there may well be some biological prey programme telling soldiers to 'sit very still', it has been very difficult to pin down.

Researchers have had more luck with a socially determined

aspect of freezing which plays a major role in conflict between animals of the same species. This appears to have a biological basis but, for people, at least, it is heavily reinforced by social hierarchies, corporal punishment and playground fights. Through childhood and adolescence, people learn that passivity is a reasonably effective response to the violence initiated by others: not least because the fight is usually started by someone who knows they will win whatever our response.

People crouch or bow their heads to make a smaller target and put their hands to their heads to ward off blows, but these actions also serve to communicate submission to the attacker. The 'hands up' action of surrendering is an extension of this and the so-called defensive wounds that are popular in television crime shows are often due to victims signalling submission.

The submissive side of freezing is most relevant when aggression has been triggered to assert dominance or seize resources. In same-species fights, there is usually a point where doing nothing is the option with the best survival value for both parties. Most of the time, when one man or animal admits defeat, the other stops beating him. The beating might not stop straight away but natural same-species fights are rarely lethal. It is usually far more useful for the winner to let the loser live on to become his bitch.

A lot of armed combat fits the theme of controlling resources through dominance and submission. Although a fair amount of killing is usually involved, deliberate operations are almost always designed to do something other than kill. Raids are often designed to seize intelligence, fighting patrols aim to dominate ground and deliberate attacks usually try to grab key terrain. A passive response to this kind of aggression is not unreasonable for individual soldiers on the receiving end, with high survival value for a soldier, even if it means his unit loses the battle.

These lead into the common-sense aspect of Marshall's 'is it worth it?' calculation, where sitting very still is clearly the rational choice. Many soldiers have reported firefights where they were caught in a ditch or behind a wall and able to calculate, very roughly, that trying to return fire meant maybe a one-in-ten chance of being shot in the face. These men rationally chose to freeze, but they were frozen all the same.

After this, there is a half-deliberate 'sleep of fear', as seen in some Argentine conscripts in the Falklands. This builds through different types of clinical response until it reaches a catatonic stupor, where the sufferer is completely unresponsive and either rag-doll limp or completely rigid.

The layers of paralysis are partly due to physiological powering-down following, and sometimes during, a period of high stress. This is the thing that makes a unit most vulnerable just after a successful attack; this is a favourite fact of platoon sergeants and is the body's attempt to regain control of an over-stretched system. But this can develop into a holding pattern where brain and muscle get locked into a feedback loop. One part of your nervous system is saying 'run' and another part is saying 'nowhere to run to'. When this happens the body can shut down all alternative responses, even when these alternatives have greater survival value than freezing.

Overall, freezing can be seen as having five layers: an instinctive layer, where it is just that automatic cognitive blink response; a reaction layer, where things pile on too quickly for us to respond any other way; a habitual layer shaped by previous experience; a sensible layer of deliberate choice; and a clinical layer where a man is hammered into paralysis. There is no science behind this list, and it would be easy to add different layers or change the labels, but these five seem to be the best fit to soldiers' accounts of freezing.

When the layers are combined, they help explain some instances where common sense has failed to work. A few minutes after an artillery barrage lifts, common sense usually causes defenders to leave their artillery-proof bunkers and prepare to defend against infantry assault. But this does not always happen. The clearest example comes from Japanese forces in the Second World War, who got to be very good at building bunkers but tended to stay in them long after the threat had changed.

In Burma and the Pacific, attacking Allied forces repeatedly walked over unoccupied but reasonably sound Japanese trenches because the men who should have been in them were still in bunkers hours after the bombardment lifted. Following days of pounding from air, artillery and naval gunfire, most of the defenders were unable to apply common sense and move to fortifications more suitable to repelling an assault. They stayed in shelters where they could offer little resistance and were easily killed with flame-throwers and explosives.

This has often been ascribed to Japanese fanaticism, as if the desire to kill for the Emperor was so intense that men sat patiently in bunkers waiting to be burned alive. The few survivors tell a different story; a story where the layers of freezing and the unique hierarchy and bullying of wartime Japan played a key role. There were other factors involved which have echoes in Afghanistan today, but for now the important thing is the way the different layers of freezing work together.

Imagine a man in a ditch and under small-arms fire. The first bullet to crack the air above his head causes that instinctive cognitive blink. A few more bullets make it common sense to sit tight for a while. Just as he works his way out of this and decides to put his head above the parapet, another round cracks past and he is back to instinctive freezing. More bullets, an explosion and some screaming start to overwhelm him and now his inactivity has been reinforced: the bullets and explosions have not hurt him because he sat tight. If he is really unlucky, a soldier will tip into a clinical response and he will probably be stuck there until someone captures or kills him.

The layers of freezing make it the most natural response to the unnatural situation of intense armed combat. Freezing is not always the most sensible response, but it is not as simple as just being scared and it is not something that can easily be trained out of a soldier. But freezing has some stiff competition from fleeing and fighting.

*   *   *

When sitting tight looks like a bad idea, then legging it is usually the next best thing. So, if a threat does not push someone through the layers of freezing, that initial moment of stop, look and listen almost always leads to immediate consideration of the flight option. In a fight between animals of the same species, fleeing gives the loser roughly the same chance of survival as freezing. When the fight is between different species, fleeing is usually by far the best option.

Running away is especially useful if all the signs point to a bad thing on one hand and a closing escape route on the other. This is like the situation where an elevator door starts to close and people on the outside suddenly rush towards it. Some fights work this way too: the realisation that this might be your last chance to get away seems to force a stronger flight response. It has been estimated that this closing door might account for half of the psychological bonus in encirclement battles, with resistance crumbling much more rapidly when it looks like a unit is about to be surrounded. From the Zulu buffalo horns to the Falaise Pocket and the Basra Road, that promise of a last chance to escape can turn withdrawal into rout.

Just like freezing, fleeing gets much of its attraction from the way it works in other situations. Whether the threat is an angry bull or a gang from a different school, running has almost certainly worked in the past, and people tend to apply learned rules to other situations.

As with freezing, there are layers of processing which start by whispering 'take a step back' and eventually shout 'run!' so loud that no other message can get through. Fleeing has the same root as freezing and it starts with that cognitive blink. If things still look bad after the automatic stop, look and listen, then fear and common sense might suggest stepping back into better cover. This can then translate into a plausible-looking trip to the rear, perhaps to help casualties or fetch ammunition. With enough of a push, stepping back becomes running back and running back becomes a mindless rush. Instinctive, reactive, sensible, habitual and then clinical.

Once fleeing starts in earnest, all the body's resources are directed to putting space between man and threat. Heart, hormones and legs pump like mad; senses narrow their focus onto the escape route. Another feedback loop builds up, so it usually takes a marked change in circumstance, exhaustion or a sergeant waving a carbine, before the internal calculation will trigger an alternative activity.

*   *   *

In nature, the fight option appears to be selected only after freeze and flee have been examined first. Some researchers say that fighting is considered only after the first two options have been checked and found unworkable, thereby making a fight the only course of action left. This idea may have grown from researchers spending too much time looking at prey animals, whose best possible outcome is to survive unscathed. Hunters work in a different way, but they still tend to pick their fights carefully. They will freeze or flee if the prey turns nasty or the costs start to obviously outweigh the rewards.

Most animals will fight under the right circumstances. Fighting might be the last option considered, and it often has the lowest personal survival value, but it is still governed by some very powerful programming. Trap a mouse in a corner then poke it with a stick and it will run up the stick to bite your face.

Fighting can also be seen to have layers. Firing one or two rounds in the general direction of the enemy can be seen as an instinctive response that is little more than asking the attacker to go away. Aimed shots from long range and cover are a deliberate effort to hit back but are closer to common-sense self-protection than true aggression. The ultimate of closing with the enemy to kill or capture him is where a man really risks all to win, and this is where things look like a hard mix of sensible and habitual responses.

Whether a man is firing at indistinct blobs on a screen or sticking a knife into a human being that he can smell, fighting has its own feedback loop. Like freeze and flee, once a man gets into fight mode, it can take a lot to pull him out again. Once again we have layers feeding on each other. The final clinical layer can be glimpsed in many war crimes and 'blue-on-blue' fratricides. In these situations, it appears that people get stuck in the fight response and cannot work their way back out of it. This is most evident when the men who lead an assault find that they have fought right through an enemy position and are stuck out on a limb with no support.

Some researchers have proposed a 'three Fs' theory of freeze–flee–fight as a model for armed combat. This is a useful theory because, rather than waffling about morale or how men feel, it focuses on what they do and what makes them do it. But it does not fit what is seen in a real battle. The main problem is that it fails to account for many things that happen when fighting involves complex social groups and complicated equipment. These complications give us fussing: a fourth F to be shoehorned into the list. Fussing is such a crucial part of armed close combat that it needs a chapter of its own.

EIGHT

FUSSING

LIEUTENANT DEVERELL, KOREA, 1951

I am reminded of a similar episode when we were fighting the Chinese last year. They had managed to infiltrate a large body of troops to get in around and behind the battalion before they launched their attack. They had used the night and foul weather to get to within a few yards of our outposts before we became aware of their presence. The long and the short of it was that we were taken unawares and unable to use our artillery trump card to best advantage as it was difficult to use heavier guns so close to our own line. In consequence we had to rely far more on our organic weapons than would normally have been considered healthy and we had some difficulty using our heavier machine guns and mortars with effect. As usual, the two-inch mortar was neither use nor ornament and the whole battalion had no more than a few dozen of the new Energa rifle grenades.

I should point out that I was at that time a freshly minted full lieutenant, just back from sick leave and with no real job to do, so I was, if you will excuse the term, a 'spare prick' at battalion. Somebody else had been given my old platoon so the colonel thought it best that

*I just hang around, shadowing the adjutant until a suitable job
came up.*

*I was in battalion HQ at kick off and while everyone did their best to
imitate the stiff upper lip, it was quite clear from their bustle and tone
(as well as the very loud noises outside) that we were quite suddenly
pressed hard from all sides. I soon found myself commanding what
passed for the battalion reserve and was sent off with Sergeant Major
Barstow plus a few cooks and bottle washers to help out D Company,
who were defending forward right and, by the sound of it, were getting
quite a hammering. All around the battalion, the Chinese were doing
something like those 'human wave' attacks that the old hands talk up
but, as ever, there was a hard core that were using ground in a professional fashion and causing all the real trouble.*

*There was quite a commotion in this set-to, with parachute flares
being launched, tracer arcing around and various types of explosion
in concert with all the usual cracks and burps of small arms. Were it
not for all the flares and some of our adopted huts that had been set
ablaze, the night would have been absolute pitch. The moon had not
yet risen and there was a thick overcast, in retrospect an ideal time for
the Chinese to attack!*

*There was a short exposed stretch where we had to cross open
ground to reach D and we lost a couple of men on the way. Happily, I
was later to find that two of these had merely 'mislaid themselves' and
turned up unharmed back at battalion HQ once things had quietened
down. There was minor Bedlam around the company dug-out when
we arrived but we got ourselves sorted with a couple of Bren guns
and one of the borrowed .300 Browning machine guns. We headed off
toward Charlie Spencer's platoon which was already down by eight
men and seemed to be bearing the brunt of it. The sound of bugles and
burp guns certainly seemed loudest in that direction. Charlie was*

himself suffering from a painful-looking hole in the arm but when we arrived he was continuing to lead the defence with something danger-ously close to élan. Rather than trying to flex my meagre rank, I offered our little party, now down to four men plus the sergeant major and yours truly, to act as a fire brigade. Charlie immediately found a use for us but pinched our lovely Browning.

The platoon position was laid out around us with a mix of trenches and sangars awkwardly clustered around Sherman Rock, a large boulder resembling the tank of the same name and which the pioneers had been unable to budge. To make up for this weakness the dead ground around the rock was thick with mines and wire. By the time we arrived, the Chinese had pushed a gap through all this, overrun one section position, slightly to the right of Sherman Rock, and had been into the other forward trench before being winkled out again. Now they were using the boulder to provide a covered approach and as a place where they could form up to launch attacks in either direction. After helping deal with the initial threat we pushed right a little into a cosy hollow in the rocks from where we would be able to fire on anyone who put his head around our side of the rock. Their next attempt was a bit of a rush and was not pressed very hard. Rounds rapid from our Brens stole most of their momentum then Charlie's boys lobbed grenades to push them back around the ragged rock.

Now we get to the part of the story that you'll be interested in and the part that I'm still somewhat ashamed of. Once we were in position it turned out that I really didn't have much to do but fetch and carry. The men manned the guns and knew their way around them far better than I, the Sergeant Major was an old war horse who took charge of the gunners' immediate needs and Charlie was handling the next level up so I was left to help out as best I could.

I began with the best intentions by going back for ammunition from Charlie's stash and then I brought up another gun for spares. On my third trip I went back to the company area to fetch more ammo and some water bottles, and on my fourth or fifth trip I went all the way back to battalion for yet more ammunition and a spare barrel.

Between foraging expeditions I took a bit of a breather, charged Bren magazines from a huge sack of loose .303 and asked banal officer-like questions about everyone's comfort. Yet most of my time between trips was taken up with stacking and counting my lovely hoard of ammunition. I made sure that there were six magazines and a replacement barrel neatly stacked within easy reach of the gunners, a small pyramid of grenades beside the sergeant major and a larger cache of ammunition and spares neatly arranged in a small alcove in the rocks. I should point out that this was most uncharacteristic behaviour for me, for although I take pride in my appearance when out of the line, I am quite deliberately the most slovenly man when it comes to the detail of 'proper' military matters.

There were two failed attempts by the Chinese to creep up close to Charlie's boys and one attempt on our own little nest. This was a more organised affair with fire from the captured trenches and the top of the rock but it was soon smothered by our fire and then driven off with some welcome support from the battalion mortars. Between these events there was the odd exchange of fire and some attempts to push forward but nothing that really pressed us or made even a dent in the mountain of ammunition that I brought forward. By the time the Chinese broke off, maybe four hours after we first set up shop by the rock, I had built up a treasure trove of nearly fifty charged Bren magazines, 400 loose rounds and a score of grenades.

It seems amazing to me now but once I started serving those guns I never thought about doing something more useful. I must have heard when I was back at company and battalion how the other companies were much harder pressed. I could hear the fire to all points and should have worked out that either I or the whole of our little team should have headed off somewhere we could be of more use. Everyone was very kind about it, of course, I was even considered for another gong before suggesting someone more worthy to the adjutant, but I really ought to have been reading the battle and fighting it rather than flouncing about charging Bren magazines.

Lieutenant Deverell's account came from another dusty box that popped up unexpectedly. In this case, a regimental museum was closing down and my old boss was given half a dozen boxes full of war stories and knick-knacks. Deverell's account was in a box file marked 'Korea lessons'. Old Boss faxed it to me with a scrawled note on the front page saying: 'Retired to Aus. Near you? Track him down.' He was never one to waste words or set easy tasks.

To be fair to Old Boss, I was on secondment in Australia at the time and did have a possible address for Deverell. All I had to do was track down a complete stranger and travel a few thousand kilometres to ask him embarrassing questions about a war which had been over for forty years.

I need not have worried. The address was correct, I found a phone number in the book and Deverell answered on the third ring. A few weeks later he drove halfway across Australia to meet me. Granted, his trip was part of an extended touring holiday and he was very keen to poke around the base where I worked, but this was still an indication of what a charming man he was. Instead of the fragile old codger I was expecting, Deverell was the spit of David Niven in his prime: a true gentleman, dapper, sporting and with just a hint of rakishness about him.

He brought with him a stack of notes which his old adjutant had compiled for an unfinished book on the regiment's Korean experience. This included transcripts of interviews with many of the men who fought alongside Deverell that night. There was enough juicy stuff in that stack of papers to fuel the tactical psychology hunt for a year. I was in war geek heaven.

Deverell accepted that, even at the time, his grasp of the wider battle was a little vague but he was certain on two points. The first was the amount of ammunition that he gathered. He and Sergeant Major Barstow made a point of totting this up and it must have taken five trips to collect it all.

His second point was how little he and his miniature 'fire brigade' really contributed to the battalion defence. Maybe Charlie Spencer's platoon would have been overrun without Deverell's support but, as Deverell found out just after the battle, the initial assault on D Company was most likely a Chinese deception. Other companies had a much harder fight that night. Deverell's fussing seems to have stopped him from noticing this during the battle.

It is worth repeating the message that Deverell really had no reason to feel ashamed. Not only did he do something far more difficult than most men will ever do, he did it with style. His comrades still recall the cheerful way he dashed around the battlefield as though he was 'at a rather hectic cocktail party'.

Another fact Deverell fails to mention is how he helped ferry casualties back towards the regimental aid post. A more career-minded young officer would have been awarded a medal for the risks he took but we can maybe understand his embarrassment about not doing something more suited to a newly minted full lieutenant. When I met Deverell, he was still very bashful about the events of that night, but eager to flesh out his story once I convinced him that my aim was to understand the psychology of combat: 'The Adj and I were supposed to compile lessons from our bit of the war but you know how it is when you get back home. It's only proper that I should help you finish the job.'

To modern ears, Deverell's account sounds as if he was suffering from a temporary bout of obsessive-compulsive disorder. This may be true, but his experience reflects one side of the fussing that has started to dominate many aspects of battle.

Combat has come to be full of complex tasks that are not directly involved with engaging the enemy, and these activities can often take over when men are under pressure. Jobs like assisting crew-served weapons, carrying ammunition, repairing equipment, fetching water, manning radios or helping casualties can all slip into being displacement activities: simple jobs that a man can do instead of the really hard job he is supposed to be doing.

Fussing is important because of its attraction and the way that it makes the simplest things difficult. At its heart is a tendency for people under pressure to focus on what is manageable rather than what is important. It is unlikely that anyone actually rearranged the deckchairs on the *Titanic*, but it is the kind of achievable thing that people do to make themselves feel better when everything else is going pear-shaped.

Fussing in combat is driven by the same process that sees people spending money on fripperies or working on home repairs while their houses are being repossessed. Civilian work studies have found that people under pressure are drawn to details and feel more productive when they focus on trivia. In balanced tests comparing workers allowed to manage detail with others who were not, the detail group rated their satisfaction much higher, even though they proved to be far less effective than the no-detail group. In combat, the effect is sharper and the negative impact more immediate.

*   *   *

There are two types of fussing. One is centred on personal equipment and actions, like Sergeant Johansson worrying about where his arms should be as he got to the door of the C130. The other springs from the complications of organisation, like Lieutenant Deverell being side-tracked by doing support tasks.

At the personal level, even well-drilled soldiers are far less effective at basic tasks when they are in contact with the enemy. A neat series of American and Canadian studies found it takes a man nearly 50 per cent longer to repair a radio when he thinks that artillery is accidentally dropping short around him. No surprise about that, but the effect is amplified when the drill is clouded by some extra source of confusion.

The soldier subjects in these studies were sometimes deliberately given a radio slightly different to one they had been trained on. When this happened without the artillery dropping short, it took slightly longer to make the simple repair but, with added fire, it took nearly three times as long and they repeatedly made the same mistakes. Like Johansson being sent out of the 'wrong' side of the plane, the men with the 'wrong' radio had stress and confusion piled on top of each other and this is what made them fuss.

Old soldiers are right when they say that drills take over in contact, but under stress it can be difficult to escape from the drill if it is the wrong thing to do. At the personal level, most fussing only has to last a few minutes before it drifts into a feedback loop; a soldier starts by clearing a weapon stoppage, then charges a magazine, but soon finds himself repeatedly repacking his kit. The attraction of fussing at the personal level seems to be down to the links between the main components of memory.

It is worth noting here that there is a big difference between what normal people and psychologists mean when they talk about memory. Most people judge their memory on its ability to accurately store and retrieve facts, faces and so on, but that is only half of what memory is about. A large chunk of it is actually about making sense of right now and about using information to make decisions quickly. So, while there are large parts of memory that are set up to remember things, there are other parts that remember only as a side effect of processing information for other reasons.

Memory can be seen as having four components. First there is sensory memory, the bit that turns the mass of data from eyes and ears into useful information. This works like an input buffer, throwing most of the data out and remembering things only for a few moments. Sensory memory will often filter out everything but the image of a fist rushing to your face, the taste of blood and a sudden pain below your nose; it sometimes filters out the pain too. In this respect it is like the cognitive blink we saw earlier, in the way it blocks irrelevances like the smell of cut grass or the kind of hat your attacker is wearing. It is the main reason why mugging victims often only remember seeing a big knife pointed at their face.

The filtered data is quickly passed on to the next component, working memory, which remembers things only as a side effect trying to make sense of the current situation. In the example of seeing a fist and tasting blood, it works out that you have been smacked in the mouth. In a way, working memory produces the situation report for the rest of the body to work with and it provides the main link for turning information into action.

The next component, long-term memory, is perhaps the only bit that we would recognise as proper memory; it is the bit that stores facts, faces and the outline plans of what has worked in the past. In this case it offers up a general response to being smacked in the mouth. It might suggest grabbing the attacker because, having been smacked in the mouth, you cannot see well enough to block more punches.

The final component, muscle memory, fires up the drilled sequences of actions that get the job done. Muscle memory is the bit that remembers the moves needed to change a radio battery or perform an emergency stop in a car. So, when working memory says 'smacked in the mouth' and long-term memory says 'grab the bad guy', muscle memory might fire up the sequence of moves you need to get your attacker into a headlock.

This four-part division of memory is clearly a simplification. The brain does complex parallel processing and is not divided into neat boxes, but these four faces of memory generally work along these lines. All the components pull together with working memory as the hub to try and turn information into action quickly enough to make a difference.

That 'quickly enough' line is important. The brain is not a super-computer that can process huge amounts of data very quickly; it is a smart-but-quirky meat sack that makes up for being a bit slow by processing only the most important stuff. Much of the rest has to get thrown out and mistakes are sometimes made.

The links between memory components usually work well enough, even in stressful or complicated situations, but when things are both stressful and complicated, such as mending a radio under fire, working memory gets gummed up and overloaded. When this happens, the other memory components try to talk to each other directly and they are not very good at doing this. So, even when long-term memory says something sensible like 'check the power and signal cables then reconnect the battery' our muscles do the wrong moves because all they can hear is sensory memory yelling 'somebody's shooting at us!', and they perform the drill for the equipment they are most used to.

Most of the time, the results are merely annoying. People used to driving cars with a manual gearbox often do double-footed braking when they drive an automatic: the drill takes over and they go for the clutch but stamp both feet on the brake. When the wrong response is pulled out of the bag in combat, the stress is redoubled and a soldier can be pushed further away from winning the fight.

*   *   *

Remember those muskets collected after Gettysburg with multiple unfired charges? While Chapter 5 was concerned with aversion to killing, the other big reason for men loading and presenting without firing came from a combination of stress and an overloaded working memory. Muscle memory took over and reverted to the habitual dry-firing drills: drills that often skipped over details like fitting the percussion cap. This was one of the most fiddly and easily forgotten of the essential steps needed to load and fire a rifled musket. So, in addition to avoiding killing, these men were automatically repeating what their fingers and thumbs were most familiar with doing. They left out the important tricky bit.

As technology has improved, the basic drills for loading and firing have become simpler. A Western soldier in Afghanistan today is most likely to have an assault rifle with only three or four essential steps for loading and firing, rather than six or seven for a musket. But everything else has become far more complicated.

A Gettysburg infantryman only had one piece of complicated kit to worry about and all his mates carried the same thing. Loading, presenting and firing were pretty much all he had to do with this weapon unless it stopped working. When this happened, there were only two things he could do to put it right before he threw it away and picked up an almost identical weapon.

While an assault rifle is simpler to load and fire, the variety of things that can go wrong with its ammunition feed mean that a soldier often has to check six options rather than two when a weapon stops working. Then there is a one-in-four chance that his rifle will have a grenade launcher attached; he also has two or three types of hand grenade, maybe a pistol and often a radio. There is a one-in-eight chance he has got two radios, a one-in-four chance he has night vision goggles and a one-in-four chance he has a computer, a mine detector or an electronic signal jammer. Soldiers are festooned with gadgets that can give them a lot of things to fuss with under fire.

Then, if a soldier has to discard his weapon and pick up another from an injured buddy, there is a good chance it will be a belt-fed weapon that works quite differently to his rifle. In a ten-man patrol there can be six or seven different weapon systems. Things get increasingly complicated in a platoon-sized group, where two men might have a missile launcher, two more operate a grenade machine gun and two might have a light mortar.

With a few woeful exceptions, all of this kit is kept as simple and reliable as possible. But most soldiers have to learn how to use nearly all of it. No matter how thorough his training, the complexity of equipment options increases the chances that a soldier will do the wrong drill under pressure and get stuck fussing with his kit. The last fifty years have shown an increase in the number of soldiers repeatedly conducting radio checks, changing barrels or stripping magazines when the enemy is almost on top of them.

*   *   *

This brings us up to organisational-level fussing, which is tied to the kind of necessary but less essential jobs that have plagued commanders for centuries. Many examples mirror Deverell's experience of becoming mired in unnecessary administration.

The most obvious is the understandable tendency for too many men to get involved in casualty handling. Even in the Falklands, where the motto was 'save your casualties for the re-org', and injured mates were supposed to be ignored until the enemy were defeated, attacks sometimes stalled because a whole fire-team would stop fighting to take an injured man to the rear. Then the rest of the platoon took more casualties because they had too few men to win the firefight, lost more men tending to those casualties and were sometimes defeated as a result.

In the days when it was possible to see whole battalions fighting, the best units were those who used the fewest fighting men to manage casualties. In the musket era, poor units often had four men moving each casualty out of the firing line; better units only had one man per casualty. Rather than being hard-hearted, these units' commanders realised that more of their men would die if there were fewer to face the enemy.

There are a few examples of men digging mortar pits, filling sand bags or laying mines when the enemy were getting near bayonet range. With modern equipment and organisation there are far more chances for a battle to get bogged down by this kind of friction. Even in field training, where none of the casualties is real, nearly a third of failed attacks are the result of units getting overwhelmed by their own administration. It is not uncommon for a small-unit action in Afghanistan to stall because of the effort required to supply water, ammunition, radio batteries and air support.

Unpopular 'wars of choice', where each casualty seems to be the subject of an inquiry, have exaggerated this effect. The enemy in Afghanistan can hold up our troops with only a fraction of the fire that was needed just thirty years ago. But thirty years ago, armies were simpler, more focused on winning and their enemies would batter them with artillery if they sat still for too long. Thirty years ago, soldiers might have liked to stop and deal with their injured friends, but they knew this would get them killed. A few decades of fighting ill-trained, ill-equipped insurgents has let armies be seduced by the luxury of attending to every casualty.

There is little hard data for how this organisational fussing works (and it is mainly a problem for colonels rather than corporals) but we have some idea how it impacts on the chance of soldiers fussing. When a complex organisation tries to follow complicated orders, the 'hurry up and wait' of a mission includes more waiting than hurrying. In these situations, when a soldier does his 'is it worth it?' calculation he is more likely to err on the side of fussing because he has already been encouraged to fuss by the orders he was given.

* * *

Any effort to categorise armed combat is bound to be an awkward compromise, but the four Fs of freezing, fleeing, fussing and fighting provide a simple basis for understanding a man's basic responses. Each type of response is primarily governed by what happens in a fight but, once a response is forced or chosen, it generates its own gravity. These gravity wells can pull a soldier in and then make it difficult for him to break free.

The four response types and their gravity wells can make a soldier's responses work something like a Christmas cracker puzzle: those twiddly pieces of tat where a ball-bearing has to be navigated around a maze of bad holes to get to the good hole at the end. If the ball goes into a bad hole, a lot of tipping and rattling is needed to get it out again but, once the ball is out, it can shoot off in any direction and land in another bad hole.

It is the same with the four Fs. It is difficult to avoid the non-fighting holes and, once in one, get back out again. This is exaggerated by feedback and stresses acting like magnets under each hole, making it harder to break out the longer you are in.

All those high-level factors – good training, not being dicked around and so on – aim to make sure our own soldiers start on the edge of the puzzle that is closest to the fighting hole. Then, once the fighting starts, leadership is about tipping the puzzle the right way to roll men into the fighting hole and keep them there until the battle is won. But the aim of tactical psychology is to tip the enemy's puzzle towards the non-fighting holes and make it easier for our guys to win by turning up the attraction of the magnets for freezing, fleeing and fussing.

Surprisingly, the trite ball-bearings-and-magnets analogy has been accepted by some of the most stubbornly attritionist commanders. The real hurdle has been to get them to accept that tactics can make the enemy stop fighting. I have worked with dozens of very bright people who cannot seem to get their heads around this fairly basic idea.

The Tank Colonel had a hard time seeing past the glamour of super-soldiers, but the real barrier to understanding tactical psychology comes from people who have no ability to empathise with men under fire. One of the worst offenders for this was an unpleasant but influential US staff officer, known to many as Colonel Catfu.

Master Sergeant Johansson told me how Catfu (an old-school acronym for Completely And Totally Fucked Up) got ahead in the US military by backstabbing his peers and blaming failure on subordinates. I had heard similar bad things about him from a dozen people, but my own glimpse into Catfu's world came when I was tricked into briefing him while he was a junior general at the Allied Rapid Reaction Corps.

The briefing started well enough, we sat in Catfu's office and I talked while he nodded in most of the right places, but it became clear that he could see no benefit in even trying to make the enemy fight less. As far as Catfu was concerned, the enemy were targets who existed only to be shot down. Instead, he was fixed on the idea of making our own soldiers into fighting machines, either through psychometric testing or pill-popping.

Catfu's lack of combat experience was not a problem, but it became obvious that he had tried to fill this gap with computer games and war movies; he had the unnerving habit of referring to both as if they were accurate reflections of real war. When I tried to show him how making the enemy freeze, flee or fuss was more efficient than killing them, he could not see past double-tapping every bad guy in the style of a shoot-'em-up game. He seemed quite happy with the four Fs but missed the point that these were behaviours seen in every soldier. He wanted 'a personality test to weed out the freezers and fussers'.

In my time, I have met plenty of people who believed black or Hispanic soldiers weakened the US military, but this man's bigotry extended to everybody but himself. Catfu was convinced that he was some kind of naturally heroic archetype who, if he ever saw combat, would fight like John Wayne or Jason Bourne. Marshall's non-firers were all cowards as far as Catfu was concerned.

He accepted the mechanics of suppression but saw this working only on the enemy and *'untermenschen'*, a particularly unfortunate phrase given the German officer in the room with us. At the centre of Catfu's belief system was the idea that a chemical cure could keep our soldiers fighting even under the heaviest fire.

What Catfu lacked in empathy he made up for in ambition. At the end of the brief, he let me in on his plans for his next job as military head of one of the US research centres. He was going to launch a new era of military science, where he would 'finally crack that shit they were doing in *Jacob's Ladder* and *Universal Soldier*'. I have to admit, I suffered from my own cognitive blink at that point. It took a few moments to process the idea that a man who was about to take over one of the world's most influential research positions drew his inspiration from a Jean-Claude Van Damme film. The German officer's raised eyebrow spoke volumes.

I have no idea how far Catfu took his dream (any politically incorrect research is instantly covered by the highest national security rating), but I do know that he engineered the scrapping of three useful research projects and the early retirement of two excellent analysts.

Military research is notoriously hamstrung by the 'preferred answer' and the seemingly narrow-minded world view that comes with it. For the armoured corps, the answer to any problem is more tanks; for the navy, the answer is pointier ships. The preferred answer sometimes springs from an influential oddball like Catfu or from lobbying by missile makers, but it is more often due to people like me not explaining themselves clearly enough. The ball-bearing analogy tells us nothing about the magnets that make freezing, fleeing, fussing and fighting so attractive. So, before we look at the tactical tricks that tip the enemy's ball-bearing puzzle, we need to look at the main things that control the power of those magnets.

NINE

COHESION

PRIVATE HALDER, FRANCE/BELGIUM, 1915

Cowardice took hold of me in an English ditch. As our barrage moved forward we left our line and advanced within the cover of our machine guns and trench mortars. English strong-points gave fire from left and right as we rushed over the broken ground between the lines but we lost few company men: Bremer, a particular friend, dropped in front of me with gore gushing from his face; Feldmann, another good soldier, fell dead to my right though I saw no wound. We then fought hard into the forward trench with grenade and bayonet to kill and capture the defenders there. Very many put up their hands once we dropped into their lines.

There was then a great press of our men mixed in together without any order or control but we pushed toward the reserve trenches with vigour. I found myself in a shell hole with men from another battalion. After a short pause I took these men forward in a bound to get behind a strong-point, but this made us very exposed to the very rapid fire coming from the English reserve trenches. I think two men fell to rifle fire as we ran into the fall of our own mortar bombs. Four of us took cover in the ditch where I was later found. It was part crater and part

*defensive work so it gave reasonable cover while we waited for the fire
to slacken.*

*As we hunched up in that hole unable to move forward or back, the
English bombs landed around us and fire from all points cut the air
above our heads or kicked into the lip of the ditch. I busied myself with
my pack and boots as we waited for the fire to ease and exchanged
mouthed encouragements with those other men but my mood soon
turned from Grim Duty to life and family. With no friendly face near
me, it took my mind that behind me my company was scattered and
smashed; retreating through a deathly fire, leaving me trapped alone
with strangers. At some point the others in that hole went forward but
I stayed behind shaking and waiting to die from an English bullet or
from the hard fear of death's certainty. I knew I was alone and I knew
I would die.*

Austrian General sent me a translation of Halder's account along
with a collection of background notes. This all came on a floppy
disk that only a stone-age Mac could read, but a useful handwrit-
ten note was included. The note ended with a Germanic attempt
to inspire me to greater efforts: 'COHESION is the key! You must
find this. Keep working.'

I had a vague idea that cohesion helped retreat turn to rout
or pursuit turn to massacre, but the true value was lost on me
for a long while. The drawn-out death of the Sennelager Club
and immovable obstacles like Catfu had combined with a half-
divorce and a series of foreign postings to drag me away from
tactical psychology.

In my absence, battle morale had swung in and out of fashion
again. A new project had been started, another wet-behind-
the-ears analyst had been tricked into taking it on and then, just

as he was starting to understand the problem, he was told to look at something completely different. He was not pleased about this. Within a few days of my return to the UK, he started to bombard me with emails. He wanted his project back and thought I could help. Curiously, he seemed to think that the best way to get my help was to criticise my ten-year-old battle morale study.

His criticism was sound enough. In fact, his argument was similar to Austrian General's. The trouble stemmed from the dynamics of this telling-off. I was now a department manager with underlings and a reputation, yet I had a mouthy whelp from Liverpool criticising my work. Things came to a head when this Gobby Scouser sat on my desk, invaded my space, and told me how my old battle morale study was hollow without cohesion.

He was far too brash to be a civil servant and he kept jabbing his finger towards me as if he was looking for a fight. As his argument became more animated, his accent thickened. After a while, I had to pay close attention just to make out the words; every fourth word appeared to be a profanity. He didn't have the look of a civil servant either. He was bulky, pimply and his teeth had a mahogany inlay from the roll-up cigarettes he chain-smoked.

I had two options: pull rank and shoo him away, or listen to what he had to say. Thankfully, I roped in my ego and let him tell me why cohesion is so important. He then went into overdrive and proceeded to remind me of the psychology I had forgotten over the past decade. Gobby Scouser told me, in far too much detail, how the power of cohesion can be seen by welding civilian psychology research to combat accounts.

When he had finished spouting, I performed a master stroke of delegation. I gave him Austrian General's floppy disk, a stack of papers on the four Fs, and told him to crack on.

'Am I getting paid for this?' he asked.

'Sorry, son,' I replied as I pointed to the door, 'defence research is too busy looking at overpriced planes and boats to spare you any cash. Do it in your own time. If it's any good, I'll buy you a curry.'

It was four years before he got that curry. In that four years he gave up trying to be a civil servant and moved into the murky world of freelance defence research. When he sent me his reply, I was delighted to find he had included a detailed assessment of Private Halder's battle.

*   *   *

Halder was a solid, dependable soldier who had received commendations and would do so again. His qualities were recognised later in the war with a promotion and a transfer to his regiment's storm company. But on this day he simply stopped fighting and stayed in his 'English ditch' until he was found by his friends.

He came under heavy fire and saw comrades fall, but he had seen worse in previous actions without any noticed effect on his combat performance. The notes attached to Halder's account suggest that his main problem was down to being separated from his friends: he came unstuck when he found himself in a ditch full of strangers.

Withdrawn and 'nervy' when his friends found him, Halder recovered after a visit to the battalion command post. His therapy consisted of a hot meal, a pipe of tobacco, some looted British rum and a little conversation. He was back with his platoon later that day. Two days after that he told his story to a staff officer writing a report on trench tactics.

Halder's company commander believed that the break-in battle, the fight for those forward trenches, lasted around forty minutes. Despite steady and controlled supporting fire during the advance, the company lost a dozen men as they bounded across no man's land. They managed to break into the forward trench but then they were fixed (prevented from moving) by a British counter-attack until this was driven off by a flanking German company. Halder was in his ditch for another two or three hours while the counter-attack was repulsed and the British were cleared out of the next line of trenches.

Unknown to Halder, his company was not scattered and smashed but held onto the trenches that they had seized. By First World War standards they suffered very few casualties while doing this. The attack captured a section of ground that strengthened the German defence and was held onto until a strategic withdrawal was ordered later in the war.

Halder's problems started when he set off on the extreme left of his battalion's advance. Nearly every man to his left was from another battalion and a stranger to him. He was mixed in with these strangers when the advance was channelled into choke-points by barbed wire and shell craters. Contrary to the popular view of British early war tactics, the defenders had many of their men and heavier weapons in strongpoints behind the forward line. German troops crammed into the British forward trench to escape the fire from these depth positions. In the confusion, Halder was further separated from his friends.

Being isolated like this clearly had little effect on its own, because Halder led a scratch squad over open ground to get around a block between the first and second lines of trenches. But the pause in the attack had allowed the weak British reserve to counter-attack just as Halder was doing this. Suppression and sitting still were all added to the loss of cohesion. In addition to pinning Halder, British fire inflicted heavy casualties on the German second echelon as it advanced over no man's land to reinforce the attack.

Effectively becoming the tip of the spear for this attack, Halder's small band had gone out on a limb and found they were outflanked and outgunned. Initially pinned down by a conscious common-sense decision, Halder switched to fussing with his pack and boots. This was a sensible soldierly decision to engage in concurrent activity, but it slipped into the feedback loop of being frozen. Halder lost the weak bond he had with the men around him and, no longer stuck to his company, it was easy for him to get stuck in the ditch.

*   *   *

Cohesion is a cornerstone of tactical psychology, but we need to be very specific about what 'cohesion' really means. Military definitions are not just about men sticking together (lateral cohesion) they also include sticking to the chain of command (vertical cohesion), sticking to the job (task cohesion) and cooperation between units (organisational cohesion). Very often, cohesion is used as an alternative label for the equally woolly concept of morale.

This flexible definition makes it difficult to pin down cohesion's effects. At one extreme, 'loss of cohesion' has been used to describe the problems in a NATO logistic company in Afghanistan, where everyone got so bored and stoned that they could not do their jobs properly. In this example, cohesion was used as another word for professional competence and had nothing to do with tactical psychology.

At the other extreme, the German Fourth Army was said to

have lost cohesion during the Soviet Bagration offensive of 1944. This included the progressive loss of vertical, organisational and task bonds, prompted by the complete destruction of seventeen divisions and the deaths of 300,000 men. In this example, loss of cohesion was a euphemism for defeat.

To avoid any ambiguity, tactical psychology only uses the word cohesion to describe the lateral bond that makes a small group of fighting men stick together. Cohesion is the thing that makes the men in a fire-team, a section or, at a push, a whole platoon tend to fight or not fight more like one entity than a collection of separate individuals.

There are two sides to this simpler version of cohesion. The first is that, like Halder, men very often stop fighting when separated from their mates. Armed conflict is a team event and there are few people who fight alone. In modern combat, the section or platoon is what most soldiers fight for, so when the link is severed, men lose much of their reason for fighting.

Despite the unhealthy side effects seen at battles like First Ypres, standing people close together makes it easier for them to see their mates, and this usually means they are more likely to carry on fighting. The need to maintain cohesion was one of the two main reasons why close-order battle, where men are packed into tight ranks, outlived its physical usefulness. But, by the time of Halder's battle, the tight ranks had been abandoned almost completely and armies had just started to look for ways to counter the resulting loss of cohesion.

Wigram and Marshall both noted the old adage that men should not be allowed to lie down in combat because they lose sight of their comrades. This is a risky rule to apply but it has been tried many times, particularly in jungle wars, where it is all too easy for men to become separated from their mates. Once men lose sight of their mates and take cover they are immediately subject to the gravity of the not-fighting options and, as Sergeant Dawson found in Chapter 1, once this happens, it is difficult to break the spell of freezing or fussing.

But it is remarkably difficult to attack the cohesion of an enemy unit. A lot of effort is needed to kill or wound most of a section or to separate its members and break the bond. The firepower needed to do this means that the psychology of suppression usually kicks in before a loss of cohesion.

It is has proved to be much easier to fracture cohesion in your own force by constantly reorganising units so men fight alongside strangers or by putting men into isolated foxholes so they fight alone. US Army and Marine Corps policies did this for many years and often produced the same symptoms that afflicted Private Halder. One reason for Marshall's low fire ratios was that men like his Saké Night soldiers were mostly freezing and fussing in isolated foxholes.

There is little tactical value in knowing what happens to an enemy when he is separated from his mates. The more useful side of cohesion comes from understanding the power of the herd instinct when it pulls against fighting.

Stripping cohesion down to a simple bond between a small team lets us see that it can cut both ways. Cohesion makes it likely that a man will follow his mates when they fight but the downside (or the upside if you are thinking about having an effect on the enemy) is that he is also likely to follow them when they freeze, flee or fuss.

Cohesion is like a volume button for the magnetic attraction of all the four Fs. It is the single biggest magnet when men can see their mates. It makes men move into and out of fights as groups rather than as individuals. It is the reason why close order was great for getting men into a battle and keeping them there. It was also the reason why close-order units collapsed so quickly once the tide of battle turned against them. The way men fight and whether they fight is dominated by what they see their mates doing: the more comrades a soldier can see, the stronger the effect.

*   *   *

As Gobby Scouser was kind enough to point out, cohesion is best understood by looking at civilian psychology research. Every few years there is a public outcry when a crowd of people witness a mugging, rape or accident but fail to come to the aid of the victims. These bystanders are often more motivated by group cohesion than self-preservation. Their initial cognitive blink becomes a more drawn-out 'stop, look and listen', where each bystander sees a lot of other people who are doing exactly the same thing: nothing. They then interpret the inaction of others as an indication that no action is needed so, in effect, every bystander does nothing because every other bystander is doing nothing.

Bystanders provide a host of reasons for doing nothing. These range from 'I thought it was a domestic' (so it was OK for a woman to be raped outside my flat) to 'it looked like street theatre' (so I watched a man being kicked to death in a shopping mall). But these statements are largely rationalisations for following the crowd. A bigger crowd tends to have a stronger effect because it spreads the responsibility for inaction and provides more evidence that doing nothing is the best option.

Back when I learned about group psychology, this was as far as bystander research went: in all matters, a person's decision was overwhelmingly influenced by the action, or inaction, of others. This made the behaviour of groups more consistent and predictable. But, in my days as a psychology student, there were no numbers for the strength of the effect. Since I shoved the cohesion problem to Gobby Scouser, he filled his spare time finding cohesion facts and figures.

Luckily, some mugging victims have found that there are usually one or two people who do not follow the bystander crowd. Crowds appear to have a built-in counter-pressure that makes some of us less sheeplike. This is fuelled by another strange mix of biology, psychology and sociology, which drives some people to display a degree of deviance from the bystander norm.

This appears to have an evolutionary benefit, with deviant behaviour being a kind of mutation that stops tribes and families from getting too stuck in a rut. In the same way that a tribe full of natural fighters would have low survival value, a tribe of natural sheep would soon get killed off too. Even actual sheep sometimes react in ways that are un-sheeplike, because it is useful to have some deviation from the norm.

No one knows the real details of how this works, but it means that crowds, tribes and infantry sections have something in them that opens up the chance of an alternative response. This can be seen when one person goes against the grain to help the mugging victim. Once someone in the crowd bucks the trend they can break the spell for everyone else, reverse the bystander effect and start a rush to stick one on the bad guy.

Yet, despite counter-pressures, the drive towards following the crowd is far more powerful, and the resulting consistency makes it easier to understand how small units react to combat.

* * *

People tend to follow the crowd in non-threatening situations too, and these give us an idea of how strong the cohesion effect is. The power of following can be seen in experiments that give a straight choice between almost identical options, whether it is a choice between brands of breakfast cereal or shopping mall exit doors. In these experiments people are about four times as likely to take the option they have just seen someone else go for.

This works even if people have no idea why the other person picked that particular option. The effect is stronger when the choice is confused by more options or by some kind of distraction. Even the vaguest familiarity with the other person increases the effect considerably, so when it comes to the tight-knit groups that make up most military units, the bond can be extremely powerful.

The same numbers apply in combat. Combat videos from Afghanistan and Iraq show men going into and out of cover like the Mexican wave that Sergeant Dawson mentioned in Chapter 1. This usually happens without orders and with no obvious physical change to the level of threat.

Imagine combat as a choice between four doors, with a door for each of the four Fs. Now assume that the first soldier to reach the decision point has an equal chance that he will choose each door. Whichever door the first man picks, the next man to decide (assuming he knows and trusts the first man) is about eight times more likely to choose the same door. This could go on with a gradual increase in probability: as each soldier reaches the decision point and sees more people picking Door A, he is slightly more likely to follow them. In some simple computer war games, combat works just like this.

Sadly, for people paid to use computers to understand war, the real world gets in the way. The four options never start with an equal value. Base-level motivation gets in the way, but tactical factors like ground, weather and weapons have an even greater impact. When two opposing patrols meet, one usually has better cover, or better weapons, or sees the enemy first, making it more likely to fight.

Despite these real-world problems, the cohesion effect does work a bit like the four-door decision. In a small-unit 'meeting engagement', where two patrols just bump into each other, the theory is not too far from the truth. Nearly a quarter involve no fighting at all, with both sides just walking away as if they had never met. In a third of engagements, a few rounds are exchanged (little more than saying hello; Napoleonic soldiers called it 'bickering') before both sides withdraw. Most of the rest have one side withdrawing or surrendering after a short exchange of fire. Only one in ten small meeting engagements leads to a stiff fight where both sides take casualties before the outcome is decided.

Most battles, even the small ones, are more complicated than this, so the mix of psychological and physical factors really twists the way that soldiers react. For example, most Afghan engagements are actually ambushes with one side pre-prepared to catch the other out. Despite this messiness, Gobby Scouser's combination of psychology and combat data provided a fairly clear picture of how cohesion drags people into freezing, fleeing, fussing and fighting.

* * *

It has been said that small-group cohesion is the key to winning and losing battles, and now we can start to see how this really works. Without the power of following, it would be almost impossible to win a firefight in anything close to an evenly matched engagement. Each man would be pinned by fire only while it was passing close to him and for a short while afterwards. Soon after the fire stopped or moved on, he would reconsider and, if he had not been sucked in by the magnets of freezing or fussing, could go back to fighting. But he sees his mates pinned and so he is pinned too. Like those civilian bystanders or the people picking breakfast cereal, a soldier's responses, whether passive or active, are heavily biased by what everyone else is doing.

In the Second World War and Korea there were dozens of examples where men who ran to the rear to fetch a bazooka or satchel charge caused a chain reaction and a whole company ran from the fight. At My Lai and in a score of less famous massacres, cohesion helped fix men in a fighting response until they had killed every prisoner, civilian or farm animal they could find.

Soldiers need to understand how cohesion works on their own unit but its most useful feature is the way that enemy cohesion helps win a fight. The power of following is evident when firing-range trials are compared with real combat data.

Back in Chapter 4, field data showed that small-arms suppression was twelve times as powerful as range trials suggested, and cohesion plays a large part in this because a man is indirectly suppressed by fire that directly suppresses his mates. The effect of cohesion on suppression is now being relearned in Afghanistan. One reason why some veteran units were starting to win battles with a fraction of the fire is that they had, almost by accident, learned how to exploit cohesion.

There are similar differences between the firing range and the real world for other tactical tricks that we will look at later.

Once a tactic convinces half of the enemy to stop fighting, nearly everyone else follows them. And most of the difference between range trails and operational experience comes down to cohesion: it is the strongest magnet under those holes in the ball-bearing puzzle. Men tend to follow the example of others and, as in smaller versions of old close-order units, cohesion reinforces whichever behaviour is currently dominant.

The only reason cohesion promotes a fighting response is that it tends to be shaped by compulsion from corporals, sergeants and commissioned officers. The next chapter looks at how these fighting commanders compel men to fight.

TEN

COMPULSION

BOMBARDIER FIDLER, SOUTHERN ENGLAND, 1940

I made to jump into the dugout but the major goes 'Stand still man. Stand still.' So me and Major Peabody we just stood there watching them bomb the town. You could see the bombs falling past us. And then the noise and smoke and dust flying up when they hit down in the town. And the firebombs; thousands of 'em they dropped. I'll never forget that fire. Oh I was frit alright but I wasn't going to let him see that after he'd told me. So we just stood there.

We were there to defend Southampton from the bombers but we had no ammunition do you see and they came in too low for us to do much of anything in any case. There'd been alarms all week and the odd plane but that night there must have been hundreds of them went over us to bomb the Spitfire works. And there was nowt we could do about it. No ammo for the guns and no Spitfires to defend their own factory.

I think the major's idea was that at least we could show we could stand with town against the bombers. So we stood.

He was the proper sort of officer, if you know what I mean. If we'd had more like him in Belgium and France we could've stopped the Germans there maybe.

He was posted off somewhere else when the battery went east but he came to mind a lot when we were on the run after Singapore and Palembang and then when we were took up by the Japs in Java. Whenever things got a bit brown I'd remember old Peabody telling me to 'Stand still man.' It wasn't about playing the big man, the Japs and Koreans soon learnt anybody as tried that. It was more of a quiet thing inside you that said if you hold on and do your bit you'd be able to hold your head up once it's all over.

Bombardier Fidler did not have a good war. Often in the combat zone without a rifle, let alone an anti-aircraft gun, he did not have the sexy job that attracts medals. As a survivor of the Battle of France, the Dunkirk evacuation, the fall of Singapore, defeats in Sumatra and Java, then slavery in Japan, he did what countless others have done: he endured.

Good leaders can show a man how to endure but there is a lot more to leadership than can be squeezed into a few words. Most of it cannot be measured. But whether it is old-school leadership like Fidler experienced or the more hands-on approach of today's corporals and sergeants, no book can tell a soldier about real leadership. Although this may be a cliché, all my experience talking to combat veterans has convinced me that the only way to understand leadership is to live it.

So, while Gobby Scouser was trying to pull his cohesion facts together, I delved into the mass of books and journal articles that claimed to say something useful about leadership. These ranged from the delightful but often misty-eyed recollections of old generals to the nauseating evangelism of management gurus.

There turned out to be only a few hard facts at the edge of leadership that could be seen to have a real effect on close combat. At the top of the list is the way that section and platoon commanders give everyone else a physical example to see and to follow. Like Wigram's 'guts and movement' commanders, they are most often the first to opt for a fight response and by doing so they increase the power of the cohesion magnet that pulls men into the fight.

Leaders can be designated and given stripes or pips by higher command, or they can be emergent and rise to the challenge only when things turn nasty. When things are going well, leaders increase the chance that men keep on fighting, but when things turn bad, leaders are the ones who buck the bystander trend. In this situation both types of leader can be seen as the deviants who create the reverse bystander effect.

While leaders pull men into the fight-through example, they also act as the bridge that links our simpler version of cohesion with some elements of that broader military definition. But sticking to the chain of command and making sure men stick to the job in hand can be more accurately described as compulsion, because this is not the glue that binds men, but a force that drives them on.

A platoon sergeant's battlefield job has sometimes been described as 'moving from flank to flank, driving on'. They push men into fighting. So, while it has become fashionable to emphasise how soldiers fight for their mates, we should not forget that men also fight because somebody tells them to. And then stands with them to make sure that they do.

Compulsion is a constant theme in war. We have already seen in Sergeant Dawson's story how junior commanders directly compel men into the fight. Then, in Provost Skobelev's letter, the mere presence of an officer seemed to double the accuracy of firing squads.

Unit tradition, debt to country, corps or regiment and an ephemeral bond with higher commanders combine to provide an undercurrent of compulsion. Unfortunately, these are ambient effects that cannot be properly measured and cannot be controlled in combat. For our focus on the close tactical level, such strategic factors form part of a soldier's baseline motivation to fight. In a tight spot there is also a tendency for these out-of-sight bonds to slip from the mind so, in a hard fight, most compulsion comes directly from the corporals, sergeants and commissioned officers who represent higher authority in a close battle.

Compulsion sometimes needs blatant threats but it is more often an unspoken drive to work harder when the boss is near by. S. L. A. Marshall sometimes suggested that company and battalion commanders were unaware of the supposed fire ratio problem because, wherever they went, their presence compelled men to fight. While there is reason to doubt some of Marshall's work, there is certainly an element of truth in this point. The mere presence of an authority figure is powerful on its own and has a direct impact on a soldier's 'is it worth it?' calculation.

The strongest evidence we have for this comes from research led by David Rowland, a British historical analyst who examined many aspects of tactical psychology long before it was called tactical psychology. Rowland came to be the granddaddy of historical analysis, but he was originally tasked with working out the best balance of tanks and anti-tank weapons needed to face the armoured might of the Warsaw Pact. For years, armour fans had been saying that: 'The best thing for killing a tank is another tank.' Rowland proved this to be wrong: in fact, anti-tank guns were far more efficient tank killers. He also found that anti-tank gun crews appeared to be up to ten times more effective when they were watched over by commissioned officers or senior sergeants.

The classic example of this is from the battle for Point Snipe, which formed part of the Second Battle of El Alamein in 1942. This critical point in a pivotal battle had the battle-winning six-pounder anti-tank gun manned by a corporal, a sergeant, a lieutenant and a lieutenant colonel. Together with the private soldiers around the gun, they managed to destroy at least seven German and Italian tanks: more kills than many armoured regiments were able achieve that day.

In other battles, two-pounder guns mounted on the back of small flatbed lorries, perhaps the most vulnerable anti-tank weapon ever invented, were used against German Panzer IVs with three or four times the firepower and twenty times the protection. In these circumstances it is hard to understand why any of the gun crews fought at all – but they did. Rowland found that they were most likely to fight when they were helped out, or simply watched over, by someone with at least three stripes on their uniform.

As usual, Rowland's work was subject to the 'preferred answer' syndrome. The powerful pro-armour lobby in Western armies at the time brushed over the finding that anti-tank guns were a more effective way of stopping Russian tank divisions. In those days, 'buy fewer tanks' was not welcome news, especially after the Berlin Wall came down and armoured regiments were likely to be disbanded anyway.

Other facts about the nature of anti-tank weapons were also lost in the noise and bias of military procurement, but everyone latched onto Rowland's compulsion findings, which seemed to say that what armies really needed was a lot more officers. To work out how true it might be, we need to take another quick look at some civilian psychology studies.

*   *   *

In the early 1960s, Stanley Milgram, a psychology professor at Yale, recruited people to take part in a learning experiment. He got pairs of volunteer subjects to draw straws to see who would play the teacher and who would play the learner. The 'teacher' watched while the 'learner' was strapped into a chair and attached to a machine that dished out electric shocks. The teacher was then taken into a separate room and seated at a desk with a microphone, a list of questions and the control panel for the electric shock machine. A professor sat near the teacher to give directions if they were needed.

The teacher was then required to ask questions and give the learner, out of sight in the other room, an electric shock every time there was a wrong answer. The shocks started at fifteen volts and increased by another fifteen volts for every wrong answer. As the shocks became more intense, the teacher heard the learner yelp, demand to be let out, scream and eventually fall silent. Most of the teachers were clearly uncomfortable, suggested stopping and fumbled a lot. But when the professor issued his stock phrase of 'please carry on', most of them did. Two out of three teachers went all the way to the highest-level shock: a clearly fatal 450 volts.

Once the experiment was finished, the teacher was let in on the act. In case you have not guessed, the apparently random selection of teacher and learner was rigged, the learner and the professor were actors, the shock machine was a fake and the answers or screams were all pre-recorded. The experiment was actually aimed at finding out how far people would go when someone in authority, in this case the professor in his lab coat, told them to do something risky then waited around to watch them do it.

The Milgram studies can tell us something about how compulsion can overcome aversion to killing but not how it works against fear and common sense. Soldiers do things that are simultaneously dangerous to others and to themselves. In combat, the teacher can get zapped just as easily as the learner, so Milgram only gives us half the story.

To work around this, a series of unofficial variations of the Milgram study have compelled test subjects to do things that were more like combat. Two of the American Sennelager Club members conducted a firing-range trial, where soldiers were tricked into thinking that their shots were ricocheting back onto the firing line. In another trial, which pretended to examine parachuting accidents, soldiers were led to believe their jump was set up to test the effect of air steals. (An air steal happens when a parachute sucks the air out of one above it. The chance of an air steal was one of the many things that played on Master Sergeant Johansson's mind when he lay awake between jumps.)

Similar studies used risky military training or extreme sports. Each study, deliberately or accidentally, compared the level of risk that soldiers would accept for themselves or others when they were, or were not, compelled by men of higher rank.

The results of these little studies were clouded by all sorts of unforeseen factors. In one instance, a respected junior sergeant could get men to do much riskier things than the 'pencil-neck' major who was supposed to be doing the job. Many soldiers were willing to do something that risked themselves or strangers but would do nothing to endanger their mates. One white-water rafter hit the experimenter with a paddle rather than do the risky thing. This kind of thing often happens when staff officers and researchers try to mess with soldiers' heads.

While these studies all involved risks, they were a good few steps away from actual combat. Other trials comparing painful marking ammunition with painless laser-weapon effects simulation showed how it can take a lot more compulsion to get soldiers to break cover when getting shot really stings, but, once again, they are a long way from real war.

Yet, when all these studies are combined with historical analysis, particularly the work of David Rowland and his colleagues, they give us a fairly good idea of how compulsion changes the 'is it worth it?' calculation. When compulsion is added to the mix, a soldier is no longer asking: 'will the possible effect on the enemy of my active participation be worth the possible adverse effect on me?' With the boss beside him, the soldier pays much more attention to the adverse personal consequences of not fighting; these range from social embarrassment to being shot in the back of the head. The threat might not be stated openly, but it is there nonetheless.

When the boss is present, there are extra rewards for fighting too. Medals, ribbons and booty play a part, but the social and self-esteem rewards seem to have the biggest effect.

There is a fairly clear upper limit to the power of compulsion. No matter what romantic nonsense West Point, Saint-Cyr or Sandhurst instructors sometimes feed to officer cadets, even well-led soldiers will not jump into volcanoes to order. When any boss, no matter how good, jumps up for an obvious death or glory charge, soldiers almost always choose not to share in the experience.

The few exceptions to this come when the designated leader is right on the man's shoulder. Physical proximity greatly increases the effect and can trick men into doing things that look extremely rash. A series of small-unit actions have been examined in detail to look at the effect. In many of these examples, the senior rank revved everyone up to rush the enemy but only the two or three men right next to him actually joined in. At the time, these men were considered to be the most gutful; in fact, they were simply closest to the boss.

* * *

In practice, it is almost impossible to separate the compulsion and cohesion effects of leadership, because the man who says 'follow me' is mixing push and pull. While there is an academic debate about the interaction of cohesion and compulsion, we have to consider the pull and the push from leaders as being the same thing. This combined compulsion works when trading fire with the enemy at a distance and during the intimate violence of assaults. But the effects can be seen best in the mid-range of combat intensity, when men have to move towards danger but are not yet really close to the enemy.

In a textbook section attack of the kind taught by Lionel Wigram, and still taught at infantry schools around the world, everyone has a reasonable idea of the enemy's location and strength. The enemy is a few hundred metres away and suppressed by another section. This puts the chance of each attacker surviving at better than 90 per cent, though a soldier might consider it closer to fifty-fifty. As far as can be seen from those small-unit actions, these attacks almost never get off the ground without the presence of higher rank, and this is usually someone from outside the section.

Without this compulsive presence, the section stays where it is
and trades fire but very rarely tries to close with the enemy.

When private soldiers are left on their own to start something
that involves high-risk violence, fewer than 20 per cent of them do
it. When a low-authority leader is present, the chances increase
to 40 per cent. A high-authority figure (and this could be Fidler's
Major Peabody or Skobelev's adjutant, but could equally be a well-
respected corporal) raises the chances of soldiers closing with the
enemy to 70 per cent. The effect is moderated by the proximity
and visibility of soldiers and leaders. Darkness and close terrain
reduce the effect considerably.

Compulsion has to push against all the degrading factors we
have seen so far, and a few we have yet to see, but it has a profound
effect. Those closely examined small-unit actions were combined
with the Milgram-style studies and historical analysis, including
David Rowland's unclassified data, to derive a 'practical maximum'
effect. This practical maximum is something less than having
General Patton on the shoulder of every man in a unit: more
like the effect from a senior sergeant or respected junior officer.
In daylight and open country during that moderately intense
engagement, it will make a soldier six times more likely to fight.

By itself, this figure is of little use to a combat soldier. A section
or platoon commander can put himself in a position to compel,
but he can never be in all places at once. He can try to target enemy
leaders, but this is even trickier. In any case, these decisions are
bread and butter for junior commanders.

Curiously, compulsion is one of those things that works best
when everyone, not just the designated leader, understands how
it works and accepts the need for someone, almost irrespective of who it is, to be the leader. This can be seen in units which

encourage the ready acceptance of a leadership role, where a junior rank steps up and says 'follow me' when there is nobody else to do the job. Whether it is a Napoleonic grenadier with a marshal's baton in his pack or an Israeli paratrooper who has been fed the 'follow me' spirit all his life, units where all men are expected to lead suffer far less combat degradation than others. A leader is needed to get the job done, but at the sharp end this leader can be any good soldier who has the respect of his mates and the will to take on the job.

In the small number of attacks where a section went in without a designated leader, the men always came from a unit where there was a 'follow me' tradition. In each instance, a private soldier looked at his mates and decided it was up to him to get the job done.

As with all the other factors we have considered so far, cohesion and compulsion will only be of real use when they are combined with everything else. Fortunately, now that most of the basic psychological processes have been outlined, we can have a good look at the nitty-gritty of battle.

ELEVEN

PROXIMITY

COLONEL ARDANT DU PICQ, FRENCH WARS OF THE 1800S

Physical impulse is just words. It is the worst mistake to believe in the physical impulse. If the head of a column wants to stop then it will fall to the ground rather than be pushed forward. Anyone who has truly experienced and understood the infantry battle of today knows that this is what happens. The physical impulse was dominant in the days of the Empire and still is today, so strong is the force of routine and prejudice, yet the attacks in close column are absolute disorder, outside a leader's control.

This is what happens. If your battalion is eager and the men fresh from barracks, if their load is light and they think only of the manoeuvre, then I have to admit, it marches in narrow columns with its sub-divisions separated by four measured paces as the companies shape and order their men. However, as soon as the pace increases or the ground becomes uneven or the guide stops marching with math-ematical precision, is it not true that your narrow column battalion will become, in the blink of an eye, a disorganised herd of sheep?

But let us move on. Though no one will ever see this order in the days of the rifle, let us assume that your battalion is now 100 feet from the enemy and in good order. What is going to happen? Nothing: it is ten to one that your enemy will already have fled the field.

But let us again assume that the enemy does not flee. Man, naked against iron and lead, cannot control himself. The instinct of self-preservation has absolute power and there are but two ways for the man caught in the middle to reduce the risk: to run away or to rush forward. Let us rush forward!

Oh well! Even if the distance is short and the enemy only a moment away, it is again the instinct that takes over. We rush forward, but most of us will rush forward with caution in the back of our minds, allowing the rash to pass us and the daring to rush ahead. It is peculiar but absolutely true that the closer we get to the enemy the further we get from each other. Goodbye to the theory of surge. And if the head of the column is stopped those who are behind it will fall to the ground rather than push it forward. Even if this stopped head were pushed it would itself fall to the ground. I make no outcry; this is just the way it is. There is a surge but it is to the ground and to the rear.

But the enemy does not stand, the moral pressure of approaching danger is too strong for any waiting, any force that can stand in the aim, even with empty rifles, will never see the enemy charge reach them. The first rank of any attackers would feel dead and no one wishes to take a place in that first rank. So the enemy never stands unless it is you that is running away. Goodbye to shock.

All the peoples of Europe are saying that no one can stand against a bayonet charge made by them, and they are all correct.

When I eventually paid off Gobby Scouser with that promised curry, I also brought along Old Boss. Old Boss insisted we go to a Nepalese place in Aldershot where, being a veteran of a few small wars and a vague relation to a Gurkha, he was treated like a pop star. We were indulged with a four-hour banquet featuring the full range of Nepalese classics, Gurkha pork specials and the restaurant owner's personal collection of strong drink.

We had a lot of catching up to do between mouthfuls. Old Boss had moved up the greasy pole in Whitehall, so his waking hours were filled with shady preparations for the Iraq War. Gobby had just landed a big contract to have another look at that white elephant of a light tank. I found myself admitting that I was managing a former government research department that had been privatised against its will and was likely to dissolve in the next few years.

There was a tacit realisation that we had sold our souls to the dark side: Old Boss for his gold-plated pension, Gobby for his tax-efficient dividends, and me for my stack of free company shares. Day to day we plodded on, trying to convince ourselves that we were bringing some integrity to the job, but it was clear that we had lost our zeal and principles.

For a second or two, I think we all wanted to talk about this. There was an exchange of tight, flat smiles and a sigh or two, but then we did the blokey thing and made a joke of it. We came close to broaching the subject later but Old Boss distracted us with the details of how the Sennelager Club eventually ate itself.

From outside the Sennelager Club, the Gulf War had sparked a technology obsession which created a wedge of acronyms and wishful thinking. Missile makers and military parochialism then hammered this wedge between research and combat. After a few cycles of seeing soldiers as weapon platforms or as nodes on the tactical internet, it was hard to find any analyst or staff officer who could speak squaddie. It was as if a memo had gone around saying that everyone below the rank of captain had to wear a badge marked 'does not understand the big picture'.

Then the War on Terror was invented and everyone started to mistake dissent for defeatism. It became career suicide to question anything, whether it was the strategic sense of invading Iraq or why the army really needed quite so many outmoded computers. Old Boss told us of a promising young major who questioned a particular mix of technology and doctrine too loudly in the wrong company: 'It was as if he'd been caught taking a shit on the Cenotaph. Two weeks later he was counting paperclips in South Georgia.'

Inside the Sennelager Club, patronage got out of hand when members started to ask their bosses to meetings. Then speakers and hangers-on started to be selected for entertainment rather than insight. The final nail came when someone tried to make a club tie. In the end, the Sennelager Club turned into a slow and boring version of Facebook.

It was only when we were tucking into the third or fourth course that we worked out we represented three generations of failure in tactical psychology. Just as Gobby Scouser repeated my failure from ten years earlier, Old Boss had failed ten years before me. After a round of mocking each other's howlers, Gobby and I took turns to prattle on about cohesion and compulsion.

All the while, Old Boss hid his smug grin by shovelling food into his face or taking sips from his magic whisky tumbler. When we had finally tied cohesion and compulsion together into what looked, to us, like a tidy package, Old Boss dropped his bombshell: 'Of course, all your clever sums and social psychology mumbo-jumbo come to nothing when it gets down to sticking bayonets in people.'

We complained that he had broken Sennelager Club's rules by reminding us how he had seen 'proper' war. Granted, the Sennelager Club had no list of rules, but we had decided that Rule 3 should be: 'No member shall try to win an argument by using combat experience as a way of pulling rank.'

In his defence, Old Boss offered a half-drunk, half-serious suggestion that he had, in the true spirit of the original Sennelager Club, reached his higher state of consciousness by combining his combat experience with many tedious trips to the Public Records Office. Above all, he claimed to have achieved nirvana by thoroughly absorbing the writings of Ardant du Picq.

Unfortunately, Old Boss proved too incoherent, and too easily distracted, to provide a reliable account that night. The next morning we met up and, with the aid of a whiteboard and a little caffeine, he told us about his discovery.

*   *   *

Colonel Charles Jean Jacques Joseph Ardant du Picq knew a lot about fighting. He saw action in Syria, Algeria and the Crimean War, where he was captured by the Russians while storming Sevastopol. So he knew all about the things that stopped men fighting too. He is recognised as one of the great military theorists but, before he could pull his ideas into a coherent whole, he was killed leading his regiment in one of the first battles of the Franco-Prussian War of 1870–71. His death allowed many of his ideas to be misinterpreted and then, with disastrous consequences, misapplied in the First World War.

That small quote from *Battle Studies* includes an incredible amount of tactical psychology. And, like Ardant du Picq, we have reached a point where we can no longer examine the forces of tactical psychology in isolation. The proximity effect is so wrapped up with fire, fear, common sense and aversion to killing that we now have to look at how all these things work together when men fight at close quarters.

The critical point of Ardant du Picq's work is that one line which says: 'The closer we get to the enemy the further we get from each other.' It refers to the way units physically and emotionally fragment as they approach the enemy, losing much of the reverse bystander effect that comes from cohesion and compulsion.

The best way to understand this is to trace the evolution of that physical impulse that Ardant du Picq was so worried about. This needs another step back to a time when firepower was less dominant, when most men fought toe-to-toe, and when the physical impulse was more than just words.

*   *   *

The phalanx is most often associated with ancient Greek combat but it crops up throughout history with different names to reflect variations in weapons and tactics. The Greek idea was for armoured men with shields and long heavy spears to stand in tight even files, ten or twelve ranks deep. Variations of the phalanx did away with shields or armour, or had men armed with halberds, billhooks, sarissa, naginata, pikes up to seven metres long, and sometimes swords or sharp sticks.

The phalanx hung around, in one form or another, until Ardant du Picq's time, when the men in them were armed with rifles and bayonets. At that point it started to become obvious that bullets and shrapnel shells made standing upright and close together very unhealthy.

The unifying theme of the phalanx variations was for a tightly packed hedge of spikes to hold off enemies or make hard physical contact with blade, mass and muscle power. Military psychologists love the phalanx because it boils close combat down to the basics. The evolution and eventual demise of the phalanx let us examine the proximity effect and the way this has influenced the physical and psychological forces of modern close combat.

The Greek phalanx was slow and inflexible; it could suffer terribly if the enemy had effective missile weapons or had the means to attack its vulnerable flanks. But it delivered an incredibly powerful physical and psychological shock to anything it hit. When it did make contact, it tended to roll over the enemy or force them to quit the field, unless they too had some form of phalanx.

This system of warfare originally evolved, and then kept on re-emerging, because of the problems of getting loose bands of skirmishers to close with the enemy. The earlier tribal way of fighting in an open line or loose crowd could rarely build up enough cohesion and compulsion to get the whole force to close with the enemy.

In Ardant du Picq's language, the closer a band of skirmishers got to the enemy, the further they got from each other. When men in a loose formation come close to interpersonal violence they start to look out for themselves and this separates the few most gutful or most compelled men from the majority. This type of fighting was sometimes called heroic because it broke down into islands of one-on-one violence where the born, trained or compelled fighters did all of the work, while the rest floated around the edge of the battle. This looked a lot like an adolescent gang fight, where most of the kids hop about on the edge of the action, doing little more than egging on the main protagonists.

The phalanx exploited cohesion and compulsion to make much more efficient use of manpower. Each man could see and rub shoulders with his mates and leaders until he made physical contact with the enemy, so the physical impulse of being surrounded by men who were all moving forward combined with the reverse bystander effect to keep everyone in line.

Before contact was made, this combination usually quashed any urge to flee or freeze, while the simplicity of walking forwards carrying a big stick minimised fussing. This made the phalanx the ideal way to get men from the edge of a battle into the thick of things. Then, once in contact, the extreme close order of the phalanx gave it the emotional and physical weight to keep men in line until the fight turned really nasty.

All that tightly packed social pressure plus, with a few exceptions, the relatively modest missile threat, meant that unlike Ardant du Picq's men having holes shot through their ranks, nearly everyone in a Greek phalanx could move at a uniform pace. If rank and file did become disordered while moving, there were few penalties for pausing to realign the phalanx before the final approach to the enemy.

At that time, the true face of battle only appeared in that first physical contact. Most young men (the front ranks of phalanxes were filled with the younger men) fail to realise the horror of war until they see someone they know being killed or injured. In a phalanx war, this often happened only when the enemy were close enough to spit at. By that point, a soldier did not have much time to think of ways out of the situation: he was arm's length from danger and his physical options were limited by the press of men all around him.

But, when contact was made, there was suddenly an incredible amount of violence packed into that tiny space too.

The simplicity of phalanx combat and the popular term 'push of pike' can make people on the sidelines mistake its basic slaughter and manoeuvre for a game of rugby or American football. Granted, there was a lot of shoving, but the language of push and scrum tends to obscure the fact that both teams were armed with long poles tipped with metal spikes. When phalanxes clashed, many soldiers in the forward ranks were instantly maimed or killed. With a spike through the thigh or groin, a man would drop unless he was held up by his comrades; with one in the armpit or neck, the weapon might help to hold him upright. But otherwise he would drop and be trampled.

To avoid this fate, even an armoured and well-drilled soldier would use up his limited wiggle room trying to reverse, sidestep or twist away. Some men who had not yet been injured would drop to the ground despite the danger of being crushed. Then the forward ranks tumbled and slipped over the fallen. Helmets, shields and weapons could be torn away. Combatants on the forward edge entered a morass where knife work started to take over.

The first three ranks of a phalanx were a very unpleasant place to be. But there was no way out, as long as the rear ranks continued pushing forward. Yet, seven or eight ranks back there were few benefits to be gained from shoving, as the effort was as likely to crush your own side as the enemy. Rear ranks might then be peeled off to extend or protect the flanks and men would begin to ease off to conserve their strength or to allow the forward ranks a little manoeuvre space.

The fight was often decided near the sixth rank of a phalanx. With the pressure on their backs eased, these men began to contemplate the mincing machine that was chewing up the forward ranks. With no hiding places and the enemy not yet in a position to accept surrender, freezing was unlikely to slip into the sensible, habitual or clinical layers. Then, just as in the advance, simplicity meant minimal fussing. The men in the sixth rank had a fairly straight choice between fighting and fleeing.

Their dilemma was particularly intense because the social and physical pressure of the phalanx did not just clash with the normal levels of fear, common sense and aversion – it smacked head-on into the psychological wall of enemy proximity.

*   *   *

In modern war, the psychology of proximity makes all the difference between the long-range firefight and that especially personal bit of fighting in an assault. This intimate kind of fight shifts the balance of power in tactical psychology.

Dave Grossman, a retired US colonel and modern combat theorist, suggests that there is a universal human phobia towards interpersonal violence. This label is a little confusing because a phobia is an irrational fear; being afraid of being battered or killed by another man is far more rational than a fear of beards, clowns or paper clips. Yet there is clear merit in what Grossman says.

People have a much more coherent understanding of toe-to-toe violence than they do of a long-range firefight. Most men have taken a beating at some point, so interpersonal violence puts fear, common sense and aversion back on familiar ground. This makes their combined effect much more intense. As a result, proximity works against cohesion and compulsion, to have a marked effect on a man's choice between the four Fs.

Grossman has suggested that perhaps 2 per cent of men do not suffer from the aversion to close personal violence. Another 5 or 10 per cent acquire some immunity through repeated experience of winning and some others seem to work around the problem some of the time. Despite this, almost all soldiers are still much more averse to getting into an interpersonal fight than they are to trading fire at a distance.

Hints of this can be seen in dozens of combat accounts. A good example comes from a Pacific veteran saying how 'the line gets drawn when you're close enough to really smell 'em. Plenty of men would shoot a Jap from fifty yards but there's not so many who'd get close enough to stick a knife in him.' Others speak of the way a defensive line starts to fragment as the assault gets closer, with men firing into the air or looking to the rear just before the enemy get close to bayonet range.

An assessment of battles during the First World War campaign in Palestine sheds some light on the proximity effect. One of General Allenby's staff conducted a detailed study of casualties that Old Boss managed to find in a mass of forgotten paperwork. He turned the result into a tidy-looking graph where casualties to small-arms fire increased as the attackers got closer and easier to hit. Starting at 400 metres, there was a predictable increase in attacker casualties, with more than twice as many being killed at 200 metres, and nearly four times as many at 100 metres.

But then, from around fifty metres, defensive fire rapidly loses its effectiveness. By the time the enemy is twenty metres away, defensive fire has less effect than at 200 metres.

The figures needed careful interpretation to account for effects like machine guns being unable to traverse at close range and defenders being killed, injured or suppressed by fire. There was also a chance that the body count may have included some men killed by artillery and friendly fire. On top of this, fussing seems to have had a direct effect for some of the Palestine battles, with the defenders sometimes failing to adjust their rifle sights and therefore firing over the heads of close attackers. But, once these effects are subtracted (a tedious process combining maps, war diaries and ballistic tables) there is still a clear proximity effect on either the quality or quantity of fire from the defenders: as the attack got closer, more of the defenders were either firing wide or not firing at all.

Another staff study combined these Palestine battles with a selection of similar attacks from other wars. This study concluded that the drop in effectiveness was due to a shift in the behaviour of defenders once the attackers got closer than fifty metres. At around 200 metres, two-thirds of defenders were seen to be fighting, one-third of defenders were fussing or freezing and about one in twenty were doing something that looked a lot like fleeing. This shifted by the time the attackers got to around twenty metres, with one in five fighting and nearly half of the men either freezing or fussing. The rest of the defenders, about a third, were clearly starting to flee. (The original assessment did not separate freeze and fuss; men were said to be either 'attempting to surrender', 'dazed' or doing 'nothing of use'.)

Both these studies were based on successful attacks, so they included only passing reference to the effect on attackers, yet proximity clearly has an impact on both sides. Wigram, Marshall and Ardant du Picq all reported attackers simply stopping just at the point where it was most dangerous to do so. Rather than push on into the close fight or run back to a place where the fire is less intense, these men stayed at the edge of interpersonal violence.

The effect on attackers caused a lot of headaches for Old Boss. Some men die while frozen in the killing area; others stay hidden until the battle ends. Sometimes soldiers flee but are cut down; at other times they manage to make it to safety. Very often, both sides will stop and trade fire rather than close the distance to bayonet range. There was an echo of this in the attack on Corporal Rabuka's platoon house, when the insurgents fought all the way up to about thirty metres from the platoon house but then stalled and withdrew rather than press the attack. Marshall's 'Fight on Saké Night' has the same feel and we will get other glimpses in later accounts. But the psychology of the failed assault is one of the true mysteries of combat.

It is unlikely that anyone will be able to unpick all of the details underlying the proximity effect. Maybe, as Grossman suggests, it is some kind of phobia; maybe, as the Palestine staff study suggested, it is pure 'fear of the bayonet'. It is probably a potent mix of fear, common sense and aversion to killing. What is known is that a man has a much greater tendency to stop fighting at the point where he can see that his battle is about to become personal and he still has a chance to get away. At this 'last safe moment', the pressure from comrades and commanders is suddenly countered by proximity, giving soldiers a much clearer understanding of combat.

*   *   *

The collision between cohesion, compulsion and proximity can be seen in the way this last safe moment has come to be further from the enemy and to have its effect on smaller groups of soldiers.

In those Greek phalanx battles, a fight usually involved physical contact with a drawn-out period of shoving and slaughter before one side or the other gained the upper hand. Then, often around that sixth rank, enough men passed into freezing and fleeing for a Mexican wave to infect a whole phalanx. Two or three men would stop fighting, then ten or twelve; then nearly everybody would stop. With an army often composed of only two or three massive phalanxes, the whole battle could collapse in a matter of minutes and shift to rout and pursuit.

In the pike-and-shot battles of the 1600s there was more fire from muskets or artillery, so casualties came at a greater distance from the enemy. The phalanxes were smaller and men sometimes fought in a more open formation, maybe a metre apart rather than rubbing shoulders, so cohesion and compulsion tended to lose their reverse bystander effect earlier. Compared to its classical predecessor, a phalanx in the 1600s was more likely to collapse before it made physical contact with the enemy.

But pikemen generally moved to close order for an assault, so there was usually enough psychological and physical pressure to get them to make contact with the enemy. The period of slaughter in the pike push, with proximity at full effect, tended to be shorter but the rout was more localised. The gaps between phalanxes acted like circuit breakers to stop the Mexican wave from spreading. Battalions disintegrated rather than whole armies, with other battalions able to plug the gaps.

There was more fire and less close order by the time Ardant du Picq and the breech-loading rifle came along. The loss of impetus was starting to become obvious because the phalanx had thinned to three or four ranks deep and men stood even further apart. The front ranks were no longer physically pinned by the men either side of them, and this made it very difficult for them to be shoved forward by the men behind.

As a result, an attack nearly always stalled or collapsed before there was physical contact unless, as Ardant du Picq noted, the defence had already started to collapse instead. Smaller phalanxes, and more space between the people in them, increased the number of circuit breakers so, once again, the rout became more localised, with companies fleeing and other companies stepping forward to take their place.

By the end of the First World War, battlefield dispersal had reduced the impetus from cohesion and compulsion, greatly reducing the impact when they collided with fire and proximity. The circuit breaks from dispersal meant that a rout could be limited to a platoon or section. Companies and battalions would still collapse, but this was rare; the rout of a whole army developed more slowly and usually happened at a greater distance from the enemy.

Where a classical spearman might have his last safe moment five metres from the enemy, it was nearer twenty metres for a man with a musket and bayonet and is maybe fifty metres for a man with a modern assault rifle. In modern battles between balanced forces on open ground, fire and dispersal have removed the physical impulse and greatly reduced the psychological impulse that came with it. Many factors help decide the distance at which the last safe moment takes effect, but the most obvious of these is terrain.

Marshall's description of 'Saké Night' had most of the killing within ten metres. Accounts of failed attacks in woods and forests tell a similar story, with a mass of dead attackers often only a few metres short of a defended position. At first glance this seems to contradict the assessment of those successful Palestine attacks, where the killing peaked at around fifty metres.

Close terrain makes for close engagement ranges (it being difficult to shoot someone when they are behind a tree) but it also puts the last safe moment much nearer to the enemy. On Saké Night the Japanese attackers were revved up by booze and banzai, then, in close order and out of sight of their enemy, they rushed forward. But by the time they could see the enemy, or at least tell by muzzle flashes and shouting that he was very close, the ground and the dark had stolen the reverse bystander impulse. The attackers were suddenly in clumps of three or four men, facing a close enemy and mostly out of sight of their leaders.

Many fought, some fled but a lot of them stopped moving forward in those last ten metres and died there. Those that fled were given more booze and banzai then sent back in to repeat the process with diminishing chances of success. Meanwhile the defenders had all the physical advantages of defence, despite their cohesion-breaking foxholes. Analysis of attacks at night, in woods, in towns or over very rough ground tends to show the same effect. The attack falters very close to the enemy positions unless the defenders can be overwhelmed locally, and then it is the defenders' turn to rout or surrender.

*   *   *

If men pass through the last safe moment, they appear to reach a 'point of no return'. Like those men in the front ranks of a phalanx or the soldier who turns a corner and is face-to-face with a Taliban gunman, they have gone past the last safe moment and this steals any survival advantage from fleeing or fussing. It is very clear that running or stalling will probably get them killed, so their only options are to fight or try to surrender. With only two viable options, this greatly increases the chances that men will fight once they get to within a few metres of each other.

This is where tactical psychology reaches its murkiest point. Sometimes two men come face-to-face, both fight and one dies; or one freezes or tries to surrender but dies anyway. Sometimes both men sit down to smoke cigarettes and trade family photos. Unfortunately for us, these men are always overtaken by events before a staff officer can show up with a notebook and try to work out what happened. The tide of battle turns; other men kill them, capture them or drag them back into the fight.

For tactical psychology, the point of no return is like dark matter in physics: something extremely important that no one really understands. Extreme proximity changes the rules of tactical psychology and hides most of the hard data. This has caused staff officers and analysts to brush over what happens between the last safe moment and the point of no return. But vague muttering is not an option; if tactical psychology is going to help soldiers win wars, it has to get a grip on what happens in a close battle.

*   *   *

When all the scraps of evidence were combined and savoured with a pinch of salt, Old Boss found that there are two fairly sound numbers. The first is that, at the last safe moment, the number of men who actually fight drops to a quarter of that for a long-range exchange of fire. But then, at the point of no return, the number of men fighting jumps back up to the level we see in a firefight.

For the fighting soldier, these figures highlight the danger and the opportunity that comes from men faltering in the crucial zone just before an assault. This is particularly important because the chaotic interaction of proximity, fire and close terrain is one of the defining characteristics of the fighting in Afghanistan.

Engagement ranges are very short in the Afghan green zones or in villages that are a maze of alleyways and compounds. As a result, the men at the front of a fighting patrol are often making contact with the enemy when they are already past the point of no return. Meanwhile their comrades just ten or twenty metres further back realise there is a close personal fight ahead of them and stop short around their point of no return. A few men are doing most of the fighting because they have no other option. Their mates cannot help them because dispersal has stolen the means to push them past the point of no return.

This is another example of soldiers having to relearn old lessons. Like those 'guts and movement' attacks seen by Lionel Wigram, men in Afghanistan are forced to fight with tactics that do not suit the psychology of war. We will see later how this is having an effect on soldiers walking the line in Helmand, Kandahar and Paktika provinces.

TWELVE

WEAPON-PULL

CORPORAL BOHR, ITALY, 1944

Our machine guns open up; one, then another, then another all across their front, pouring fire into them as they pick their way over the broken ground. Flares go up and then the mortars switch to fire for effect. There is some fire in return and some firing of our snipers and riflemen, maybe even some of our scarce artillery, but most of the noise in our little zone is Hitler's zip fly, the MG42, pouring death and fear into their ranks. In the gaps between firing all the shouting would be from the Three Grenadiers demanding more ammunition or warning us to cover them.

Did anyone tell you about those crazy men the Three Grenadiers? These are the guys in our squad that look after the machine gun and they're known through the whole regiment for this silly showing-off game that they play. They style themselves after The Three Musketeers, wear silk flowers in their lapels, curtsey to each other and speak with bad French accents. They like to wear big felt hats when the drink gets passed around. One of them is always half cut. And there are usually five of them, not three.

Our officers tut but tolerate this 'exuberance' because everyone who's been in the Three Grenadiers has turned into a real war-hound. It started months before with the original cast of clowns and that gods' blessed gun of theirs which they treat like a little prince. It has a name: 'Shouty' they call it. And it gets all kinds of special treatment. They make presents for it like a specially adapted tripod and home-rigged changes to its parts. It even had a bullet shield for a while, and that was to protect the gun as much as the men working it. They treat its camouflage like decoration: 'Shouty's party clothes' they call it.

This game is played as a childish thing, the kind of thing boy scouts or recruits do, but they've exaggerated it all and pretend it to be a piece of fun; Christ, especially as that gun's had so many new parts it's a different tool twice over. They're all old hands now and they know this is silliness but they love and pamper that gun like a prize calf.

In battle it is 'well done Shouty', 'steady now Shouty' or telling the rest of us to 'hurry now, bring Shouty's bullets' or 'make way! Let Shouty through!' Normal squads abandon guns when things get too tricky but we've had to risk our lives carrying lumps of that precious gun for them. When we really had to leave it behind they brought back a spare barrel or something and then built another gun round that so they could imagine it was still Shouty.

For sure we let them do it: when the rest of us are beetling about trying to keep our heads on our necks they are up there firing off belts as if they grow on a magic bush. Brrrp! Brrrp! Brrrrrrrrrrp! Ten, twenty, fifty bullets a time. Hot, loud, lethal lines of fire that shield the whole company and chop down Yanks and Poles and Indians and whoever else they throw at us.

We know why they do it too. That gun has killed many brave men over the last half-year (away from this madness, you would cry to see the sacrifice); it has given power to the gunners without making them killers. You see, if Shouty is real like a person, then all that the Three Grenadiers are doing is serving him while he does the murder. Brrrp! Brrrp! Yes.

It helps that Shouty and those less exalted machine guns are the most powerful weapons that the squads have to hand. One of them can do more pinning and more killing than all the company's rifles and machine pistols combined. The panzerfaust [an infantry anti-tank weapon] *and such can come in handy but for much of the fighting they get in the way. Whether we have to move or stay put, the machine guns are our backbone and they give extra backbone to the men that work them. We work and fight around them but they and the mortars do all but the smallest fraction of the killing.*

Although we pretend to sneer at the Three Grenadiers, every time one of them is replaced, the new man changes from a mud-crawler to a war-hound. After a day or two he pins on a flower, puts on a bad accent and starts shooting for a medal or a glorious death.

Who says the Germans have no sense of humour? Retreating up the mountainous backbone of Italy, being hammered by air, artillery and men from a dozen nations, these soldiers fought from one rubble village to the next in a war that they knew was lost. But somehow, the Three Grenadiers bucked the Prussian scowl to make fighting into a dressing-up game. It might not be very funny now, and even at the time it must have smacked of psychosis, but at least they gave it a go.

The only record of Bohr's squad is this interview transcript and a few scribbled notes that went with it. These were passed on to me by a grinning Danish major one afternoon when I was being shown around a large NATO field headquarters. After we were introduced by my chaperone, the Major fumbled in his desk for a moment then handed over a bulky padded envelope with my name on it. He claimed this was from his uncle, then stood smirking but offering no further explanation.

I opened the package, expecting some impenetrable European practical joke, to find it contained a small sheaf of papers, a variety of tasty treats and what turned out to be another almost unreadable floppy disk.

'Is your uncle by any chance an Austrian General?' I asked.

'Yes he is.'

'Did he include a note?'

'No. He said you were to enjoy the biscuits. Oh, and you were to "keep working".'

Austrian General's notes stated that the Three Grenadiers had four new members in two months and, by the time of the interview, there were no original cast members left in the team; the others had either died or moved on due to injury, illness or promotion. But somehow, each new man became more aggressive when he joined the Shouty crew.

Shouty was an MG42, arguably the best machine gun ever made and still used in a few nasty places around the world. It could lay down ten times more fire than all the riflemen in Bohr's squad put together. We are told that the sword itself incites to violence and there is hard evidence to show that better swords incite more violence. This effect is called weapon-pull.

There is a marked difference between how much riflemen and machine-gunners fight, but the Three Grenadiers look to be at the extreme end of the scale. The general trend appears to be close to what Marshall noted, with men on crew-served weapons four times more likely to fire as riflemen, even though they attract more fire. This effect can be seen in all kinds of battles: heavy-tank crews fight more than light-tank crews; six-pounder anti-tank gunners win more medals than two-pounder anti-tank gunners; snipers hold out longer than riflemen. A large part of this is down to the weapon-pull, but not all.

*   *   *

To uncover a weapon's power to make a man fight more, we need to consider the other pressures working on a machine-gunner. Background factors play a part. Machine-gunners tend to be bigger and smarter than the average rifleman, and natural fighters generally have both these qualities. There are also the simple physical facts that machine guns get more ammunition and can engage at longer ranges so they are always likely to fire more. Then, at least in planned battles, the proximity effect is reduced by that longer engagement range.

Tactical training places great emphasis on crew-served weapons and most battle drills are based around using a machine-gun team to suppress while riflemen assault or protect the gun's flanks. The Wehrmacht's version of battle drill was even more extreme, with most riflemen being worker bees that served the machine gun. This is perhaps why there were five men in the Three Grenadiers.

Cohesion comes from being able to see your mates, and mates around one gun have to stick together, work together and talk to each other more than riflemen. While cohesion can cut both ways, encouraging men to stop fighting as well as start, there are other forces that push weapon crews to fight more. Most compulsion comes from being watched over by senior ranks, and battle-winning weapons attract this attention. Anti-tank guns and machine guns are often commanded by sergeants or corporals and, like that anti-tank gun at Point Snipe, which was manned by a lieutenant colonel, machine guns usually draw the attention of commissioned officers. It is more noticeable when battle-winning weapons fall silent; a rifleman can hide in the crowd or behind a bush, this is a lot harder for a machine-gunner.

Aversion to killing is considerably reduced through diffusion of responsibility, whether this is through following orders, following the crowd or following drills that make behaviour robotic. Weapon crewmen are not solely responsible for doing all of the things needed to kill another person. The burden of killing is spread around the crew and often, like The Three Grenadiers, it can be passed on to the weapon.

Automatisation, the process of making behaviour robotic through constant training of fixed drills, is more pronounced for crew-served weapons where one man loads, one man fires and another picks targets. Crew actions are often so tightly drilled that they will be continued while a man draws his last breath. A weapon crew is directly dependent on each man doing his bit of the job and is therefore more likely to spot any useless fussing. But then the job is a kind of rote repetition anyway, so if a man needs to do something over and over again, a gun crew is the place to do it.

When we strip away all these factors, we are still left with the pure weapon-pull, where the potency of a weapon encourages a man to fight, but this is an effect that has two sides. One side comes from the half-conscious 'is it worth it?' calculation. When a man asks himself this question, the answer is more likely to be 'yes' if his weapon is more effective than the others in his squad. But part of it is more primal and comes from the raw power of a weapon to promote aggression. A weapon acts like a magnet, drawing a man towards a fight response, and a bigger gun has a bigger pull.

The primal side of weapon-pull has been noted in armed police officers; when they are given a pistol, a baton and a taser, they are more likely to use any one of their weapons than if they have only one of the three. A similar effect can be seen in range firing too: even people shooting at paper targets fire more often when they have more guns or bigger guns.

Weapon-pull is not restricted to firing. While crew-served weapons are usually held back in the assault (with flame-throwers being the obvious exception), heavier individual weapons are usually expected to move forward with the riflemen. When they do go forward, the men who carry them are more likely to go past the point of no return.

When Second World War and Korean War accounts are unpicked, we see that whenever BARs (Browning Automatic Rifles, the standard US squad heavy weapons at the time) became personal weapons, the men who carried them were more likely to be at the point of an assault. In the Pacific, there was usually a man with a BAR, or with a .30-calibre machine gun and an oven glove, on the position when it was taken. (The 'oven glove' was a thermal mitten designed to be worn when replacing an overheated barrel but sometimes used to allow one man to carry the gun and fire 'from the hip'.)

Those few 'gutful' men whom Lionel Wigram saw driving home an assault usually included a large proportion of the men who were armed with Bren light machine guns. All those selection and compulsion factors are at work too, but informal trials in training exercises show men with bigger guns fighting more, even when weapons are issued randomly and designated leaders are kept out of the game.

One aspect of weapon-pull is the perception of quality, with the look and feel of a weapon shaping this perception. Anything too tinny, too plastic or too light is usually distrusted way beyond its actual reliability or killing power. Once a weapon acquires a reputation for being unreliable, it gives the soldier a ready justification for not fighting. But if a weapon can prove its reliability, it will be cherished by its soldier.

Glamour picked up from war porn comes in handy, whether this is Robocop or the Iranian embassy siege, but soldiers are usually practical people who can see past any spin once they have their hands on a weapon. The Old Boy network that helped with this book includes a British corporal who dumped his semi-automatic Self-Loading Rifle for the sexier Argentine full-auto version, then swapped back after firing a few rounds and deciding for some reason that 'it was a piece of shit'.

But soldiers are always drawn to weapons that seem to be better than the one they have. A pikeman would ditch his weapon if he saw a musket handy, even if he was not sure how to use the new-fangled gadget. Even today, troops in Afghanistan are stealthily trading in 5.56mm weapons for 7.62mm. Thirty years of propaganda have been shaken off, even though there is some hard evidence that, as far as making holes in bad guys goes, 5.56mm is at least as good for most Afghanistan fighting.

If we cut through this fog, we see that the psychological effect in combat is quite profound. When rates of fire and available ammunition are balanced out, patrols in Iraq using both 5.56mm and 7.62mm fired nearly 20 per cent more 7.62mm rounds. There looks to be a similar effect in Afghanistan. The weapon-pull effect is usually hidden by the fact that no army will put up with mixed-calibre or mixed-quality weapons for very long. But, while NATO forces try to work out what infantry weapons they really want, their men have their backs against the wall and gun geeks are able to compare the relative psychological effects of different weapons.

* * *

Yet weapon-pull is annoyingly relative, and it is relative to a lot of things. When a sister battalion or allied army has a coveted, new or sexy weapon but you have something inferior, it gives an excuse for not fighting quite as hard. Weapon-pull is also relative to the weapon a soldier used to have, with his 'is it worth it?' calculation altered up or down by the quality of the new weapon.

The most telling aspect of relativity lies in mixing weapon quality within a platoon or section. Giving some men better weapons probably makes those men fight more but it also makes their less well-armed comrades fight less. On top of compulsion and the rest, there is also an influence from a slippery group process called social loafing.

Social loafing studies tell us that ten men pulling on a rope only give 80 per cent of the effort that they would if they were pulling on their own. Put enough men on the rope and they will barely be bothered to pick it up. This is a complicated business for psychologists, but for soldiers social loafing is simply down to men being lazier when they work in a bigger team. In combat, social loafing and reduced compulsion mean that the man with the rifle is more likely to keep his head down if there is a friendly machine gun near by that can see off the enemy by itself.

No one has yet got a good grip on exactly how all this relativity balances out, but the heart of weapon-pull is the fact that less effective weapons promote freeze, flee and fuss, while more effective weapons promote fight. The basic facts are fairly clear but I have to admit (and this is a terrible admission for a war geek) that weapon-pull is something that is difficult to put a number to. Even then, while the figures are valid reflections of combat data and fit well enough into a spreadsheet or graph, they are not the best fit to plain English.

Overall, weapon-pull appears to provide a 50 per cent boost to the chance of a man fighting. So, giving a soldier a weapon that is twice as good as all the others in his fire-team (for example having a 7.62mm assault rifle with greater range, accuracy, lethality and robustness than the standard 5.56mm offering) does not make the combination of him and the weapon twice as effective, but two and a half times as effective.

There is a commensurate increase and decrease in overall effectiveness if the weapon's relative power changes, but at the edges of the graph this relationship starts to fray. Small increases in weapon effectiveness are often apparent only at very long or short engagement ranges. Large power increases tend to add weight, slowing a man down and sometimes keeping him from the fight. At its heart, weapon-pull, while a genuine combat phenomenon, is incredibly difficult to work with.

Even forgiving its ropy edges, this 50 per cent boost might be useful to defence accountants, but front-line soldiers must work with the weapons they have to hand. For soldiers to exploit the psychological power of weapons we need to understand the other side of the coin. In the next chapter we will see how the power of enemy weapons can push soldiers away from fighting and how this has an effect which is dominated by tactical decisions to have an enormous impact on the outcome of battle.

THIRTEEN

WEAPON-PUSH

TROOPER BROOKS, GERMANY, 1945

After the breakout the regiment was supported by a troop of Crocodiles again, special Churchill tanks with built-in flame-throwers and a petrol bowser hooked to the back. As Recce Troop our job was to work our way round the village in our little Honey tanks to attract fire from any 88s in there, report back on what we'd seen and look out for any Jerry trying to slope off before our boys went in.

There might be some artillery to get any anti-tanks and SPs, that's self-propelled guns, buttoned and then the Shermans might put a few rounds into the village, then in would go the Crocodiles and the bloody footsloggers. Before anybody got in range, the Crocodiles would fire off a few jets of flame to let Jerry know what was coming and then they'd walk with the infantry up to the edge of town.

Meantime Jerry was having a quick chat about their prospects, and ten-to-one they'd be waving bed sheets before the Crocs got in range. There was the odd time when they'd chance a few shots at the Crocs or fire a Spandau at the infantry, but that would just draw fire from the Shermans and they'd get a few squirts from the flame-throwers before we'd let them surrender. They mostly couldn't wait to throw the towel in. Didn't matter who they were: SS, para-troops, it didn't matter. Once they'd had the carrot and the stick waved at them, they packed it in. Then we'd all have a brew and a fag before heading off to round up the next lot.

There was a couple of times that the old bush telegraph had been at work and their officer flagged us Recce boys down and the whole lot surrendered before the rest of the outfit even got there. Sixty-odd of 'em with an SP and bazookas and they were all sat chatting and smoking our fags by the time the Crocs turned up. But we'd usually have to wait for the big stick – the Crocs – and the big carrot – the infantry that they felt they could surrender to.

The trick didn't always work. We got cocky once with it once and went off half-cocked. Sent the Crocs in before the infantry caught up with us. Didn't work at all. Jerry knocked out one Croc and damaged another and we had to pull out 'til the next day before going in again. No carrot, you see. Very messy when we went back in, too. Arty boys smashed the place to bits but we still lost blokes and we had to burn out the whole lot. There was no 'handy hock' on that bloody pig of a day I can tell you.

Trooper Brooks is one of that breed of veterans who are more than happy to talk about the war but only go beyond the superficial with people who pass muster. In a way, his criteria were as strict as Master Sergeant Johansson's. Like many Old Boys, he thought anyone who spoke too freely about their war was a braggart, trying to paint themselves a hero or denigrate their old comrades. I finally convinced him to let me use his account, heavily edited to make it doubly anonymous, by explaining the whole story of tactical psychology.

Brooks's account reflects the other side of the psychological power of weapons. While a man is pulled towards the fight because he has a weapon that is superior to his mate's, superior enemy weapons will push him away from fighting. Weapon-push is something beyond simple suppression. It can come from weapons that might not be firing at you and from weapons that might not be firing at all.

The effect is based around the way enemy weapons compare to whatever your own side has, from a weapon's reputation and from the way it is advertised in combat. Before we look at the way Brooks's unit used the Crocodile, there are a few other status weapons to consider.

Corporal Bohr's account, in the previous chapter, skipped over the psychological effect that Shouty had on the enemy, but it was considerable. Allied infantry were in awe of the MG42 with its high rate of fire and distinctive firing note. In the sustained fire role it spat out up to 1,500 rounds a minute: that's twenty-five bullets leaving the muzzle every second. This was usually limited to a more reliable 1,100 or 1,200 rounds a minute but was still far more bullets in the air than was necessary for a purely physical effect on the enemy. Crews would often fire off a belt of 100 rounds in one screaming burst. This produced tremendously effective suppressive fire, but its weapon-push effect could be felt way beyond fall of shot.

Sydney Jary, a platoon commander we will meet again later, recalled how fire from an MG42 'would rip the air with the most terrible screech. Even those outside the beaten zone would go to ground whenever they heard it. We estimated one MG42 to be worth nine Brens or three Vickers.' Allied companies were usually stuck with the 500 rounds per minute of their BARs and Brens that were fed through magazines holding twenty or thirty rounds. Compared to the short, steady burp of these Allied weapons, the ripping sound of Hitler's buzz-saw was distinctive and intimidating. As Allied soldiers went forward, the distant firing note of the MG42 reminded them of the imbalance.

Even approaching the direct fire zone, the sound of an MG42 firing at someone else could force men to the ground. Once this had happened two or three times, soldiers were very unwilling to get back on their feet and move forward. While many units came to rely on artillery and armour to beat German machine guns, others moved towards infiltration: sneaking up to and around the enemy rather than trying to batter them. One of the benefits of infiltration was that it meant advancing troops might not have to hear an MG42 firing until, like Wigram's platoons, they were very close to it.

But the weapon-push effect can start long before contact. Some old hands had faced the MG34 (the MG42's predecessor) on the retreat to Dunkirk and others had met both weapons in North Africa. They were not shy about telling recruits the bad news. Allied authorities made some clumsy attempts to play down the reputation of German machine guns. One training film described the MG34 as firing only 120 rounds a minute; another dubbed the sound of a Bren firing over the German machine guns. A young volunteer who saw the first film recalled 'a lot of coughing and some cat-calls from the old hands at the back of the theatre'. The downside of hiding the truth, as we will see shortly, is a rude awakening in contact.

Most machine guns have an effect approaching that of the MG42, but the biggest and noisiest ones have the greatest weapon-push, even though small and quiet weapons can be just as lethal. Unless bullets are passing very close to them, many Afghan insurgents 'ignore 5.56, are wary of 7.62 but pack up and leave once a point five joins the fight'. Pure suppression is playing its part in this, but the distant sound or rumour of a status weapon like a .50-calibre machine gun can push men away from fighting on its own.

This effect has been multiplied by using anti-aircraft weapons to shoot at people on the ground. In Korea, the quad fifty 'meat chopper', four .50-calibre machine guns bolted together, seems to have had more than four times the effect of a standard .50. The quad fifty 'kept them pinned way outside its beaten zone and had far more morale effect than any other weapon we had'. North Korean and Chinese soldiers were reported to be instantly torn between running and hiding whenever it fired. The intense numbing crack of a near miss or the sight of rounds hitting anything had an intense effect, but even when firing nowhere near a man, the heavy rattle and thump of the weapon could be enough to force him to the ground.

German 20mm cannons and Russian 14.5mm guns have also claimed a profound weapon-push effect, but the prize for most feared ground-role anti-aircraft gun has to go to the German 88. Firing a large, high-velocity round a very long way with a high rate of fire, the many variants of the 88mm Flak 18 had an effect on infantry, but their real psychological bonus was most evident when they were used as anti-tank guns.

*   *   *

The evolution of the battle between tanks and anti-tank weapons has been subject to a lot of detailed analysis and this gives us a clearer picture of weapon-push than the messier, more confusing

infantry battle. Trooper Brooks's account provides a useful introduction to the way comparison, reputation and advertising have
their effect.

Brooks and his comrades were all too aware of the limitations of
their little Honey tanks. The nickname 'Honey' was first given to
the M3/M5 Stuart by Commonwealth tankies and cavalry because
it ran as sweet as honey: it was faster and more reliable than the
British-built tanks of the time. But by 1944 its thin armour and
light gun had made it unsuitable for much of anything but reconnaissance, and Honeys were considered to be 'little more use than
jeeps when it comes to the fight'. By the time Trooper Brooks was
fighting, the joke was that the nickname came from things getting
very sticky in a Honey.

Almost any anti-tank ammunition could pierce the Honey's
frontal armour at maximum range and its tiny 37mm gun was of
so little use in European fighting that some units cut off the turret
to make the Honey faster and less visible. Sometimes the Honey's
only defence was German unwillingness to give away their
position by firing at such a low-value target. But units still had
difficulty pushing Honey reconnaissance forward: some were
forced to switch the crews to less risky jobs securing rear areas.

Sherman tank crews had a similar problem. The smokescreen
put out by the authorities meant that most men were unaware
of the weaknesses of the Sherman before their first battle. Their
opinions quickly altered. Just a few miles from Trooper Brooks,
the 4th/7th Royal Dragoon Guards soon came to accept the
Sherman's limitations:

We had a nasty shock although we did not realise it for a week
or two after D-Day, because we were still too full of confident

enthusiasm to be easily deterred; but it was not long before we realised that our tanks were outmatched by both the enemy tanks and anti-tank guns, and that in a straight fight at anything over point-blank range, we were backing a loser every time. The armour of the Shermans rarely resisted any armour-piercing shot, except at extreme range, and when pierced usually burst into flames almost spontaneously, adding burns to the other ways in which members of the crew might become casualties.

The 75mm gun, though an accurate weapon, and excellent for H.E. [High Explosive shells used for shooting people or buildings rather than tanks], had no powers of penetration to deal with Tigers or head-on Panthers. The 17-pounder of the Sherman Firefly was indeed a match for the German guns in penetrative power, and we treasured the five that 'A' Squadron had like the most precious stones, but even here the tank was at a disadvantage, as its armour was so inferior to that of its opponent.

The realisation of Sherman vulnerability is reflected in the way tank and crew casualties changed over time. For US armoured divisions, the first week in combat saw four crewmen killed or wounded for each tank that was destroyed. Crew casualties dropped sharply after the first few weeks then bounced along, gradually declining until, by the fifteenth week in combat, only one crewman was lost for each tank destroyed. This was a remarkable survival rate given the Sherman's tendency to burst into flames.

Some of the drop in crew casualties came from modifications like fixing track plates or railway sleepers to the hull, or from improved escape drills and better casualty handling. But most change came from crews being more likely to abandon their vehicle once they suspected that it was outmatched. Many crews would abandon their Sherman as soon as it was engaged, or even before it had come under fire. Veteran tankers have told how their immediate action on contact with an 88 was to fire all their weapons as fast as possible in any direction while reversing quickly into cover, then dismount and get away from the vehicle before it was hit.

These reactions were encouraged by the legendary status of the 88. But while the MG42 had its distinctive firing note to advertise its presence and status, a tank crew would not usually hear or see an anti-tank gun until they were engaged. Even then, it could be difficult to tell whether they had been fired on by an 88 or a less prestigious weapon.

It turns out that the 88's advertising came by word of mouth rather than any firing characteristic. It had such a reputation that when orders said there were anti-tank guns in the area, the 88 instantly sprang into everyone's mind. Then, as soon as someone got on the radio to say a tank had been fired on, this was used to confirm the initial assessment.

Throughout the war any unidentified anti-tank gun was usually counted as an 88. The awe inspired by this weapon was most noticeable in North Africa, where its incredible range could be used with best effect. British Eighth Army bingo callers dropped the 'two fat ladies' line in favour of 'driver reverse ... 88'. Whenever they were engaged in the desert by an 88, or by any other gun that they suspected might be an 88, smart tank crews often dropped into cover and stayed there until dark.

The same aura surrounded the Tiger tank, which was almost twice the size of a Sherman and armed with another variant of the 88mm gun. One Normandy veteran recalled 'a grumble to our front that sounded like a half-track to me, but some fool shouted

"Tiger" and our tanks just buggered off behind the hill, leaving the company to face it alone'. Variations on this story were repeated right across north-west Europe. Tiger crews instantly turned into elite fighters, with Tiger aces like Michael Wittman getting benefits of weapon-pull and weapon-push that far outstripped the physical advantages of their tank.

The same effect can be seen, but so far only just glimpsed, with the new breed of vehicles being used in Afghanistan. If they manage to get around or through the screen of mines and booby traps, their armour and heavy weapons often combine to push the enemy away from fighting very quickly. If well handled, they can even cause an insurgent to try surrendering.

The psychological bonus for the side with better weapons has confused many military analysts. Trained to apply simple rules of attrition, which have more powerful weapons gradually wearing down less powerful weapons, their sums are upset when a force suddenly collapses in the face of a better-equipped enemy.

Physically, three Shermans should have been able to beat a Tiger, but in reality a Sherman force would have to outnumber Tigers by more than five to one or call in support from other arms. Similar effects have been found for imbalanced tank-on-tank action in the Yom Kippur, Korean and Gulf Wars. Once the side with the worst tanks realises they have the worst tanks, a lot of crews get out and walk, or spend so much time thinking about getting out that they cannot fight effectively.

*   *   *

There is considerable variation around the average weapon-push effect. The side with better weapons usually wins with an easier fight than can be explained just by looking at the physical effects, but sometimes they win without a fight and sometimes they are beaten despite their physical advantage. Many factors play a part in this but the most profound is the way units choose to advertise with their status weapons. To understand this we have to put ourselves in the shoes of those men facing Trooper Brooks's pals in the Crocodile flame-thrower tanks.

Like poison gas, napalm bombs and white phosphorus, armoured flame-throwers have had a bad press. But unlike these area weapons, the reputation for armoured flame is not entirely justified: in practice, a flame-thrower tank can be a surprisingly moral weapon for attacking morale.

The Crocodile provided a potent mix of common sense and fear. The real difficulty of finding protection from rods of burning fuel combined with the intense primal fear of fire. The difficulty of getting a telling shot on a heavily armoured target like the Crocodile was easily exaggerated to the beast being seen as invulnerable. This combination made armoured flame a very potent stick, but on its own it had no carrot: it could tell the enemy that fighting was a bad idea but it did little to encourage him to surrender.

Field research teams found that attacks supported by Crocodiles were twice as effective as those with normal infantry support tanks and two and a half times more effective at night, when the rods of flame were more obvious. Over 90 per cent of attacks supported by Crocodiles were successful and half of these attacks met little or no opposition. When opposition was encountered, five times as many enemies surrendered as were killed or injured.

But the level of opposition depended on how closely the Crocodiles were tied in with the infantry advance and when they chose to project their first rods of flame. In actions that applied the trick described by Trooper Brooks (standing off and advertising the stick of the Crocodile and the carrot of infantry), twenty-seven men were captured for each man killed. So while status weapons push the enemy away from fighting, this is one situation where how you use it matters more than how big it is.

This trick was not used by many units because they were trained to not project flame until the Crocodiles were well within their effective range of about eighty metres. This was because 'every effort was being made to obtain the maximum shock and surprise'. Holding fire until you can get the best physical effect is usually the best way of maximising psychological impact, but armoured flame is one of the weapons that does not fit with accepted wisdom. This is because of the way it can be used in a variety of tactical advertising campaigns.

Successful advertising relies on a mix of stick and carrot. A television advertisement might wave the stick of 'your family will suffer when you die', but will only sell life insurance if it shows the carrot of how insurance can solve the problem. The men facing Brooks were shown the stick when flame rods were fired at a distance, but they were also shown the carrot of supporting infantry: real people who could be surrendered to. The target audience for this advertising also had time to agree their decision among themselves and find some white flags before the Crocodiles closed in.

In those attacks where the Crocodiles rushed in close to torch buildings and trenches, the proximity effect tended to be flipped from 'last safe moment' to 'the point of no return'. Then there was no carrot because the tanks overtook the infantry in the rush to get into killing range. The attacking infantry (with minimal

weapon-pull and concerns about being accidentally torched by
their own side) tended to hang back a bit anyway.

Men have difficulty surrendering to tanks and tank crews have
difficulty accepting surrender. Concerned about their poor vision
and the danger of enemy infantry getting into their blind spots
with anti-armour weapons, tank crews like to keep infantry at a
distance, usually by shooting them. Infantrymen know this and it
twists their four-Fs decision. Running and surrendering are not
viable options when you are close to a tank, so the defenders have
a greater tendency to fight if they have something to fight with.

Just a few miles from where Brooks's regiment was fighting,
there were Crocodile battles where large numbers of enemy
troops were killed rather than captured. In one attack where
Crocodiles were used without carrot-and-stick advertising, the
ratio of enemy captured-to-killed was 3:8 rather than 27:1. (This
example is used to highlight coordination problems later, but
for now it reflects the way the carrot-and-stick trick was a fairly
local affair.)

Carrot-and-stick does not seem to have spread to other theatres
or other wars where armoured flame was used. In the Far East and
Pacific, flame-thrower tanks were said to have an intense morale
effect but rarely caused large numbers of the enemy to surrender.
This was usually put down to the fanaticism of the enemy, but
there were several other factors at work. Fanaticism certainly
played some part but, as we have already seen, the Japanese soldier
suffered from the Allied perception that he would not surrender
or did not deserve to live.

The Japanese started that cycle of barbarity to create a war
which partially smothered aversion to killing. But this smother-
ing of aversion was exaggerated by the Japanese bunker-based

defence and their limited anti-armour weapons. This usually made driving up close to a bunker and burning out the Japanese defenders much quicker and simpler than trying to offer terms of surrender.

Language also played a role in extending this loop of the barbarity cycle. At that time, there was no Japanese word that really fit our word 'surrender'; but the problem ran deeper. One psychological warfare study relates how shouting through a loud-speaker, 'You @$*! Japs get out of that bunker or I'll #$%^ burn you out!' did not work. What did work was, 'Attention, honourable Japanese soldiers! I am the authorized American commander for this area, and I have been ordered to make it secure. Attention! I have flame-throwers. I will use flame-throwers to carry out my lawful orders. I regret the unfortunate consequences resultant on the use of flame-throwers! Japanese soldiers! I order you to come out and assemble properly at (some designated landmark).'

The war with Japan was nearly over before that trick was learned. There is evidence of a similar oversight in Afghanistan.

North Korean, Chinese and North Vietnamese soldiers were no more likely to surrender to armoured flame than the Japanese. Men with no weapon that could hope to have an effect on a flame-thrower tank usually chose to stay hidden or risk running. The few who had something to fight with still had to get through a wall of fire to have any chance against armoured flame. This was an option that was very unlikely to get a 'yes' response to the 'is it worth it?' calculation, but it did not encourage men to surrender either.

The closer terrain of these eastern wars (often fought in moun-tains and jungles unlike the rolling country of north-west Europe) also helped to force the flame-thrower tank into lethal range. At this point the tank crew's safest option was to burn out the defenders then shoot them with machine guns if they ran. On top of this, most flame-thrower tanks in the Far East campaigns did not use a fuel trailer like the Churchill Crocodile, so crews tended to save what they had for close-range killing blows. These factors cut down on the opportunity to advertise the carrot and stick, drastically reducing the ability of armoured flame to induce surrender.

Armies turned away from armoured flame when this reduced effectiveness was combined with distaste for the horrific alternative of burning people alive. This was bolstered by a corporate aversion to using tanks in close support of infantry, and the many difficulties of building and supplying flame-thrower tanks.

No armies currently admit to having armoured flame in their arsenals but many have found other nasty sticks to take their place. But, just as in Trooper Brooks's time, it is rare for a unit to wave both the carrot and the stick before the killing starts.

*   *   *

Weapon-push goes back to the earliest warfare, with a base effect that reduces the chance of men fighting if they have weapons that are less effective than the enemy's. Before armoured flame, Greek fire was known for its morale effect; before the machine gun, the repeating rifle made the enemy less likely to fight.

The base effect is boosted by efforts to highlight the difference in weapon effectiveness. Before Stukas and Warthogs exaggerated a soldier's vulnerability, biplanes were having their timing and exhausts altered to advertise their dominance. Drums, chants, war cries, shiny breastplates and a variety of unfeasibly large hats were also a staple before camouflage came back into fashion.

The advantage of these exaggerations has often been boosted by presenting the enemy with a credible offer of the chance to surrender.

By combining the analysis of armoured combat with the smaller, scrappier infantry data set, it has been possible to generate a workable conservative estimate of the weapon-push effect. When the enemy have a status weapon, the chance of a man fighting is reduced by 30 per cent.

This effect is greatly increased if the side with superior weapons advertises the imbalance and offers the enemy a viable alternative to fighting. With advertising from a firepower demonstration, loudspeakers or cutting into the enemy radio net, plus a viable carrot such as a lull in the fight, visible infantry and a believable offer of surrender terms, the chance of an enemy soldier fighting is reduced by 90 per cent.

Advertising carrot-and-stick is not easy to do in the confusion of battle, especially in close country, and many wars reach a level of barbarity that make it almost impossible to offer a credible carrot. But, when advertising can be used effectively, the winning side will take far fewer casualties, use far less ammunition and will capture a lot more of the enemy. As a result, units that combine weapon-push and advertising have been able to roll up or roll through an enemy force because they are better able to maintain their fighting power and momentum.

FOURTEEN

SEEING STRAIGHT

LIEUTENANT JARY, HOLLAND, 1944

Running across the level crossing, I suddenly found myself face to face with a German platoon complete with MG34. Fortunately the gun was mounted on a tripod, which was unusual, and could not be traversed in our direction. From a drainage channel on the left of the road a parachutist leaped up swathed in a camouflage veil. Pointing his Schmeisser at me, from about ten yards' range, he fired a whole magazine of about thirty rounds. It was like watching a slow-running silent movie. I didn't hear the chatter of the Schmeisser but I do remember seeing the stream of empty cartridge cases fly from the German gun. Miracles do indeed happen. One 9mm bullet went through my beret, missing my head literally by a hair's width. Another went under the epaulette of my jacket, penetrating the webbing cross-brace of my equipment and grazing my right shoulder. A third bullet ricocheted off the surface of the road and disintegrated, the jacket finally lodging in the palm of my right hand. Then came the anti-climax. The German looked at me in amazement, threw away his Schmeisser and, with a shrug of the shoulders, surrendered. My natural elation was

*short-lived. Behind me lay Lance-Corporal Porteus shot through
the heart.*

*Some of the German platoon ran away across open fields to our left
and were cut down by rapid rifle and Bren fire by Sergeant Kingston's
section, which now lined the railway track to the left of the road. The
remainder of the enemy came towards us over the level crossing with
their hands raised. We took fifty-seven prisoners.*

Unlike Trooper Brooks, Lieutenant Jary is not one of those veterans who put a fence around his wartime experience. Instead,
driven by the knowledge that mistakes in the next war come from
not understanding the last one, he has helped new generations
of soldiers by sharing his experience openly. Although he was
a professional soldier for only four years, his war involved the
possibly unique experience of commanding the same platoon
from deadlock in Normandy to victory in Germany. His book, *18
Platoon*, is a model of not bragging and not denigrating comrades.

The point of interest from Lieutenant Jary's quote is the
way he experienced events when he bumped into that German
paratrooper. We have already seen how perception can go awry
with the instinctive side of freezing and how memory problems
increase the impact of fussing. These were specific instances of
how the brain's limitations can reduce the likelihood of fighting,
but the way a soldier perceives and thinks in combat can influence his response in other ways too. This chapter and the next
show how problems with seeing straight and thinking straight
can be exploited to make the enemy think he is losing, even when
he is not.

Jary's perception of silence, slow motion and enhanced vision
matches reports from soldiers throughout history. Whether

someone is firing a machine pistol at you or trying to stick you
with a pike, your perception of events will be guided by programming that is older than mankind and contains bugs that can crop
up in combat.

There is no handy number for the size of this effect is but there
are some figures on the kind of perceptual weirdness that takes
place. Dave Grossman used a survey of US police officers who
reported perceptual distortions in gunfights, which found that 85
per cent of them blanked out the sound, 65 per cent experienced
time passing in slow motion, 70 per cent experienced increased
visual clarity and 80 per cent reported tunnel vision. Less common
effects include intensified sounds, time speeding up and feeling
detached from events.

If we step back from the sharp end for a minute, everyday
life includes huge differences between reality, what sense
organs detect and what people perceive. We do not perceive the
world as it is but through an elaborate mechanism which, every
second, translates millions of photons into thousands of data
points, compresses these data points into dozens of images, then
combines the images with data from other senses to help fill the
blanks, make guesses and attribute meaning. This bewilderingly
complex system is best understood through a clumsy analogy.

Soldiers used to be trained to detect, recognise and identify
the enemy. To detect was to spot something worth looking at,
to recognise was to realise it was a tank, and to identify was to
work out the tank was a command vehicle used only by the Iraqi
Republican Guard. Brains lack the time and processing power to
detect everything that happens, recognise everything they detect
and identify everything they recognise.

Stage magicians and street conmen play on these limitations to draw the eye with one hand while they fix the cards with the other. This is well documented in experiments using contrived illusions or real-life events, and it is surprising how much people can miss. There is an 'invisible gorilla' test where people are asked to count how many times players pass a basketball. Six players pass two balls and test subjects are asked to count only the passes using one of the balls. Most people get close to the right number of passes but about half of them miss a man in a gorilla suit walking through the middle of the game and stopping to beat his chest.

Daily life works in the same kind of way, but if stress and fatigue are added, the effect is increased as the brain tries to get a clearer picture of what it thinks is the main event. If two things look to be equally important, the brain often lacks the time and space to take them both in. So, like the magician or conman, combat can trick people into focusing on the wrong thing.

It is almost impossible to get psychologists to put a number on this, and even when they do, no two will give the same number. This is because pure perception is guided by expectations, assumptions and a series of mental processes that evade accurate measurement. But perception is guided by working memory and its limitations can be measured.

*   *   *

The classic figure for working memory capacity is that the average person can only hold about seven things in their head at any one time. In combat, this capacity is reduced because a considerable amount of brainpower is assigned to other jobs. Jobs like sphincter control and not falling over are normally automatic, but they can require conscious effort when someone is in a tight spot.

On top of threat-based stress, a combat soldier has usually not slept properly for weeks, might have been carrying fifty kilos in fifty-degree heat for the last eight hours and has a sweaty sergeant shouting at him. These things eat up yet more brainpower and cut down the number of things a soldier can concentrate on. Core processing power is reduced and perceptual systems either limit the amount of information they pass on, or risk what they send bouncing off a block in working memory.

The level of stress does not have to be too high; even the threat of being hit by a paintball can make a difference. Threatened with a little pain from marking ammunition, soldiers give after-action reports that are far more disjointed than when they train with blanks and lasers. Even with blanks and lasers, there is usually a big gap between perception and reality. Military observers, who run alongside platoon command teams in training, give much more accurate descriptions of events, even though they were in the same place, seeing the same things and doing nearly as much physical work.

The command teams and the observers are both trying to make a meaningful picture from what they see and hear. Yet, time and again, observers report that Sergeant X or Lieutenant Y is an idiot because he did something that was completely inappropriate. In most cases he was not an idiot; he simply had a reduced understanding of the situation because his brain was far busier than the observer's. Observers are under no pressure to get a job done, so they have far more spare brainpower available to understand what is really happening.

A similar thing happens in battalion command teams. In their after-action reports, headquarters staff miss about a quarter of the facts picked up by observers. When command teams' perceptions are compared to the real battle picture, it is also apparent that they unconsciously add in a few extra facts to make a more coherent story.

The gaps in perception and the leaps to make a complete story can make for a bad day in the unit. When radio reports say enemy tanks are near Bravo Company and artillery is falling on Delta Company, nearly a fifth of command teams put the two reports together and leap to the conclusion that both things are happening to Bravo Company. The battalion reserve is unleashed but misses the enemy tanks, which have driven right past Bravo and overrun Delta while it was still recovering from the artillery bombardment.

This will sound implausible if you have never spent time in a battalion headquarters under pressure, but headquarters have a lot of people in them and a lot of radios throwing information at them. Each person in a headquarters has to do a much harder job than counting basketballs or spotting invisible gorillas. As with platoon command teams, outside observers are frequently gobsmacked by the apparently stupid things battalion command teams do in training. The easy answer is to say that, like Sergeant X or Lieutenant Y, Battalion Z is not up to the job, but this hides the fact that it can be very difficult to see straight in battle, even if it is a pretend battle.

While these command teams were under pressure and had a lot to deal with, they were only on an exercise; the bullets were not real and, in the case of battalion staff, the shooting was often a long way away. Careers can be made or broken on an important exercise but this pressure is not as intense as the imminent threat of death or injury. In close combat, a soldier's perception is far more distorted than that of a battalion command team because his physiological system is working at the limits of its capacity.

* * *

Psychologists like to plot curves for the relationship between physiological arousal and the accuracy of perception. People miss or misperceive a lot of things at the extremes of arousal (half asleep and hyperactive), but are much better near the middle ground. We get better at spotting important things as we become more alert but then get much worse as arousal exceeds the optimum level. Away from the most intense threat, some soldiers can find that their arousal level puts them 'in the zone' but in a critical fight most people are operating at the overloaded end of the scale. So a soldier can easily have a Jary-like experience, where he sees insurgents firing at him with enhanced clarity, but this can only happen because the brain blocks other inputs. These other inputs might be from another bunch of insurgents running in to throw grenades. Sometimes fire-and-movement works as much through perception as it does through suppression.

There are some gross exceptions to the rule of focusing on the biggest threat, when people get hung up on irrelevances like bootlaces or clouds as they are sucked into fussing or freezing. But even soldiers 'in the zone' suffer from perceptual blinkers and the distortions that go with them. I once worked with an American tank commander who said his only experience of real combat, against part of the Iraqi army on the road to Baghdad, happened in fast-forward Technicolor, as if he had taken some kind of disco drug. So far, his experience looks to be a one-off, but other reports come close to this.

The really important misperceptions are usually noticed only in post-combat interviews when men get together to compare what they saw and heard. These group interviews, invented by S. L. A. Marshall, show something like tunnel vision to be a common cause of 'blue-on-blue' fratricide, failure to spot enemy infiltration, or not realising that someone is shooting at you. Bombardier Fidler, the anti-air gunner we met in the compulsion chapter, was once so preoccupied with serving a gun that it took him a while to realise that the bees clicking past him were bullets being fired by a German sniper.

Remember Civil War Corporal Murphy's line in Chapter 4 about showers of lead, and not having the space to poke your cap up without it being torn away? That could have come from any fight in the last few hundred years. Yet when we look at the firing rate of Civil War weapons and the practical limits on the number of men that could have been firing at Murphy's company, his assessment appears to be something of an exaggeration. Soldiers' assessments of the chance of being hit are usually six to ten times the real figure. Most of this inflation is not from exaggeration but from genuine misperception, the flexibility of human memory and, above all, the high value people put on their own lives.

To work around these problems, army organisations and procedures are generally designed to make things obvious and simple: to limit the chance of commanders becoming overloaded, they usually control no more than four subordinate units; in defence, to reduce the chance of him missing something, each soldier is usually told to look out for enemy in a very narrow slice of the ground in front him. These constraints can seem ridiculous in basic training (there's no way I'd forget about one of my sub-units; nobody could fail to spot the enemy over to my right) but combat experience has shown these schoolboy errors happening time and again. Likewise, repetition and stating the obvious with 'Go! Go! Go!' or 'Incoming!' are habits adopted to counter problems with perception in combat.

Despite the problems with perception in combat, soldiers are rarely taught to look out for their mates who might not be seeing straight. Chiefs of Staff are taught to watch out for tunnel vision in their generals, but the tag teams of lieutenant and sergeant or corporal and lance corporal need to keep an eye on each other too, to make sure they are not missing something important. Soldiers also need to know about seeing straight should they find themselves giving evidence to an inquest or court martial. There has been an increased tendency to blame soldiers and commanders for doing things that might appear negligent or wilful in peacetime. In reality, these are often the result of the problems that result from unavoidable misperception under stress.

Problems with seeing straight in combat seem to be almost random in the way they strike and how hard they hit. They are difficult to pin down or put a number on but the next chapter will show how seeing straight really causes problems when it meets up with the weirdness of thinking straight in combat.

FIFTEEN

THINKING STRAIGHT

CORPORAL MACBRIDE, IRAQ, 2005

My thought process? You want to know about my fucking thought process? Fuck me, you fuckers would be better off poking your pencils into that prick what was driving that radio-controlled plane or the king-prick what sent us to attack that frigging shite hole in the first place.

Alright, alright. Where do youse want us to start? Orders? Fuck me that was a fucking world away; that was two days ago nearly. Alright, alright, shush now ... I'll give it a go if you'll give us minute...

Righto. The plan was for a battalion raid on a bomb factory in the machine shop at the old water plant. In, out, maximum violence, no messing; secure the site for bomb disposal and collection of evidence; lift the local big player if we get the chance; kill the twat if we don't.

The green slime told us there was the player and maybe six militia in the machine shop, then 'about eleven' (however the fuck they landed on 'about eleven' instead of saying ten or twelve or something I'll never know) but anyway, these guys were in a building next door that they'd been using as a doss house. There was supposed to be no one in the admin building to the south, where we were due to give fire support from. That was on account of it being torched back in '03.

The locals were staying well away from the whole place because the player and his cronies were a particular bunch of bastards and from some different faction or tribe or whatever. I'm guessing the locals were expecting a thousand-pounder being dropped through his window sometime soon but they got us lot instead.

We were supposed to have a Gucci Unmanned Air Vehicle as top cover, instead of the old shite drone we usually get, and some special ops blokes watching us in, and the bomb disposal and Int boffins tagging along. A big cake and arse party basically. The Warrior Company was to put in an outer cordon at the last minute, C Company was reserve and inner cordon and us in A Company were down to do the business on the objective.

Three Platoon plus some odds and sods were doing the assault, silent at first then noisy on orders or if we got spotted. One Platoon was to be right up their chuff ready to clear the buildings and us in Two Platoon were giving fire support from the admin building, with my section left, Mick's right, and the Lieutenant with LAWs and that just behind us, and Spunky's lot in all-round defence.

The big idea was to give the militias a message: 'Don't fuck with Colonel Nick's boys or you'll be getting some of the same.' So once we got the nod we were to put down as much fire as possible, then Three Platoon would dash in and kill every fucker that didn't throw their hands up.

So I guess I'd say my 'thought process' was just business as usual for orders, I suppose. To be fair, we were all quite keen seeing as this bastard was likely to blame for killing at least one of our boys, so maybe we had a tiny bit of the red mist from the off. But, yeah, thought process all business-like.

It was kind of a party atmosphere at orders 'cause we were finally getting off the leash and going to lay out some payback but mainly it was all as per usual and a lot like training. Pencil: sharpened at both ends. Mission: stated twice. Chairs, canvas: forty of. Plenty of photos and a cracking model of the objective. Best set of orders I've been to, to tell the truth. Maybe a bit detached from the reality of some real hard contact and there was quite a bit of admin to sort but just the usual drill really.

Was different on the way in, mind you: a wee stroll up to the admin building, watched in by the UAV and the special ops wankers so I was kind of on autopilot. I kept an eye on my boys obviously, but instead of worrying about the enemy or my kit I just zonked out a bit and let nonsense run through my head. It sounds arse but a lot of this was me imagining the brilliant best man's speech I'd give at my brother's wedding; all very detailed and all complete toss of course, seeing as he's only fifteen and not got round to even a sniff of skirt yet, the soft shite.

There were a few other bits of that sort and another lump of brain decided it would run Slade's 'Merry Christmas' as a backing track for the whole show. Suppose that's me fucked up with flashbacks every year now is it? Yeah, thought so. Just my fucking luck.

Anyway, we get into position, check comms and start reporting on activity round the objective. By some miracle this pretty much fit the Int brief except on thermal it looked like there were four militia boys patrolling round the works and just to the west, that's our left, which no one mentioned before. There was a lot of heat coming from the main building too and we thought this meant some of them were up and about in there.

We'd been there maybe a half-hour. Quite a long half-hour when you're lying on your belt buckle shivering and listening to Slade *going round in your head; a very fucking long half-hour when you're supposed to be doing a raid. The assault sections were snurgling up when things started going tits up.*

First we heard we'd lost the UAV, then we hadn't, then maybe we had and maybe we hadn't. Then some chat about the Warrior cordon and the patrol and maybe going loud early. Then some prick from Three Platoon fell off a wall and bust his ankle so the assault lost most of a section carrying him back out of the way. They were already a bit light through blokes on the sick and having to secure vehicles so the Lieutenant was told to peel off a section to join them. It was my section that got volunteered for the privilege of helping them out.

After very much fucking about dumping kit and tracking back and forward we got up with Three Platoon, only to find the fuckers didn't want us at all. That full-of-himself prick of a Captain who'd taken over Three made up some cock-piss intimate support job for us and we went and lay down behind another fucking wall while they sorted their shit out again.

Thought process at the time? I didn't have no fucking thought process at this time; I was too busy crawling round checking my lot knew what the fuck was supposed to be going on. I was concerned about arcs and making sure we wouldn't get spotted by the militia or slotted by our own Rupert up on the admin building. There was Slade of course, but the best man's speech had been forgotten, and I was squared away with what we had to do.

My focus? My focus was on getting sure my boys were straight so we could put as much fire on that doss-house building once things went hot.

Flanks? What do you mean flanks? You mean the inner fucking cordon? Look pal, I was told to sit tight then shoot the shit out of the barracks building. Yeah, I'd got the Company Command net. Booming. Yeah, I heard the inner cordon was moving in tighter.

No. No fucker said anything about them coming in from the right. No way, I wouldn't have missed that. Comms were good for once. If I'd been told that...

Look, I've already heard this shit from that cock of a Sergeant in One Platoon and I don't care what the Captain said, we were down to give fire support as Three came in from the left, no one said nothing about One assaulting from the right. No. No, there was no talk about the patrol changing things.

Look, maybe they were on about that at Battalion but we heard nothing at Company and if One was told to go in from the left and run straight into our arcs then some other fucker's to blame not us.

Thought process? Factors? You back on that again? There was nothing wrong with my thought process, pal. What are you trying to say, eh?

No, I've told you, no fucker told me there'd been a change. If there's been a change we wouldn't have been put down to fire on the fucking doss house would we now? Would we? Eh?

Look pal, I've had enough of this shit, stop your scribbling. We was told to fire on the doss-house building when I got the go and that's exactly what we did. Fuck it, I've had enough of your shit, pal. Stop scribbling; switch off the tape; stop fucking scribbling...

That interview didn't go too well, did it? The questions about Corporal Mac's thought process were a well-intentioned attempt to find out why he seemed to forget a complete change of plan and then fire on his own people. It is no surprise that Mac could not describe his thought process very well: the brain does not just perceive in an odd way, it can think in an odd way too.

The Slade earworm and the best man's speech are sidelines worth a quick mention. Master Sergeant Johansson had the lyric: 'The bird, the bird, the bird is the word' going round his head every time he was preparing for a parachute jump. The Afrika Korps and Eighth Army chased each other across Libya with half of them humming 'Lili Marlene'. As far as anyone can tell, this kind of thing has no apparent impact on combat effectiveness.

Daydreaming about a best man's speech or some other irrelevance is a common displacement activity. If impending threat turns brain activity to full power and there is no relevant task, the brain will invent little jobs for itself. This is perfectly healthy and usually has no negative effect. It is a bit like having fancy animated wallpaper on a computer: it uses spare processing power but usually gets kicked out of the way once real work starts. It is a sideline related to fussing, but again there is no hard evidence on how it might influence combat soldiers.

*   *   *

It was Mac who gave me a copy of his interview tape. We met in a trench on Salisbury Plain and hit it off after he ripped into me for being 'another one of those pen-pushing bastards what treat proper soldiers like the dog shite on their shoe'. This was a good few years after his embarrassment in Iraq, which luckily resulted in no one being killed and no court martial. But Mac was still barred from promotion when we met. He had also acquired an unflattering nickname, which he bore with remarkable good humour.

I was in Mac's trench because he was in pre-deployment training for Afghanistan and I was looking at some of the problems with feeding lessons from one unit into the training given to another.

At that time there were half a dozen organisations involved in the 'lessons process' and a heap of PowerPoint presentations detailing how it was supposed to work. But all this seemed to hinge on one or two people trapped in a big shed in Helmand. The lessons process was very slow and usually resulted in soldiers having to do more work and carry more kit. Mac had very firm views on this, as did a large selection of soldiers who had started to bombard me with emails.

These emails were the result of another piece of meddling by Old Boss. In his frustration with the formal lessons process, he had set up an underground alternative and was using Gobby Scouser and me as his truffle hounds. Old Boss made sure we were inundated with gripes, not just from British soldiers, but Americans, Canadians, Danes and even an Estonian. This group came to form a kind of digital Sennelager Club, with all the zest of the original but considerably less port drinking.

Most of the gripes had little to do with tactical psychology but, after a few months of staring at incident reports, listening to accounts of combat and pestering soldiers on post-tour leave, patterns started to emerge. One the boldest patterns was that, like Mac in Iraq, soldiers in Afghanistan were having trouble thinking straight.

The real problem for Mac came not from getting new information into his head but from the way his brain kicked it out again. This can have a similar outcome to not seeing straight (fratricide looks the same whatever the cause) but the mechanism is different. There are many problems with thinking straight in combat but Mac suffered from the one that is best understood.

Some radio nets were recorded during the raid and the change of plan was mentioned four times over the company radio net that

Mac was listening to and talking on. He might have missed a few of these but he definitely acknowledged the quick orders that went with them. Two of Mac's section and the platoon radio operator overheard him discussing the details with his platoon commander.

But then, by all accounts, he never mentioned the new plan again and either forgot it or never understood it in the first place. He told his section they were going to help the left flanking assault by Three Platoon, not that they were going to a new fire support position so that One Platoon could assault right flanking.

There is evidence of something like this happening maybe a dozen times on operations over the last ten years. The evidence usually gets hidden. As soon as things go sour, a man's mates will try to cover for him. Then, if the commanding officer does find out, there is a drive to keep the problem in the family. This is only right and proper at the time – no good can come from an otherwise exemplary soldier having his career ruined – but it is one reason why armies tend to forget about tactical psychology.

On the rare occasions when someone can interview witnesses and track back through radio logs, it often turns out that the soldier under investigation was told of a change and acknowledged the telling, but his head was simply too full to retain the information. Mistakes are often traced back to someone afflicted with the same kind of mental block that Mac suffered.

'Mental block' is a tired phrase which fails to convey the delightfully complex way a brain creates plans, patterns and stories to make sense of the world. But in combat the blocking is what matters: brains under pressure create barriers to accepting new ideas. The history of science gives enough examples of people paid to think and, with time to think, having trouble accepting new ideas. (Most of psychology spent forty years teaching tricks to rats and pigeons; physicists usually cling to untenable theories until the man who invented them is dead.) By compressing the thinking time and adding bullets to the equation, combat greatly exaggerates the mental block.

Examples from training exercises are easiest to see because they are observed by directing staff, recorded on tape and picked over in an after-action review where even the enemy and the 'dead' can tell their side of the story. In many cases, people hear and acknowledge a situation report or a change of plan but then just carry on as if there has been no change. In one example, a battalion commander used the cannon and chain gun on his vehicle to shoot down his unit's reconnaissance helicopter three times. He did this while he was acknowledging radio reports telling him that this was happening. Somehow, while one part of his brain was putting two and two together, another part was sticking with five.

In another exercise, an armoured squadron leader shot up supporting infantry while he was speaking to them on the radio about them being shot by his tank. Two and two were making five again. Similar examples from US and UK exercises have anyone from a rifleman to a brigade commander shooting his own side because they have forgotten that the situation has changed. Sometimes commanders even forget a change of plan that was their idea.

This mental block can be seen most often when commanders take platoons or companies to the assault start line or fire-support position they were given in orders and had rehearsed the night before. They manage to hear that the plan has changed but still move into a minefield or killing area, or attack the wrong side of a village. The same thing can happen when timings are changed close to the attack: the artillery fire plan is delayed but infantry attack on the old timings and walk into their own barrage. A soldier hears or sees new information but acts on the old information because it is more strongly wired into his head.

The normal frictions of combat play a big part in this. A corporal might be told about the changed situation while he is lying in the dark and the rain under a poncho, scribbling onto a tiny wet map with a pen that is running out, his only light source a fading red torch; he has a different radio net playing in each ear and he has been awake for two days. Despite this, outside observers are still surprised when a detailed, well-rehearsed plan blocks acceptance of the quick orders rattled out over the radio ten minutes before an attack starts. This mix of friction and mental block can be seen to play a part in nearly half of all mission failures.

*   *   *

We saw the simplified version of human memory back with Lieutenant Deverell fussing in Korea. Now, with Corporal Mac's account, it is apparent that there are four main problems with the way brains work in combat: first, information can bounce off sensory memory when the perceptual blinkers come on; then working memory can be too busy juggling to make sense of incoming information; after that, there can be an awkward link between sensory, long-term and muscle memory; now it is clear that information can be rejected by a kind of mental block in long-term memory.

Other quirks of human decision making can be seen as variations on the mental block theme. Rather than working like machines to pick the best option, people tend to pick the first adequate solution. We also tend to look for evidence that our current plan is the best option rather than trying to work out why it might not be. There is a form of mission creep where, once committed to an option such as firing at a particular building or struggling through a maze of mines and booby traps, people keep piling more resources onto that option. Decisions can also be biased by wishful thinking, trusting to luck or thinking every option is rubbish and doing nothing instead.

The full or tired brain can sometimes bias decisions towards the importance of time and physical effort rather than the chances of survival. When considering the option of going the long way round over hard ground, this can be rejected in favour of something quick and easy but much more risky. The 'straight up the middle with bags of smoke' option is sometimes the right answer, but it's usually the answer that involves less thinking or crawling, yet gets more people killed.

There is also something special about the wiring of mental maps, the internal projections of objects in time and space, which makes them particularly resistant to change. We seem to forget that mental maps are usually rough guesses about where things might be; instead we assume that, like real maps, they are accurate representations of reality. Other loops of programming are less heavily reinforced but still very difficult to shake off. Perceptions of the enemy (they will not stand), our own combat posture (we are defending) and even tactics (left flanking is always best) tend to be very resistant to change once they are wired in.

Bad decisions can also be reinforced by the nature of small groups. Groupthink is a sheeplike tendency to pick options that avoid arguments rather than get the job done. Risky shift is a slight but insidious bias towards picking a more extreme option because of diffused responsibility. Unwary teams can combine these to pick a risky option because it looks to be what everyone else wants – even though most people are actually thinking there is a better alternative.

These things can all be seen to result from the need to balance time and effort against making a sound decision. Not enough is known about how these things work in daily life, let alone combat, but some research suggests the value of one practical solution.

German staff officers found that complicated plans were much more likely to fail. People got confused by their different priorities or simply forgot what they were supposed to do, and there are inherent mechanical problems with making a complicated plan come together. But the biggest problem came when the enemy refused to follow the plan. When this happened, it was a lot harder for people to get a more complicated plan out of their heads and they were much less likely to react effectively. The fragility of complicated plans has been reported in both world wars, the Falklands and Iraq.

The effect has also been confirmed in standardised US and British training exercises. With no change in the difficulty of a battalion mission or in the forces engaged, plans with three tasks per company were nearly twice as likely to succeed as those where companies had five tasks or more.

*   *   *

The only practical way to link all these brain problems with the rest of tactical psychology is to see them as a kind of buffer that almost randomly rejects new information. It is unpredictable and might make a man do something that he would never do if he had all the information coming through and enough time to think about it.

Under the most intense combat threat, a soldier's response is most likely to be a variety of freezing, fleeing or fussing – but sometimes it will be to fight even when everything is lost. So, while armchair generals might criticise a man for doing something that looks stupid, cowardly or suicidal, the soldier is sometimes just reacting to the limits of time and brainpower.

The buffer can cut out the effects of weapon-push or suppression as easily as it can block compulsion and cohesion. Seeing straight and thinking straight sit close to the heart of tactical psychology. They are wrapped around the basics of fear, common sense and aversion, where they moderate the effects of any tactic that might be applied by either side. If we combine all the evidence on the problems of seeing straight and thinking straight, we get a conservative estimate of the combined effect: the buffer halves the chance of soldiers doing what we want them to.

The only way to limit the effects of this on our own men is to follow the old corporal's advice to 'Keep It Simple, Stupid'. This is easier to say than to do, but it is advice that can be turned around to make things complicated for the enemy.

SIXTEEN

FIGHTING FAST

SERGEANT WERTH, NORTHERN EUROPE, 1631(?)

To supplement the slight rise that the enemy must traverse we had the advantages of wind with a greater number of pike, musket and cannon to bolster the luxury of a chosen position. Though these advantages were but slight our Colonels were convinced that they outweighed the supposed greater vigour and craft of the Swede.

With a little exchange of cannon shot, the enemy to our Regiment's front came forward at a steady pace but in unusual array, having their pike to the fore with few defensive arms to be seen and but three or four ranks deep; their muskets in six ranks close behind. Few passages were seen between Companies, with a front of perhaps fifty files to each; to my eye this made their movement ungainly but no less swift for that. As they advanced on our regiment we joined our fire to that of the cannon whereupon the Swedish foot increased their pace to a brisk trot. This had a most disconcerting effect on our pikemen: arrayed to receive artillery, they began to draw together to repel their pike but the enemy's haste added to our own and there was an uncertain stumble to our movements. Our muskets gave service with ranks firing and withdrawing by turn but this was made awkward by the skittishness caused by the Swede's rapid approach.

When the Swedes had suffered but two or three ranks of our fire and received unnoticed injury to life or will, their front was nearing pistol shot and the time was upon us for musketeers to take shelter amongst our pikes. At once there arose a shout from all the enemy line; their pikemen threw themselves all upon to the ground. Their muskets most promptly stood over these prostrate men in a doubled close order; some first kneeled, some affected a squatting posture and the rear stood high. Almost immediately they loosed their shot into our array.

Our pike and musket suffered most profoundly from this shot: my own self being alongside the front rank between musket and pike, I was knocked to the ground by this tirade. For a moment my wits were taken from me but whilst I gazed upon the damage to our foremost men, the enemy's pikemen rose up and dashed into our disorder. Having shot away many in our front ranks and upset the remainder, the third and fourth ranks of musket were not set to give fire and our pikes too wrapped in one another to receive the assault. As I struggled upright I was overrun by the Swedish pike, then manhandled and taken for hostage by their mass of musketeers. Their pikes dashed through our confusion, striking down those of us who did not take flight or treat for mercy with sufficient haste. Around me our line was broken and beyond recovery. Those not broken or captured were making unseemly haste to the rear, many having discarded their offensive arms.

This account came in another one of Austrian General's comfort packages. It included the usual encouragement to 'keep working' but there was no mention of his failing health.

Those of us in his British fan club did not learn of his death until a few weeks after the funeral. The news had a curiously profound effect on us all. I had only met him twice and Gobby Scouser had never met him, but we both felt as if a pillar of wisdom had crumbled. The Tank Colonel, bless him, was almost tearful.

A group of us held a wake, of sorts, where we mainly told stories. After a suitable amount of moping, Old Boss gave a stirring speech and we resolved to crack on with the quest and keep working. At that point, we finally admitted to each other that half of our paid work was irrelevant or counter-productive. It was wonderfully cathartic to burst the bubble that had hovered around since our Gurkha curry night.

Suddenly we were able to talk straight to each other and clear the air. We reached an understanding that work came second to duty: we might be tied to the bloated defence machine by contracts, but we were bound to the Queen by the oath of allegiance. We decided that the Queen, had she known of our existence, would have preferred us to work on making the army better, rather than promoting the ambitions of our department managers or shareholders. The next day, I started to stitch Sergeant Werth's account into what we knew about fast attacks.

Doing things fast should have an effect something like Sergeant Werth's description of a pike-and-shot battle. Whatever weapons are used, attacking the enemy with lots of different things at the same time or with one or two things very quickly should make it harder for him to work out what is going on. Once this is added to the physical effects of weapons and the psychology of suppression and proximity, the rapid change in the situation should tip him over the edge. It is a trick that has been used throughout history but, as you might suspect, is quite difficult to quantify.

Werth's story ties in with the effect that psychology and military doctrine point towards but there are problems with the doctrine and with the story. The problems with the Werth account need to be dealt with up front. The main thing is that most people who have seen it think that it was made up by a grumpy Prussian officer, two centuries after the battle was supposed to have happened.

The authenticity of the account is suspect because only colonels and generals wrote about war in the 1630s and most of them were trying to reinvent classical Roman tactics or struggling with the mechanics of moving large bodies of men. While commanders and soldiers clearly understood tactical psychology, it was only written about briefly or in very general terms. Then, although most sergeants in Imperial service during the Thirty Years' War (1618–48) were literate, and must have had something useful to say, no one seems to have been very interested in their views. Some things never change.

There also appears to be no other record of this Swedish trick being used. The discussion attached to Werth's account looks to have been written in the 1860s and gives no clues as to where or when the original engagement might have taken place.

A critical problem is that the Swedish manoeuvre looks far too neat to have worked in reality. It would have needed tight control and balls of steel to run uphill towards a defended position in this elaborate extended line. Getting the pikemen to lie down, the musketeers to fire their clumsy matchlocks quickly and, most of all, getting the pikemen to get back up and into the fight looks more like a dance move than a tactical reality. Altogether, this account has the feel of a man proposing a cunning plan that he has not really thought through.

So why are you being shown a dodgy description of 400-year-old battle? The simple reason is that there is no better description of men being on the wrong end of a fast attack.

The one thing that really rings true in Sergeant Werth's account is the way it describes how his unit collapsed when fire and physical contact came in such quick succession. The same effects, or something very close to them, can be seen in pike-and-shot battles like Edgehill in 1642, with units collapsing when heavy fire is suddenly followed by pikes or cavalry rushing in. Some eyewitness accounts look a lot like Werth's but they are usually scrappy sidelines in bigger stories.

There are snippets of the speed effect everywhere – half of the accounts in this book hint at things happening too quickly for a man or a small unit to deal with – but most people on the receiving end of a fast attack do not have the chance to record their experience. Added to all the problems with seeing and thinking straight, witnesses are nearly always too busy fleeing or being knocked about by their captors to have a good look at what is going on around them.

In modern combat, dispersal and camouflage have made it even more difficult to see the effect of a fast attack. The fragments we get from recent wars often have the feel of Werth's account but tend to be even scrappier than those from the days when battle was simpler. It seems that Sergeant Werth, if he really existed, might be the only man clearly to describe the way men react when they are hit by a fast combination of casualties, suppression and proximity.

* * *

Most of the search for hard numbers on the speed effect has been focused on whole armies or very large units. It should, in theory, be a fairly simple matter to look at the effects of speed on divisions and generals, then try to draw parallels for sections and corporals. After all, operational doctrine is filled with concepts like momentum, tempo, simultaneity, surprise and shock. Armies are always trying to apply these concepts which all include effects from speed or overload. But even at the level of high command, where staff officers can record what happens when things move too fast, the accounts are scrappy and confused.

Rapid Dominance, the 'Shock and Awe' that was talked up for the 2003 invasion of Iraq, is typical of doctrine concepts in its aim to 'so overload an adversary's perceptions and understanding of events that the enemy would be incapable of resistance'. Yet no one has been able to work out whether US forces beat the Iraqi army because they moved so quickly or whether they were able move quickly because they beat the Iraqi army. Overwhelming firepower and the physical destruction of the Iraqi command system meant the effects of speed and overload could not be measured.

One study tried to account for cause and effect by looking at attacks and counter-attacks that faced similar defending forces. Fast attacks were found to be more likely to succeed than slow attacks and, when they did win, the victory came with far fewer people killed and injured on both sides. However, this study included a heavy caveat that the fast attackers who did win seemed to be doing something more than just going fast. The study could not quite pin down what this 'something more' was.

Ardant du Picq has already shown us how simply running quickly towards the enemy can have mixed results. To have a reliable effect the rush needs to come very soon after suppressive fire or, if the attackers are really keen, at the same time as suppressive fire. This fast combination of firing and moving is one aspect of the 'something more' that those fast attackers were doing.

This is where combined arms (mixing pike and shot or artillery, tanks and infantry) can show us how doing things fast really works, but it is also the point where we need to have another look at Werth's account. Before doing this, it is useful to summarise what is known about the weapons and tactics of the period.

* * *

Before Sweden joined in the Thirty Years' War, pike-and-shot battles could be drawn-out affairs and they usually followed a script where well-drilled moves were applied with only a few variations. With what looks to us like a slow technological progression, the four arms of pike, musket, cavalry and artillery tended to balance out like a long game of rock-paper-scissors.

The decision often lay in the bedlam that was the push of pike but, while phalanxes were often subject to rapid collapse, they would sometimes meet and fight themselves to exhaustion then draw apart for a bit of a rest before starting all over again. Men were being killed, maimed and psychologically battered but not fast enough to make either side give way. Meanwhile, musketeers would stand around the phalanxes, typically in open order, standing in ranks but a few metres apart to avoid killing comrades with their clumsy matchlocks; their ranks would take turns to walk forward, fire then step back and spend a whole minute reloading.

In this way 100 musketeers might be able to manage 100 rounds a minute to try and suppress or kill their enemies. A musketeer could give harassing fire at maybe 200 metres but would have difficulty hitting a barn at that range. The real killing and suppression from matchlocks happened within thirty metres.

Cavalry, typically armed with pistols, usually went through a similar routine of firing and withdrawing to reload. Artillery pieces would be scattered around the battlefield joining in where they could, but were of little value once the two sides clashed.

Generals tried to combine arms and, in effect, pull out 'rock' and 'paper' at the same time, but the limitations of technology and organisation made close integration very difficult. There was usually a big enough gap between the effects of each arm to give the enemy time to deal with them in turn and not be overwhelmed.

The Swedish army helped to change all this. With a small army, many enemies and dubious allies, they could not afford battles of attrition, so they used speed and combined arms to try and win with minimal losses. The trick was to get a pike push or cavalry charge to come very soon after fire from muskets, cavalry pistols or artillery.

The Swedes made lighter artillery that would give close support to battalions. They trained and equipped cavalry to hit the enemy with a charge just after firing their pistols, and they put musketeers among the horsemen to provide extra firepower. They made smaller phalanxes that could move around the battlefield more quickly and get better support from flanking muskets, artillery or cavalry. When they had the chance, Swedish musketeers would often close into three tight ranks to fire a more powerful volley. All of these innovations made the four arms more closely combined and brought the effects of suppression and proximity closer together than had previously been possible.

Now, while it is a bit of stretch, let us suspend disbelief for a short while. If we assume, just for now, that Werth really existed and that he got the chance to tell us what happened, his battle can tell us something about speed and combined arms.

For Werth's regiment, defending against the wily Swedes, open order was the best option when their attackers were 300 metres away. Open order was still handy for the Imperial musketeers when the Swedes were only fifty metres away. Up until this point the best place for the musketeers would be alongside or in front of the pike phalanx.

Within fifty metres, close order starts to become a better option but the appropriate response depends on what you think the enemy are going to do. Are they going to hit with a pike push, a steady exchange of fire or a concentrated volley? Then, while Werth might have been focused on the pikemen that would make such a mess of his musketeers, his commander might have been more interested in the muskets that could ruin everyone's day. One man might have been expecting a steady rotation of fire while another was worrying about a heavy volley.

Despite this uncertainty, well-trained men still responded to orders and drum beats, but not with the smooth efficiency of the drill square. The uncertainty and the threat created indecision and confusion. The result was the 'uncertain stumble' of the pikemen and the understandable 'skittishness' of the musketeers. Once this started, men entered the realm of fussing despite the simplicity of some of their weapons. They all started to consider the benefits of some version of freezing and fleeing. Then they were hit by fire.

Even if we shave off a healthy amount for things like weapon malfunctions and fear wobble in the Swedish firing line, each Imperial soldier in the front rank had one or two 20mm lead balls flying towards him from fifteen metres away. Compared to 100

Imperial muskets each firing one round a minute, the Swedish volley fired all 100 in a few seconds.

The musketeers, all un-armoured, had lumps smashed off them. In the first few ranks the casualty rate instantly got up near 30 per cent. Men who were not hit were splattered with gore, wadding, hot smoke and flying grit. Twenty seconds later they were hit with pikes.

The Imperial musketeers were never in any position to stand against a rush of pikemen. But now the front three ranks were full of gaps caused by fire and were completely unready, the three ranks at the back were still reloading and the men in the middle were probably still preparing their weapons. They would collapse the instant the pikes closed on them. If Ardant du Picq had it right, most of Werth's men were already running away before the Swedish pikemen charged.

The Imperial pikemen were little better off than their musketeers. Musket balls punched dents in breastplates (if the pikemen had them), broke ribs and knocked men down. The physical result of the volley was like that first contact between phalanxes: falling men, dropped weapons and screaming in the front ranks, the middle ranks unable to level their weapons in time and the men further back already having a look at running away. If they were in open order, the front ranks might have taken fewer casualties but the rear ranks would have caught more. Open order would have been unlikely to hold off the Swedish close-order pike rush even without the fire effect.

Werth's regiment was completely overwhelmed by this fast combination of physical and psychological effects. In a matter of minutes a force of equal strength swept them from the field, chasing, stabbing and hacking at those they could catch but did not capture. Many were killed and many maybe captured for ransom. Most of Werth's regiment survived the attack by dumping their weapons and running, but once the rout was stopped they would have been in no position to fight again that day.

Meanwhile, assuming they were able to rein in the magnetic attraction of the fight response, the Swedish force would have taken very few casualties. Despite being drained by the attack, they would have been able to re-form and be ready to fight again quite quickly.

*   *   *

We can switch off the suspension of disbelief now. It is likely that the Swedes never played this trick on Werth, but they did do very similar things to a lot of people. A fast combined-arms attack was their trump card and it is still a trump card today for units that can manage it. While this trick might sound simple, it can be very difficult to apply in a hard fight. This holds true even with more modern weapons and tactics.

In the First World War, combined arms can be seen most easily in the development of allied bite-and-hold tactics. These aimed to get infantry onto an objective before the artillery suppression hangover had worn off, so speed was of the essence. Unfortunately, coordination had to rely on fragile communications (telephones, flags and early radios proved less reliable than carrier pigeons) or on a detailed and horrifically inflexible fire plan.

In some circles it was considered acceptable to take up to 5 per cent casualties to friendly artillery in order to avoid being hacked up by enemy machine guns. Despite this drive to lean on the barrage, the risks of taking too many casualties to their own artillery often caused a gap to open between suppression and proximity. At other times, the infantry advance was delayed by small pockets of enemy.

The gaps allowed defenders to shift from the barrage response of hiding in shelters to the assault response of stepping up to the firing point. Those Second World War suppression studies suggest that a five-minute gap between artillery suppression and infantry assault had half the effect of a two-minute gap. A fifteen-minute gap had hardly any psychological bonus unless it had caused very heavy casualties.

As the First World War progressed, the gap between fire and assault was filled with storm tactics, infiltration and tanks. The more effective units on both sides had managed to crack the problem by the final year of the war and were able to combine arms more closely. Infantry, artillery and tanks had developed some simple methods of talking to each other to avoid fratricide yet still apply their unique abilities in quick succession.

Infantry platoons and sections were quickly turned into miniature combined-arms units that mixed rifles and bayonets with light machine guns, grenades, rifle grenades and specialised assault weapons. The talking needed to combine these arms was naturally simple and robust. But it is easy for armies to forget how to combine arms close enough to get suppression and proximity to happen in quick succession.

In the Second World War, both sides had to relearn the coordination skills for talking to tanks and guns in clear and simple language. The Germans had a head start in Spain, Czechoslovakia and Poland, which paid dividends when invading France and Russia, where they captured millions of soldiers who had not learned how coordinate arms. The Allies eventually managed to catch up, but they had particular problems getting their tanks and infantry to cooperate; they tried clumsier options to fill the gap.

Early in the war, the British experimented with driving tanks into their supporting artillery barrage rather than trying to dash in after the fire lifted. This was only a partial success. It was clear that driving into the barrage meant that fewer tanks were destroyed than if they waited for it to lift and faced enemy anti-tank guns as they dashed toward the objective. But, once on the objective, the barrage lifted and the tanks were left surrounded by enemy infantry without any friendly infantry to protect them.

At close quarters, tanks are surprisingly vulnerable to infantry. They can be destroyed or immobilised by short-range hand-held weapons that they would normally stay well clear of. Each crewman views the world through a slit in the armour, which is very like looking at the world through a letterbox, leaving many blind spots. Then the main gun cannot depress to ground level at close range and the turret seems to turn impossibly slowly, making it very easy for infantry to get up close without being detected. The absence of peripheral vision is particularly unnerving when the crew suspect they are surrounded by camouflaged enemies carrying explosive charges. In these circumstances, a tank crewman does not see himself riding an invulnerable behemoth but trapped in a tin can filled with explosives and petrol. These physical and psychological disadvantages led the British to abandon the idea of driving tanks into their own barrage.

Soviet armies were also concerned about losing tanks on the objective, but they had plenty of infantry so they sent them into the barrage too. Although appearing callous, this practice grew from a rational assessment of risk and reward, but it also met with mixed results. Sometimes enough infantry survived to seize the objective, but even men driven by threats to their lives and families have difficulty running into an artillery barrage, and there were many problems coordinating tank and infantry units.

In the 1960s the Russians invented the infantry fighting vehicle to get around this problem. Half personnel carrier, half tank, the BMP-1 let Soviet infantry drive onto an objective and into the barrage firing all their weapons from portholes and then dismounting to assault the instant the barrage lifted. This simple solution put suppression and proximity into one neat package.

Western armies copied elements of the Soviet solution but everybody had difficulties when it came to testing the effects. The Russians had problems in Afghanistan and Chechnya; Western armies had problems in Kuwait and Iraq. In the 1991 Gulf War, brigades had difficulty linking any artillery or air support with their ground manoeuvre, so the gap between suppression and proximity could sometimes be measured in hours rather than seconds. Smaller units usually had tanks and infantry fighting separate mini-battles. These problems were hidden by a month of preparatory bombardment and weapons that were ten times better than those the Iraqis had.

The fast combined-arms trick is really hard to do. It is still difficult to control a tank or grenade launcher firing onto a compound while infantry get close to it. Missiles and bombs might be more precise these days, but no one is willing to risk fratricide in a war of choice. This makes it very difficult to get infantry close enough to rush in just after the fire has lifted.

*　　*　　*

Despite the dearth of detailed accounts, it is clear that speed works by exceeding a small unit's collective brainpower: a kind of compound effect of not seeing and not thinking straight. Quick moves by the enemy mean the situation changes more often, giving the defenders more information, conflicting information and more response options to pick between.

Combined arms works in much the same way: two or more threats create too much information and cause a conflict between response options. But combined arms cannot be separated from speed or they would, by definition, be un-combined arms. With enough of a gap between suppression and proximity, tanks and infantry or grenade and bayonet, the enemy have time to respond to each threat in turn.

This brings us back to the study which found fast attacks more likely to succeed than slow attacks. The 'something more' used in the successful attacks was actually three things. The first of these was a close combination of arms, with speed only having a marked tactical-psychology effect when it shows its face along with combined arms. But the psychological side of speed and combined arms is still hidden by the physical effects and the problem unpicking causation.

This created a blockage in tactical-psychology research which lasted nearly forty years, but it has been possible to look at some small engagements where units had artillery, tanks and infantry yet failed to combine them. When these are compared to similar attacks but with the tanks and infantry working together, or with tanks and infantry close behind the barrage, the combined-arms attacks are more than twice as likely to succeed.

When combined-arms attacks that advance quickly are compared with un-combined attacks that advance slowly, the effect is magnified further. A fast combined-arms attack is equal to a slow un-combined-arms attack with four times the firepower. Half of this is the physical effect, but the rest is almost entirely down to the problems of divided attention and overload. With the usual conservative pinch of salt, we find that the psychological effect of a fast or combined-arms attack halves the chance of a man fighting.

These studies of fast combined arms were never meant to be stitched together like this. The results are clouded by two other aspects of the 'something more'. One of these is tied in with the advertising we looked at for weapon-push; the other is the age-old trick of outflanking the enemy. As we will see in the next chapter, getting around the side or around the back has a much clearer effect than speed and combined arms.

SEVENTEEN

FIGHTING FLANKS

CORPORAL LONDON, FRANCE, 1918

We were all very tired but everyone in the battalion was in high spirits as we'd been pushing the Germans back all over the place and though it felt a bit strange after three years of trenches, the end of the war was in sight. Both sides had got used to grafting at night and laying up in the day, so the brass were pushing for us to do some daylight raids when the other side weren't expecting it. So Gaskell, he takes me and Scott and Warren and plenty of spuds (that's Mills bombs to you) to go have a poke around this old farmhouse by the rail line. We aren't sure there's anyone in the house. We'd fired a few rifle grenades at it before and reckoned they'd been flushed out, but we know there's plenty more in holes roundabout.

We creep along by the embankment with Gaskell in front till we get to the house, then Scott and Warren go in while we keep cover. There's no one home and no one out the back so we creep on back towards our line, checking the shell holes in this here barley field. We know Jerry's close as there's pipe smoke in the air and they've been doing their business in a little hole that Warren puts his hand in. We creep right up behind the first hole and there's a machine gun in it and a couple of old hands. Gaskell coughs to get their eye, waves his revolver and they stick up their hands and start jabbering French at us. Warren waits with these lads and tries to clean the muck off his arm while the rest of us go on to the next hole.

This second lot are jumpy as they must have heard the first lot jabbering. They fire off a few shots but once we reply they throw up their hands. By now the third lot, the ones closest to our line, are on full alert. Straight away Gaskell goes on at them; this is by himself with just a revolver and a few bombs as he's had to leave me and Scotty with the second lot. There's a quick shooting match and they put up their hands too.

So now there's four of us with fourteen or fifteen of them and their three machine guns plus all the papers and what have you all in the front crater trying to get back without getting it off our boys or theirs. So Scotty goes over and tells the company we're coming then we just jump up and scamper back with Gaskell waving his revolver and scowling at the prisoners. By now I'm about blown with all that crawling but all I get is a quick breakfast and sent back out again.

That's how it was with the cutting-out business in those days. We spend years getting ourselves slaughtered going at it head-on as we'd been taught, then it turns out that the Aussie way of getting round the back was the best all along.

Corporal London's cutting-out tactic was named after the drover's trick for separating livestock from the main herd. It was a favourite of Australian infantry in the First World War, but units from both sides used variations of it to sneak or fight their way around the side or round the back of the enemy.

London went out on another raid within the hour and helped

bring in another eighteen prisoners. Small bands of men from his company used cutting-out to capture sixty-eight men and seven machine guns that day. With only light casualties on both sides, a dozen men collapsed the German defence and a whole battalion was able to advance.

This was the day when the official history noted that 'peaceful penetration found its climax'. Whatever label sex-starved staff officers used, this kind of sneaky outflanking was such a marked improvement over earlier First World War tactics that headquarters had difficulty keeping up. Flanking moves by small units changed fronts so quickly that formal planning came to be almost irrelevant.

It has been argued that cutting-out only worked because German morale had collapsed and the continuous front had been broken. A fair point perhaps, but it confuses cause and effect a little. By 1918 the continuous front had been made irrelevant by four years of artillery, machine guns and raids. Bite-and-hold, infiltration, storm tactics and tanks had made the solid line irrelevant at the close tactical level long before this. Meanwhile, German morale was certainly collapsing in places but cutting-out worked before the rot set in and it helped to start the rot.

First World War flanking variations used a few men to round up an enemy platoon, or battalions to defeat battalions. Sometimes these tactics developed intuitively because they were 'the Aussie way' but they usually grew from bitter experience, experimentation and copying the enemy: finding a flank was 'the German way' too.

The contrast between the 'walk towards machine guns' tactics of 1916 and the various flanking methods units were trying just a year later could not be more stark. Learning these techniques was a painful struggle. The penetration was not always peaceful and men often had to fight hard to find a flank then exploit it. But overall, even the hardest-fought flank attack seized ground with a smaller force, captured more of the enemy and caused fewer fatalities on both sides.

The history of war is said to be all about finding a flank. Schlieffen, the German master planner, spent his whole life trying to find the French flank, tactics courses begin with a lesson on flanking, and even switched-on ten-year-olds know of the magical effect from getting round the side or back of the enemy.

But, as with most tactics, the detail of how to actually do a flanking attack is largely forgotten between wars and has to be relearned. Tricks that seem to work at Fort Benning or on Salisbury Plain cannot easily be applied in the Normandy bocage or the Afghan green zones. Training pamphlets and exercises give a general idea but the detail of what force to use, what kit to take and how to pull everything together usually has to be picked up the hard way.

As noted back in Chapter 1, a soldier can weigh up all the physical things involved in a flank attack but he can only guess at the psychological effects. This chapter aims to put a rough number on the psychological effects so he does not have to do so much guess work.

While Corporal London's account is a useful start, we need a more balanced and recent comparison to get an understanding of the flanking effect.

*   *   *

If we return to the Falklands War, two nights before Sergeant Dawson and 2 Para attacked Wireless Ridge, there were three battles fought to break the outer ring of Argentine defences. Two of these have been compared by war college students to try and understand the flank effect.

As night fell on 11 June 1982, Dawson's half-brothers in 3 Para were preparing to attack a reinforced company of the Argentine 7th Infantry on Mount Longdon. Seven kilometres further south, 42 Commando Royal Marines (42 Cdo) were about to strike elements of the 4th Infantry on Mount Harriet.

The forces available for each attack were roughly equal, with both 3 Para and 42 Cdo based on three rifle companies with direct support from machine guns, anti-tank missiles and snipers. Each had indirect fire support from their own 81mm mortars, a battery of 105mm guns and a 4.5-inch naval gun. Though paras and marines would obviously argue otherwise, both attacking units were picked men with similar levels of training and baseline motivation.

The defending forces were fairly balanced too. The company facing 3 Para on Longdon was reinforced by combat engineers, elements of a marine support company and some snipers. All told, Longdon was defended by 220 men with .50-calibre and 7.62mm machine guns and anti-armour missiles. On Harriet, the defence had nearly twice as many men but no marines and fewer heavy weapons. There were 120mm and 81mm mortars on both positions. Both defensive positions consisted of half-finished trenches and sangars perched on rocky ridges with most of their minefields, registered artillery shoots and direct fire arcs running from northwest to south-west.

While both positions had options for fire support from 105mm and 155mm artillery, the Longdon defenders were able to make better use of it on the night. Most assessments agree that, on paper at least, 42 Cdo 'had the toughest nut to crack' but this was balanced by the fact that 3 Para could not use one of their rifle companies due to the tight angle of attack.

The angle of attack made all the difference. While the ground forced 3 Para into a frontal assault from the west, 42 Cdo were able to carry out a wide flanking move and assault from the south-east.

Both attacks were supposed to go in silent but both were sprung within a few hundred metres of the objective and instantly switched to being noisy and violent. Once this happened, higher control proved almost impossible and command decisions devolved to section and platoon commanders. Both battles degenerated into a confusing series of corporal's wars.

On Longdon, 3 Para were caught in murderous arcs of direct fire and increasingly heavy artillery and mortar bombardment. Small bands of men had to fight from one rock to another, taking casualties at every turn in what is still the bloodiest British battle since Korea. Forward movement was constantly held up by small groups of Argentine defenders fighting for every ridge and sangar. By the time they had secured Longdon, the assault force was exhausted and almost out of ammunition.

There is some variation in casualty reports but by the time Longdon was taken, 3 Para had eighteen men dead and forty wounded. They had killed maybe forty defenders and captured another forty. The remaining defenders were pushed off the position, taking an unknown number of wounded with them. After some confusion these men were reintegrated into the remains of the Port Stanley defence.

On Mount Harriet, 42 Cdo also had a stiff fight but it was far less intense than the battle to the north. Their longer approach meant their attack was sprung after 3 Para had already attracted most of the available Argentine artillery, but 42 Cdo was quickly in among the defenders and made a difficult artillery target. They were also outside the arcs of most heavy direct-fire weapons and this made it difficult for the defenders to pin down marines and make them a good target for artillery. Like 3 Para, they fought with grenade and bayonet from one small position to the next. But unlike 3 Para, their main problem with maintaining momentum came from dealing with the large number of prisoners they picked up along the way.

All told, 42 Cdo lost two men killed and around twenty-six wounded. They had killed around twenty defenders and captured nearly 300. Very few Argentine defenders escaped to fight another day.

If we consider these battles solely in terms of soldiers killed, wounded and captured, then Longdon was a three-to-one victory and Harriet was a twenty-to-one victory. In this instance a flanking attack was six times more effective than a frontal attack. Assessments of the flanking effect in other wars reveal similar figures but, while the difference between front and flank is profound, there are a few problems that need to be ironed out.

*   *   *

Flank-attack assessments, like those for speed and combined arms, tend to focus on large battles and roll the various psychological and physical effects into one big number. Analysts can sometimes get trapped in a debate about the difference between envelopment (getting round the side), encirclement (getting round the back) and some *Kama Sutra*-like variations such as vertical envelopment, eccentric movement and the golden bridge.

There are differences between attacking from the side and from the rear but these are too small and messy to be accurately unpicked. To get a clear picture it is best to count any attack that does not go through that frontal defensive arc as a flanking attack.

Sadly, most flanking research is biased by wishful thinking. One staff study used only successful flanking attacks and unsuccessful frontal attacks. This is a terrible crime for a geek to commit but is understandable when you consider how rare it is to see a successful frontal attack that does not involve an enormous advantage in manpower, suppression, weapon-push or fast combined arms.

Assessments have also been biased because unsuccessful flanking attacks tend to get forgotten. Some flank attempts bump into depth positions and turn into frontal attacks but even more seem to fizzle out when the attackers get lost or strung out and start to think that maybe they are the ones who are outflanked. Gobby Scouser did his own flanking assessment when he was new to tactical psychology. He avoids any mention of it these days because it was littered with flawed assumptions; I remind him of it whenever I get the chance.

Flanking attacks by battalions and brigades are often deliberately planned, but for sections and platoons they are almost always launched quickly and on the initiative of the men on the ground. Accidental outflanking, where men do not know they are doing it, is also surprisingly common.

The number of flank attacks that fail has been difficult to assess because, when they are reported, they are a usually single line in a battalion war diary. It is also very hard to find attacks like Longdon and Harriet that allow attack and defence strengths to be balanced out. Despite these hang-ups, the general trend from the less biased assessments is for flanking to be between ten and twelve times more effective than a frontal attack. Flank attackers suffer one-third of the casualties of the defenders, while frontal attackers take six times as many casualties as the defenders.

Even when frontal attacks succeed, the enemy usually withdraw or run away rather than surrender. When flanking attacks succeed, they tend to capture far more of the enemy than they kill or injure.

Some of the success of flanking is due to the pure physical effects. At the point of the Mount Harriet assault, 42 Cdo was able to move along the thin edge of the defended zone and repeatedly engage small groups of defenders. While 42 Cdo could only use a fraction of their force at any one time, they sometimes had double the usable combat power of the Argentine defenders.

Many flanking attacks do not have this advantage because of the problems getting a large force around a flank. It is not uncommon for a flanking force to be outnumbered and outgunned by the enemy but, like Corporal London and his mates, they still tend to win.

This is where the psychology of flanking kicks in. At the point of the attack there is something close to the fast combined-arms effect, with defenders' attention often split by a simultaneous frontal threat and too much information from flankers rushing in. An attack from the side can also have a suppression bonus because shots tend to travel along the defended line, making each bullet have a suppressive effect on more men. In platoon- and company-sized attacks there is usually a compulsion bonus too: the attacking commander can make sure he is at the point of an attack; the defending leader is likely to be a hundred metres away, still expecting a frontal attack.

The magnet of current activity plays its part too. Whether the outflanked men are having a brew or watching their front, it is a big switch from this passivity to actively firing or getting into a bayonet fight. In contrast, the attackers meet the enemy while they are moving forward in fighting mode. Proximity seems to add something too, with the attackers knowing they are at the point of no return, while some of the defenders think they are at the last safe moment.

There is also an element of organisation in there, with considerable effort needed to rejig the defence. This makes a coordinated response less likely and creates that uncertain stumble, with each man focused on a different part of the threat. Extra uncertainty comes from the enemy being where they should not be: how did they get there? Did they kill or capture everyone behind us? Have our flanking units bugged out without telling us?

With uncertainty, proximity and all the rest subtracted, the very act of being outflanked looks to have an effect all of its own. Opinion is split on where this pure flanking effect comes from. Some analysts have suggested that it is biologically programmed and has something to do with our sense organs pointing forwards, as if we have an innate dislike of being blindsided.

Others have focused on social learning to suggest that being outflanked is a culturally recognised disadvantage that radically recalibrates the 'is it worth it?' calculation, greatly encouraging the supplication aspect of freezing. This has been compared to being knocked down in a fist fight, getting your serve broken in tennis or checkmate in chess. These feeble analogies look a little bit like the flank effect, with a recognised game-changing event putting people so much on the back foot that it is much harder to see the point in carrying on.

The exact mechanism is unknown. What is known is that even

with no split attention from a fixing force or suppressive fire, men are unlikely to swing around and fight the way they do on a blank-firing exercise. Subtract the physical bonuses and all the other psychological forces and the pure outflanking effect halves the chance of a man fighting. Put all these factors back together and a flank attack, if you can do it, is seven times more effective than a frontal attack.

*   *   *

Fast and flanking attacks have always been difficult to do, but they are enduring themes in tactical psychology. Military theorists from Clausewitz to David Rowland and Old Boss have had a bash at explaining how they work. These assessments have usually been conducted under the banner of 'surprise'. Surprise is one of the principles of war and is taught at staff colleges around the globe. But like morale, itself a principle of war, surprise is an elusive concept. So much so that, despite the best of intentions, armies often do exactly what the enemy expects.

Back in the 1990s, Gobby Scouser's first job was to try and squeeze Rowland's historical analysis of surprise into a computer war game. He failed. He needed a lot of help and nearly twenty years to work out what surprise really is. He found that down in the weeds at the close tactical level, surprise is simply the physics of being strong where the enemy is weak and the psychology of fast combined flanking.

The facts only started to stand straight when our soldiers were mired in Iraq. By that point, Western armies were generally very keen to get out, and were quietly admitting that they had always suspected it was the wrong war. Despite our presence in Iraq fuelling the Afghan insurgency, there was a chance that Afghanistan could still turn out to be the right war; it was certainly closer to the real bad guy and most of the world did not seem to mind us being there.

I was not one of those who foresaw disaster in Afghanistan. Like most people, I was focused on the Iraq quagmire. We all thought, hoped, that if our soldiers could extract from that, they could go to Afghanistan and, after a few stiff fights, build some hospitals, walk around in berets and then come home healthy, proud to have done some good.

Austrian General had known it would be different. His final parcel included a one-page summary of how he thought fast and flank attacks had their effect. There was a Yoda-like comment scribbled in the margin: 'Movement is armour. Our boys will need to know this to have any chance of winning in Afghanistan.' Maybe, if he had not been so inconsiderate as to die on us, it would not have taken three years to work out what he meant.

EIGHTEEN

WEIGHBRIDGE

MAJOR STIRLING, GERMANY, 1945

The village was now encircled and the Germans cut off. It became apparent that the enemy had no SP [armoured self-propelled guns] or anti-tank guns, and as the first houses in the village were still hold-ing out and causing the infantry a lot of trouble, the left-hand Troop moved forward to engage them at almost point-blank range.

It was impossible not to admire the courage of these German paratroops, who even at this stage remained quite undaunted and continued to fire on anything that showed itself. However, they had had a pretty severe hammering, and it was thought that they might be induced to surrender, if only they would let us get near enough to tell them that their position was hopeless.

A few tanks had been fitted with loudspeakers, one of which belonged to the Troop Leader of this Troop. As he could not speak German the Squadron Leader interrupted all other business on the Regimental net to broadcast an impassioned appeal in German to the defenders for their surrender mingled with threats of what would happen if they refused. This was relayed over the loudspeaker, and almost at once white flags appeared from several windows and a German with a white flag came out of a front door. So much for the marvels of modern science. He was at once shot dead by an infantryman who had not understood the broadcast. So much for modern education.

Not unnaturally all the white flags disappeared, but not before their positions had been carefully noted down by the Troop of tanks, who then proceeded to lay about them to no small effect. So much for the sporting British.

We now played our trump card, and sent in the Crocodile flame-throwers, who proceeded systematically to burn down the village starting at the South end and working North. For the majority of the defenders this was the last straw, although one fanatic still kept up a stream of fire from his burning bedroom, but quite a number surrendered, and before long the village was in our hands.

Major Stirling's account has a useful point to explore later, but right now we need a summary of what we have looked at so far.

This book started with the observation that men fight less than most people usually think, and that this accounts for almost all of the degradation between training exercises and real combat. On average, a unit in combat is one-sixth as effective as it would be on exercise. Part of this difference is determined by a man's baseline motivation to fight: the mix of personal qualities that he was born with or had trained into him. But the main thing that determines whether a man fights is what happens during the fight and the way this alters his half-conscious 'is it worth it?' calculation.

Fear, common sense and aversion to killing underpin this calculation and generally reduce the chance of a man fighting. When combined, they mean that all men will stop fighting under the right circumstances. Yet, despite early estimates that less than one-quarter of men will fight at all, nearly all men will fight when fear, common sense and aversion are countered by other forces.

The balance between these forces determines a soldier's response, which will fall into one of the 'four Fs' of flee, freeze, fuss or fight. Each of these has a scale of intensity, with the deeper levels having a gravity that binds a man to the current response option. The most intense levels of each option usually require a considerable change in circumstance to move a man between the four Fs.

The nature and intensity of response is strongly influenced by the behaviour of a man's comrades. Cohesion is the glue that binds small units together and determines the extent to which men follow the behaviour of others. The more comrades a man can see close to him, the more likely he is to follow their lead. Cohesion tends to make soldiers react in a consistent manner rather than as a collection of individuals, making it more difficult for a man to shift between response options.

Compulsion is the pressure from designated and emergent leaders and it works through cohesion to counteract fear, common sense and aversion. The strength of the effect depends upon the authority of the leader and how near he is to each man. Compulsion can make a man up to six times more likely to fight.

Another factor that increases the chance of a man fighting is weapon-pull. This works through comparison of a man's weapon to those of his comrades. Having a clearly superior weapon, a machine gun compared to a rifle, increases a man's chance of fighting by close to 50 per cent. The weapon-pull effect is further increased by the added compulsion that superior weapons attract, and by the diffusion of responsibility that comes from serving a weapon as part of a crew.

The counter to this effect is weapon-push, which works through comparison with enemy weapons. Enemy status weapons that are clearly superior reduce the chance of a man fighting by 30 per cent. But the effect is boosted by carrot-and-stick advertising: showing the enemy what will happen if he continues the fight and offering a more attractive option. Advertising weapon-push can reduce the chance of a man fighting by up to 90 per cent.

Another counter-pressure is the physical proximity of the enemy. Proximity is moderated by weapons and terrain but generally decreases the chance of a man fighting when he approaches a 'last safe moment' between fifty metres and five metres from the enemy. Between these points the chance of a man fighting can drop to one-third of its base level. Closer than five metres, a man hits a point of no return and the chance of him fighting bounces back to its original level.

All of these effects are moderated by fundamental problems with seeing straight and thinking straight in combat. These generally reduce the chance of a man fighting, but the effect is unpredictable. They act as a filter or buffer to reduce the chance of a man doing what looks like the sensible thing in combat. Overall, the problems with seeing straight and thinking straight halve the chance of men doing what others might expect them to do in combat.

Enemy speed and combined arms give a man too many things to think about. In practice, their psychological effects are inseparable and together they halve the chance of a man fighting.

Flanking has a similar psychological bonus and also halves the chance of a man fighting. This is often boosted by all the other aspects of tactical psychology, which tend to come with a flanking attack.

This list does not include all of the factors that have an impact on whether a small unit fights. There are many peripheral effects that cannot be quantified or even described with any level of accuracy. In addition, there is the huge list of high-level factors, which could include everything from Brigadier Balchin's 'supplies of beer' to the perception of a just war. These do not only set a soldier's baseline willingness to fight, they also interact with tactical factors in ways that are too subtle to be quantified.

Despite omissions, the forces described here provide a sound basis for understanding and exploiting tactical psychology. For most of these forces, the effect shown is the practical maximum: the outcome that could be reasonably achieved in a stiff fight, rather than the absolute maximum that could come from having overwhelming combat power. Each effect has a sliding scale running down from this practical maximum.

*   *   *

To exploit tactical psychology at the sharp end, the effects need to be linked so that soldiers can see the benefits and then develop the details of tactics and procedure. To exploit tactical psychology at the blunt end, the combined effects need to be described to defence departments so they can reach appropriate policy decisions.

The next few paragraphs aim to show how the effects come together, using a hypothetical small-unit engagement. This is unavoidably abstract but it highlights important points for exploiting tactical psychology, so please bear with me. The real world will return shortly.

This engagement begins by ignoring suppression and physical

effects like casualties, though these are brought in later. Also, to keep things simple, the two sides are fighting in a war that has not descended into barbarity, so there is a good chance that any offer of surrender will be honoured and little chance that any men who withdraw will be executed by their own side.

Two identical ten-man patrols meet in a firefight at 300 metres. Both sides have good natural cover and basic assault rifles so, minute-by-minute, there is only a slim chance of actually hitting anyone once the difficulties of field firing, the fear wobble, range and cover are included. Both sides have their baseline motivation set quite high, at roughly the level of a standard infantry unit in a professional army.

With fear, common sense and aversion having only a small degrading effect in this situation, all of the men on each side will fight. However, practical constraints like changing magazines and conserving ammunition mean that even the most moti-vated man in each patrol can only fight 75 per cent of the time. The rest of the time he is doing entry-level variations of freez-ing (taking a breather), fleeing (dropping back into better cover after firing) and fussing (checking how much ammunition he has left).

Some men will be fighting more than others, but at this range and with these weapons, the natural variation is minimal and not yet a problem for the patrol leaders. Cohesion is playing its part in the background, with each man pulled back to fighting by seeing most of his mates fighting around him. Compulsion has hardly any effect because it could not push the amount of fighting much higher than the current level.

So far this is quite a lot like a computer simulation or a train-ing exercise and, still ignoring suppression and casualties for now, the fight could go on like this until one side started to run low on ammunition.

Rather than go through all the details of what might happen in this low-threat firefight, we will simply change the starting conditions to stack up the effects of tactical psychology. Flanking is a good place to start, so let us restart the fight with everything the same but one side, the attackers, magically appearing on the flank of the defenders. The defenders' chance of fighting immediately halves to just below 40 per cent. The attackers' stays at 75 per cent.

Now let us consider what would happen if the attackers also have a status weapon like an MG42 or .50-calibre machine gun. Even when this clearly superior weapon is not firing, another slice is shaved off the defenders' chance of fighting so now they are down below 30 per cent. The attackers are all still fighting near the practical maximum of 75 per cent.

Natural variation starts to tell on the defenders now, with three of them not fighting at all. Compulsion starts to earn its pay too, with the defending patrol leader trying to get some fire on that enemy machine gun. But compulsion is only at full power for the few men closest to him. So, in addition to the three defenders who have stopped fighting, three others are fighting below 30 per cent of the time. But the patrol has a good leader, so four men are still fighting nearly 60 per cent of the time.

Now let us add proximity effects, with the attackers still flanking with a status weapon but the two sides magically moved to twenty metres apart. Both sides suffer from the full proximity effect at this range and have another two-thirds shaved off their chance of fighting. But they were already at very different levels, so while the attackers are now down to 25 per cent, the defenders are not much above 10 per cent; two defenders still fight nearly half of the time but the rest have stopped fighting completely.

To draw a close to this, let us assume that after a brief exchange of fire, cohesion finally plays its trump card and all the defenders stop fighting before grenades and bayonets need to be used. Now we can try to pull this abstract nonsense back to the real world and show how easy, and how difficult, it can be to reach a point where the defenders are almost guaranteed to surrender.

* * *

Simply adding casualties and suppression would tip the balance of the fight much sooner. The chance of hitting someone at the start was quite slim, but either side is likely to lose a man at some point. Any casualty would alter the balance of power.

When casualties are taken, the weaker side loses much of its ability to suppress, especially when other men are drawn into helping wounded friends. The unit fires less often and less accurately; the chances of being hit would increase for those who did return fire.

If one side took two casualties and tried to attend to them, the compound effects of suppression could soon bring them to a point where they had lost the firefight. The attacking force could easily reach the weight of fire needed to keep the defenders pinned down. Cohesion would start to outweigh compulsion, and could even force an end to the engagement without either side moving from their start positions.

But with the enemy 300 metres away, it is most likely that the losing side would attempt to withdraw rather than surrender. This kind of inconclusive engagement is typical of long-range firefights in Afghanistan.

Things get more complicated once we consider the practicalities hidden by those hypothetical magic moves. Every time the attackers move to close the gap or get to a flank, they have to take a risk, crawl and run while lugging heavy kit from place to place. The defenders, unless they are all casualties or completely suppressed, will take the chance to win back the firefight, withdraw or surrender. By the time the attackers are on the flank with a status weapon, the defenders would almost certainly have bugged out, surrendered or died. By the time the attackers got to twenty metres, the chances of any defender fighting would have dropped almost to zero.

We also have to accept that two identical patrols hardly ever meet on a level playing field at 300 metres. Contact is usually closer; one side nearly always has some terrain, manpower, mobility or firepower advantage. There are most often a lot of other men from both sides scattered around the battlefield. The presence and actions of these men alter the balance for physical and psychological effects.

It is most likely that, even with the status weapon magically dragged to the flank, the attacking patrol leader would call up some help. The defenders would try to do the same. Whenever the attackers moved they would risk contact with other groups of enemy.

More men, movement, firepower and casualties could be added to the equation. One side could have a grenade launcher, a bunker-busting weapon or an armoured vehicle that would allow some quick combined arms to be applied. We could go as far as trying to tot up the numbers for increased suppression from flank positions and the status weapons. We might even delve into the murky world of seeing straight and thinking straight or the chances of men entering clinical levels of freezing, fleeing, fussing and fighting.

The effect of advertising also needs to be considered. At any point in this hypothetical engagement the attackers could try to get the carrot-and-stick bonus. With bullets flying and the real or imagined threats from other forces on the edge of this battle, the advertising card would be difficult to play but it could still be played and it could end the fight in one move.

If we went on down the road of detailed juggling of factors, we would also have to consider the exceptions thrown up by natural variation and that small-unit counter-pressure that makes men deviate from what everyone else is doing. There might be one or two men who would go berserk and try to fight their way out. This is highly unlikely but things like this do happen even in less barbarous wars.

War is the province of uncertainty and sometimes psychological and physical effects can come together in ways that defy analysis. In some battles, the effects combine to multiply their impact; in others they appear to cancel each other out. There appear to be anchors from training or expectation that can, on very rare occasions, trump some of the trump cards. Yet it is apparent that the vast majority of battles work by shaving off and building up effects like our hypothetical example.

Despite a few exceptions, the interactions of tactical psychology are reasonably straightforward when examined from a safe distance. Unfortunately, they are far from straightforward for the soldiers who have to exploit them under fire. Two examples should illustrate how the frictions of war can make the art of applying tactical psychology a very tricky business.

*   *   *

Our first example is Major Stirling's account that opened this chapter. It is another quote from the history of the 4th/7th Royal Dragoon Guards, and it shows how difficult it can be to apply tactical psychology even with superior numbers, firepower and the ultimate status weapon. It is full of tactical psychology but it also has plenty of the frictions that come with a battle.

The infantry started the attack without intimate tank support rolling along beside them. The close support tanks only moved in once the infantry attack was bogged down and it was fairly clear that the defenders lacked anti-armour weapons. So, rather than advertising carrot-and-stick or doing fast combined arms from the start, the attack began by, in effect, fighting with infantry and armour as separate entities.

The squadron leader tried the carrot-and-stick later, but he was not the man in charge and the assault had already bogged down. Infantry and armour were already engaged when the advertising trick was tried. Many soldiers were already fighting and past the point of no return.

Unlike the armoured flame attacks described by Trooper Brooks, this attack caused 150 of the enemy to surrender but killed 400. A surrender-to-kill ratio of 3:8 rather than the 5:1 average for Crocodile-supported attacks or the 27:1 that units like Trooper Brooks's were able to achieve with their version of the carrot-and-stick. Yet this battle happened only a few kilometres from Brooks's unit and using Crocodiles drawn from the same parent regiment.

So why did they not try the same trick? The simple answer is that the detail of tactics and procedures (when to try the advertising or how to combine armour and infantry) is rarely taught or exercised in detail and is usually only learned through personal combat experience.

* * *

The second example is from the Battle of Lone Tree in 1915: one of the sledgehammer attacks that formed part of the long and bloody Battle of Loos. At Lone Tree, twelve British battalions attacked a section of the front defended by one and a half German battalions. The attack followed a long bombardment and came after gas was released from projectors in the British forward line.

In the north, the artillery and gas had a positive effect but this could only be exploited because of the skills of the assaulting battalions. Two battalions were able to use a fast version of infantry fire-and-movement, a kind of early British storm tactics, to break through the forward line. They were able to push on to their next objective but before long they were getting battered and pinned down by German depth positions.

Things were much worse in the southern half of the battle. The gas blew back into the British line, filling up the forward trenches, and the attack stalled while dealing with gas casualties. The delay stole any benefit from the artillery suppression hangover and the Germans had time to man their defences. The assault battalions advanced but could make little headway; the few men who made it as far as the German wire were soon pinned down by heavy fire. Follow-on battalions could not move up through trenches full of gas and casualties, so they were shot to pieces as they advanced over open ground.

Higher commanders, working on scrappy, late and inaccurate reports, released their second-wave battalions to reinforce and exploit. In the confusion, all but one of these battalions were drawn into the southern killing area. Some more men were able to make it up to the German wire before being killed or pinned down but most were unable to make it more than a few metres past their own forward line.

The one unit that avoided this hell was the Welch Regiment's 2nd Battalion, who followed the northern route over ground that had been largely cleared of enemy. Having crossed the German forward line but been unable to find the two lead battalions, they turned south to try and link up with someone who knew what was going on. This mix of chance and initiative allowed 2/Welch to hit the rear company of the German battalion that was holding up the southern advance.

Attacked from the flank and rear, this company surrendered after a brief but fierce exchange of fire. Once they had consolidated on this position, 2/Welch sent a company to approach the forward German companies from the rear. The Germans saw them coming and, having held out against nine battalions in a frontal assault, they immediately surrendered.

This bloody mix of frontal and flanking attacks is a long way from the 'peaceful penetration' that Corporal London was able to achieve with cutting-out. Even 2/Welch suffered over 300 casualties as they moved up, went round the defenders and then attacked the rear German company. While the 2/Welch flanking move was instrumental in capturing over 500 German defenders, it came at a terrible cost. Altogether the British attack cost 4,500 casualties, the vast majority of these in that killing area around the lone tree that gave the battle its name.

The flow of the battle could not have been planned or controlled from above; 2/Welch did not know it but they were actually carrying out the commanding general's orders. Some of those battalions drawn into the frontal assault in the south were also supposed to be flanking or exploiting from the north, but frictions dragged them away from the plan. This costly victory was only achieved through a mixture of skill, luck and the initiative of the 2/Welch commanders on the ground.

*   *   *

Any combat veteran will recognise the role of friction in the Dragoons and Welch battles: it can throw a spanner into even the simplest plan. But, as usual, it took a while for the analysis side of tactical psychology to accept that friction screwed up our lovely graphs.

For me this came in the form of another little epiphany, this time at a 'joint fires' conference in Brussels. Joint fires are all about getting aircraft and artillery to hit the enemy without bumping into each other and without hitting our own soldiers or civilians.

To help understand how joint fires work, Gobby Scouser and I had spent the summer watching and talking to soldiers. He went out to Afghanistan; I played it safe and stuck with training areas in Europe and North America.

The consensus was that joint fires were all about talking to the right people: when the person with the heavy ordnance spoke to the person being shot at by insurgents, the fire usually landed in the right place; when fire was managed by a string of intermediaries, things usually went wrong. High-level control sometimes ended with the wrong people being killed. More often, it ended in bombs or shells landing where the enemy were not, or on an enemy that had already stopped fighting. High-level control always seemed to involve ground forces sitting tight and being shot at, or twiddling their thumbs while they waited for the big bang.

This echoed what we were seeing in our tactical psychology

work. High-level control does not suit tactical psychology because it needs a soldier at the point of contact to know the situation at that moment and have a good idea what the battle is like for the enemy. There are often only fleeting chances to use fast combined arms, where the outcome is usually down to a platoon or section commander jumping onto a tank and saying 'fire at that tree line while we dash across this open ground'. Advertising is also down to a man on the ground, and typically requires him to tell his mates to hold fire while he tries to persuade the enemy to surrender.

We failed to get this message across at the joint fires conference. Gobby had seen soldiers advertising the weapon-push of the Apache attack helicopter in Helmand province by trying to link it to loudspeaker invitations to surrender. (Like a flame-thrower tank, Apache can be a truly awe-inspiring weapon but is almost impossible to surrender to.) The effectiveness of this approach depended on the wording of the invitation and on convincing the Apache crew to not hose everything that looked like a bad guy. The trick always fell flat in training exercises. Before we even got to the psychology bit, we hit the buffers of there being no spare Apaches and no enemy surrendering in training. At the conference, we were outclassed by missile makers who were far better than us when it came to brown-nosing colonels and generals.

We decided that, once again, our geeky message was just too big and spiky for most staff officers to swallow. It was even more awkward on the ground, where no one could be expected to remember all the percentages and how they work together. The only solution is to make it simpler. The next chapter should do this.

NINETEEN

CONFUSED AND OBVIOUS

CORPORAL JONES, IRAQ, 2004

So there's fire coming in from this bunch up on the flats and rounds pinging off the sides of our wagon from high and right and there's this other bunch up the street with a bagful of RPGs so there's rounds zipping past from the front and the odd whoosh of RPG flying past or smacking danger close to the Chally. We've got one man down already and we're a gnat's flaps from it all going tits up.

Don't get me wrong, it's no Zulu Dawn. We're not being overrun but everybody can see how that might happen if we don't do something to get us out of this pickle. The boss is on the gunner net trying to whistle up some top cover, Pat is on the battle group net trying to call in some back up and I'm running backwards and forwards trying to calm down the tankies and take care of our boys. There's civvies running round all over the place and we're trying to put down fire without hitting too many unarmed locals. The tank radio doesn't work, half the man-pack radios don't work and there's not even one of those phones on the back of the Chally. It's the age of the internet and our comms are back to World War One.

No one's got a clue what to do while the boss is on the big phone. All the while there's rounds incoming and some people are starting to flap. Every now and then some prick fires some random burst round cover just to make himself feel better and I have to wind his neck in. Other blokes are clammed up in cover doing nothing and I'm having to winkle them out and give them arcs. 'Aimed shots lads, aimed shots.' Then there's this random one pip lieutenant who's come along for the ride and thinks it's his chance to get a medal. I have to grip his balls to stop him making the situation worse.

I even catch a whiff of this flapping myself. There's one point where I've got to make a dash into the open and for a second I can't make my mind up whether to have a shit or a haircut. A few deep breaths gets me to man up and I make the dash.

In between all this I'm cutting about between clumps of blokes saying 'don't panic!' like that old boy from Dad's Army. Some people don't see the funny side but I get a grin off the professionals. Some of the older hands even seem to be enjoying the whole affair. Wankers.

After what seems like an age the boss gives us the bad news of no top cover and Pat says were on our own too. Our options are to stay put and get shot to bits, push hard down the street and smash the RPG gang or put some tank rounds and 30mm into the flats. Either way, we're on the news for getting killed, losing a tank or killing half a hundred shoppers. So basically, despite having incredible firepower there's just no way we can win the firefight. So the boss says it's time we buggered off and let the militia win the day.

The wounded and useless mount up in the Warriors and the rest of us are on foot covering the wagons as we gingerly fire and move back the way we came. All the while looking out for another ambush and trying to keep up some all-round defence. That walk back out of town was the longest half-hour of my bloody life.

We could've killed 'em all. We could've maybe even done it without causing political embarrassment. But with all the civvies around and threats on two sides we couldn't see the wood for the trees. Embarrassing is what it is.

Combat is sometimes seen as an exchange of energy: putting enough kinetic, heat or chemical energy into people to stop them fighting. But history and psychology show us that it can sometimes be more useful to see combat as an exchange of information. This is not a cosy chat or swapping of emails. It is faster, more fluid and has a lot of people shouting at the same time, more like a rowdy council meeting but with bullets and death thrown in.

Like any argument, there are two main options: you either shout a lot to confuse your opponents or you give them a clear message to make it obvious you have the upper hand. So there are two aims to tactical psychology: to make the enemy's battle confusing or to make it obvious. These overlap in application because, just as battles mix slaughter and manoeuvre, they also mix confusing and obvious messages. However, the aim should be to do one or the other. Both options can involve lying.

We have already seen confusing battles with Private Halder losing cohesion in his First World War 'English ditch' and Lieutenant Deverell fussing in Korea. There have been other glimpses of confusion from Master Sergeant Johansson parachuting, Ardant du Picq's insights into war in the 1800s and Major Stirling's forlorn efforts to coordinate flame-thrower tanks with an infantry assault. Now Corporal Jones gives us an excellent example of a confusing fight.

Jones took his false name and some of his favourite catchphrases from the old boy in *Dad's Army*. Our Corporal Jones is one of those men who would prefer to stick bayonets in the enemy than back off, so as well as 'don't panic!' he is very fond of 'they don't like it up 'em'. Without the confusion in Jones's fight, he would have most likely been leading an assault rather than waiting for his boss to make a decision.

Jones's account gives a glimpse of the extra confusion that comes with fighting in somebody else's country while trying to look like the good guys. Any war has its fair share of confusion but the insurgents in Iraq and Afghanistan have been able to ramp up the uncertainty by hiding among civilians. But that trick is just a variation of something that soldiers have done for thousands of years.

*   *   *

Confusion has most of its effect on larger organisations but works well on individual soldiers and small teams. To emphasise the effect on a soldier, I have to stoop to another analogy. This will undoubtedly look lame for men who have been in a hard fight, but the power of confusion needs to be underlined for anyone who has not experienced it.

Think of a time when everything in your life was a mess: in the wrong job, in the wrong town and very short of cash. You are absolutely exhausted; as haggard and downtrodden as you have felt in your whole life. You have only managed a few hours' sleep a night for the last few weeks; your waking hours have been full of work, bills and sorting out annoying rubbish. Your family, boss and bank peck your head whenever they get the chance. You just want the world to go away and let you sleep.

Right now you have just finished a thankless fourteen-hour shift and, by some miracle, you manage to drive home without crashing the car. Walking from the car to the house you realise you left your wallet and chequebook at work. You pause mid-step, because part of you knows this is really important, but fatigue wins out and you think, 'Sod it, I'll get it tomorrow.'

After another few steps towards the house you remember that you need your chequebook to pay a bill that is way beyond a final demand. You turn around intent on heading back to fetch it. Two steps later, it strikes you that it will take ages to drive back then knock up a security guard to let you in. Too much hassle. You turn back around and head up to the house.

But then you remember a debt that will not wait another day. Somehow this critical fact got hidden at the back of your mind. You decide there is a slim chance you can get in to work, get your stuff, and still be home in time to get some sleep, pay your debts and maybe get to work in time to not get sacked. You turn around again...

This is almost, almost, how confusion works in combat. Fatigue and sleep loss play their part but instead of debt, admin and work, it is immediate and constantly changing threats to life that fill your head. The conflict of options is pretty much the same. Every time you try to start something, another fact pops into your head to say that option is unworkable. Important facts slip out of your head again and the cycle is repeated. Priorities switch and switch again, making it almost impossible to stick to one course of action.

Remember the analogy of the ball-bearing puzzle we looked at back in Chapter 8? The choice between the four Fs works like this if a battle is simple enough: a man drops into one of the holes in the puzzle and stays there until his brain cycles through response options to pick a better one.

The four-Fs choice does not work that way when a battle gets really confusing. The conflict of options creates a chaotic shift in the way brains and small units work. In a confusing fight with many threats and options, soldiers can be seen wobbling between response options. Surveillance and helmet camera videos show some men almost vibrating as they switch between responses. It is as if the puzzle is being rattled about so much that the ball can never settle in any hole.

For a fire-team or section, this rattling is compounded by cohesion. Whenever a man gets to see what his mates are doing, they are confused too and this prevents him from latching onto a response option. Compulsion can sometimes cut through this but efforts to grip the situation often add to the confusion.

There is an extra layer of complication from efforts to coordinate and control action in platoons. Whether commanders use radios or the Mk I Shout-Your-Head-Off, the information they push out or pull in gets piled on top of more pressing matters like incoming fire or moving enemy. One part of the platoon can be fighting a very different battle from another and therefore has a different perspective. So, while the platoon commander is trying to get a section to push left, the section commander is trying to hold fast on the right, but one of his fire-teams is trying to move back into better cover. In confusing engagements, platoon radio nets can fill up with ignored orders and demands for information because priorities can be very different just thirty metres away.

The side that is able to project confusing messages can greatly reduce the chances of their enemy fighting effectively.

*　　*　　*

Mixing messages without actual violence, by using feints and ruses of various kinds, can work well enough for generals. But in the close battle such tricks are difficult to apply on initiative, let alone through a formal plan that lags behind reality. Deception plans fail way more than half of the time on battalion and company exercises, and they appear to be even less successful at lower levels. Attempts in recent wars have usually fallen flat too. In many instances the enemy does not notice the feint, sees through it or has already committed to doing something else before the cunning plan is put into action.

Platoons and sections usually have too little time and too few resources to plan confusing ruses, but there are often attempts made on the spur of the moment. Yet the best way to confuse the enemy is to mix genuine threats and then exploit his problems with seeing and thinking straight.

It is easiest to see how this works in the artillery battle. When armies have seen past the simplicity of 'more fire means more suppression', they have developed tricks to increase the psychological impact of bombardment.

Leaving gaps in a barrage can have a confusing effect. Like the Argentine defenders on Wireless Ridge, some units choose to withdraw during barrage gaps. Others, like those bunker-bound Japanese soldiers, stay cooped up long after the fire has lifted. But both these extremes had taken a heavy battering. In most cases, a barrage with gaps only makes it difficult to choose between response options and adds a confusion bonus.

Confusion can also be increased by mixing ammunition types. In the First World War, fragmentation rounds were often mixed with gas shells. The shell splinters encouraged people to get into dugouts and the gas forced them out again. Defenders were often so busy getting in and out of cover that they could not respond effectively.

Confusion clogs up the 'is it worth it?' calculation. A continuous simple bombardment says: 'Freeze-freeze-freeze.' When this message ends, many defenders realise now might be a good time to step up to the firing point. A barrage with mixed messages from gaps or different fire types says: 'freeze', then 'fight', then 'no, freeze again; no wait, fuss a bit...' The confusion hangs around after a barrage lifts, imposing a suppression hangover that lasts four times longer than that for a simple continuous barrage.

*　　*　　*

Artillery suppression gives a good indication of the potential for exploiting confusion, but it is of little use to an infantry soldier. Luckily, small units have won back the selection of weapons that allow them to mix messages. Twenty years ago most British platoons had only 5.56mm magazine-fed weapons, a light mortar, a few weak bunker-busters and hand grenades. A few NATO armies were better off but years of fretting about cost and lethality had made them all tend towards being one-trick ponies.

Now platoons have multiple calibres, grenade launchers, belt-fed weapons, sharpshooter rifles and sometimes an excellent bunker-buster. This combination gives a good range of physical effects and can help overload the enemy. The variety of options can cause supply problems and, as we have already seen, increase fussing if the platoon is hard-pressed. But, if the mix is not too complicated and the platoon is free to attack, the ability to project a variety of threats is generally a good thing.

Mixing direct-fire calibres can confuse the enemy a little;

combining .50-calibre with 5.56mm looks to boost the suppressive effect by an extra 10 per cent. Mixing automatic bursts and aimed shots can boost suppression by a similar amount, by demanding a slightly different response from the enemy. (Crawling into cover might be the best response to machine-gun fire and dashing might be better for sniper fire, but this depends on the ground and the fight, so it is always a tough call.)

Firing at the enemy from several different locations, like the Iraqi militiamen using multiple firebases to attack Corporal Jones, has a greater effect and is very popular with Afghan insurgents. It appears to boost suppression by as much as 30 per cent. Fire coming from two or more directions limits the amount of useful cover and makes it particularly hard to work out which threat to engage.

Mixing direct fire with indirect fire from a light mortar or grenade launcher can be even more effective. This is combined-arms suppression on the smallest scale and seems to create the most confusion for men on the receiving end. The best responses for direct fire (getting behind something to let you fire and move about) and indirect fire (being in a trench with top cover) can be incompatible, trapping men in indecision. This dilemma is particularly evident in combat novices. There are many examples from Vietnam and Korea of green troops being caught between options and just squatting in the open. Overall, the direct–indirect mix looks to increase the suppressive effect by as much as 50 per cent.

Soldiers with the right tools and training have been mixing threats for centuries and have usually done so without thinking too much about psychology or sending messages. The Romans and Swedes did it in spades. In the First World War, confusion came from storm tactics using infantry combined arms and having small teams attack from different directions. Variations in the Second World War and a few recent operations have also confused the enemy far more than suppressed them.

Every tactical psychology factor can cause confusion. The three that have the greatest confusion effect are suppression, weapon-push and combined arms (when this takes the form of mixed fire). Gluing things together to get a combined effect is no simple matter, but basic suppression plus 50 per cent for mixing fire types, 30 per cent for multiple firebases and 30 per cent for weapon-push almost guarantees that the enemy will offer little effective resistance.

*   *   *

Is this another magic bullet? In a computer simulation it would be: ten men with all these advantages soon confuse and suppress ten men with one weapon type, no status weapon and only one firebase. In the real world it is rarely so simple. A heavy machine gun and a mortar would steal a lot of mobility, making later attempts at speed and flanking difficult. A lighter buzz-saw machine gun and rifle grenades should do the trick without slowing things down too much.

There are also plenty of nitty-gritty problems with finding the enemy and keeping them confused. Gaps in suppressive fire and multiple firebases can occur naturally but they are difficult to control. Then, as with the hypothetical example in the last chapter, things start to unravel when friction comes into play and physical or psychological factors start to bounce off one another.

Yet the numbers stand; they are practical and conservative

maximum figures, derived from effects achieved by real soldiers in the past. However, the frictions of application suggest the need for another layer of conservatism, so rather than saying confusion almost guarantees no effective resistance, we should accept that it merely doubles the effectiveness of the side that applies it. Despite friction, today's professional soldiers have the weapons and skills to confuse the enemy if they are taught the principle and allowed to develop the drills.

Once the enemy are confused and suppressed, the attackers shift from static firefight to fire-and-movement; that second firebase becomes a flanking threat once it is mobile. Tactical movement can add to the confusion, but its greatest effect comes into the other tactical aim, making it obvious to the enemy that they are going to lose.

*   *   *

In all the battles we have looked at there have been sticky situations where a fight gets confusing, but the real victories have been achieved when the benefits and costs of the different response options are made obvious. In 1944, while Lieutenant Jary was having his time-slowing hallucination, his opponents were obviously outflanked by a quick infiltration that told them they had been caught with their pants down. Later that year, the men facing Trooper Brooks and his comrades in flame-thrower tanks did not surrender because of the threat they faced but because the threat, and the alternative, were made obvious.

Other veterans have given us glimpses of how obviousness has won battles through history. If these battles had been more confusing the defenders would have been more difficult to shift.

Trapped between options, they would not have put up the stiffest resistance but they would still have needed to be winkled out or mopped up.

The biggest difference between confusing and obvious can be seen in flanking battles. The defenders of Mount Longdon were confused by a frontal attack with mixed messages that said they could fight, withdraw or surrender. Too many of them chose to fight. In contrast, the defenders of Mount Harriet were beaten by flanking and proximity, giving a clear message that surrender would be the best option. Both attacks involved killing, suppression and confusion but the Mount Harriet attack gave the clearer message and got the best result.

The four main tactical psychology factors that make a battle obvious are flanking, proximity, advertising and weapon-push. All of these can have a confusing effect (note that weapon-push was also in the confusing list) but when they are combined in the right way they tend to make it very obvious to the enemy that he cannot win.

The 50 per cent shaved off from flanking and the 90 per cent that can come with advertising and weapon-push should almost guarantee that the enemy will withdraw or surrender. But this will only work if the effects can be brought together to break through the basic problems of seeing straight and thinking straight: the message has to be very clear.

Remember those fast attacks that were said to do 'something more' by combining speed with flanking and combined arms? The final piece of that 'something more' jigsaw was advertising. In the few attacks that tried it, a clear demonstration of the carrot-and-stick was the thing that sealed the deal. When tanks and infantry went head-on against an enemy that did not have good anti-armour weapons, there was almost always a confusing bloody battle unless they advertised too.

A flanking attack nearly always won, but advertising played its part here too. When they flanked but then paused before assaulting, the rate of confusing fire dropped and the enemy nearly always surrendered or tried to withdraw. Surrender was almost guaranteed if a believable offer was made during the lull. The attackers still won if they went straight in with the flank attack, but they usually had to fight and take casualties to do it.

Although there have been some detailed assessments of battles compiled over the years, this bit right at the end, with a mass of factors involved, is the most difficult to see clearly. It is relatively easy to see if an attack has a flanking or weapon-push bonus, more difficult to spot examples where the enemy were offered a way out, but really hard to determine where all three were used. In some cases, the decision to categorise an attack as having all three factors came down to one or two lines in a war diary. These lines were generally something like: 'It was clear there was no way out for them once the tanks closed up with Dog Company men on the right. Only then did the defenders respond to the shouts from Dog to lay down their arms.'

The problems with looking at all these factors together demand another cautious interpretation. When this is done, obvious battles are seen to cause around 80 per cent fewer friendly casualties. If prisoners of war are excluded, obvious battles also cause 70 per cent fewer enemy casualties. Another layer of conservatism needs to be applied to account for friction but overall, obviousness makes an attack four times more effective.

*   *   *

The art of applying tactical psychology lies in picking when to use confusion and when to use obviousness, and in being able to shift between one and the other. A soldier can confuse the enemy enough to make him easier to kill or capture but this usually has to ease off to make the outcome obvious. If the fight is never made obvious, it sticks to being slaughter with a few random dollops of manoeuvre thrown in. But if confusion and obviousness can be applied at the right points, they save manpower and ammunition, allowing a unit to recover quickly and move on to the next objective.

It just happens to be a bonus that fewer of the enemy are killed. Morality is all well and good, but this book is about winning wars. The value of capturing the enemy comes when the tactical success pushes back up to higher-level objectives.

Great men have told us that 'an adversary is more hurt by desertion than by slaughter' but doctrine pamphlets merely parrot this without saying why and how desertion hurts more. It comes back to advertising by word of mouth. Like the big stick of the 88 or MG42, the enemy's hierarchy cannot smother the news of the bit of carrot that comes when men are captured and well treated. This cascades through the enemy force with all the advantages that status weapons accrue, to predispose men to surrendering. Like those pre-wired plans that are so difficult to get rid of, hearing that other men have surrendered will put the idea in a man's long-term memory and it can reactivate in combat. But the tactical setting has to be right or this will not be translated into him actually surrendering. A soldier needs to seal the deal every time.

It is tempting to go beyond an outline of tactical psychology effects to propose actual tactics and procedures. But, just like Wigram's battle drills, there is no template that will work in every situation. Frictions, enemy adaptation and the two-way exchange of violence could make any template unravel in the face of real bullets. Once again, the principles can be seen to have an effect but there can be no dogmatic imposition of drills.

The only way around this dilemma is to teach soldiers the principles and give them the time and space to experiment with the details. If armies stop trying to apply woolly high-level concepts as tactics, they can teach soldiers the tangible effects of confusion and obviousness. Once this happens, commanders and soldiers will work out how to get the job done.

This all begs the question: 'Why hasn't tactical psychology worked in Afghanistan?'

TWENTY

NEW WARS, OLD LESSONS

SERGEANT SPENCER, AFGHANISTAN, 2008

We had a half-dozen contacts like this on our first tour but I can remember this one in detail because we had to write it up for the Colonel. At the time the insurgency was in transition between the conventional approach and the asymmetric option. We were in transition too. By the middle of the tour it's fair to say we still had some of that Rorke's Drift mentality that suited the conventional insurgent attacks on platoon houses but we were getting wise to the mines and booby traps that were just starting to be a real worry. Most of the attacks were by locals but there was a few of foreign-trained psychos there to stiffen them up and pay the bills.

On this day the whole platoon was out with a few odds and sods hanging on. When the first rounds came in on the point section I was near the back doing my platoon sergeant's job of wandering up and down checking everyone was switched on.

When it kicked off, they hit the point section while the rest of us were out of sight a bound behind. You could tell by the fire that there was maybe half a dozen insurgents off to our front and left so I took the two rear sections on a dog leg to try and take them from the flank. We didn't wait for the boss to give orders, there was no need. I just sent two of the lads and the air controllers forward to tell him what we were doing. Give us your pencil pal, and I'll draw you a wee map.

Halfway round the dog leg we bumped an enemy surprise party of four blokes waiting to slot us from the side. We were on them before they knew it and three mags on full auto put them in the ground. Then we popped out of the trees in pretty much the ideal spot [to engage the enemy who had ambushed the point section of the platoon]. The odd round came our way but the point section had a shed-load of fire-power and already won the firefight for us.

Once I was sure everyone had caught up I pushed one section perhaps forty metres to the left. From this point on those five or six insurgents were pretty much done for. They were holed up in a rundown little compound about two hundred metres away, the crops were in so there was hardly any cover round it and we had the mortars drop the odd round onto their only chance of a half-covered escape route. We had every other route in and out covered with direct fire and we had all-round defence in case any more surprise parties tried to join in.

Now, I was all up for us closing with these poor sods but the fast air was on the way already so we just sat and waited. This suited us fine because we were all ball-bagged after a day of wandering about in full kit.

The only concerns at this point were dehydration (as usual it was roasting hot and no one had enough water) and ammo (somebody fired every time one of the insurgents showed an elbow). And whether the jets would drop one on us by mistake. This was more of a problem in those days.

After maybe twenty minutes of messing about we all got the call

and BOOM the compound disintegrates. When we went in to tidy up
all we found was rubble and bits of arms.

Old Boss, Gobby Scouser and I are sitting in the canteen at one of
the big NATO headquarters, picking over the corpse of our latest
attempt to get tactical psychology into the minds of Western
armies. The headquarters is officially the main string-puller for
operations in Afghanistan; unofficially, it is a lumbering two-brain
dinosaur and a retirement home for powerless generals. Maybe
I'm bitter, but as I nurse my coffee, the unofficial version seems
more accurate.

One of the powerless generals is having a coffee with us, trying
to cheer us up after a disastrous presentation to a roomful of
senior officers. He stuck his neck out getting us the presentation
slot but is kind enough to not mention the scuff we have left on his
polished career. A few of the senior officers are sitting with us too,
but the general does the talking.

'It looks like you're barking up the wrong tree here, guys,' he
says. 'You're talking about tactical psychology but we're a strategic headquarters.' We reply with resigned nods. He pokes his tiny
espresso with a tiny biscuit before continuing, 'No one doubts
the potential of what you've found but everyone here is focused
on running operations in Libya and Afghanistan. As far as we're
concerned, your stuff is just too low-level.' Another round of
nodding. 'And, to be fair, there's only so much you can put across
with forty minutes of PowerPoint.'

He is right, of course. But he also knows we have had similar
answers from tactical HQs ('too high-level'), training estab-
lishments ('that's doctrine') and research bodies ('is there any
money in it?'). It turns out that there is no army in NATO with

a Department of Radical Change, and no department means no action. Our only success has been with the few combat soldiers who have had time to absorb tactical psychology and think through how they can apply it.

'Well,' says the kindly general, 'you always knew this one was shit-or-bust. It's time to activate Plan B. One of you has got to write a book.' We always expected that it would come to this. The chain of facts that explains tactical psychology is too long to fit into bullet points; the defence machine is too convoluted to let the message spread from the inside. A book for civilians is needed because once civilians understand, politicians might listen and then armies will take action. But it seems I've missed out on the vote to pick the author. Suddenly everyone at the table is staring at me. Gobby Scouser's grin is showing those mahogany teeth to full effect. You are reading Plan B.

We opened our tragic presentation with Sergeant Spencer's account because it reflects many of the problems of applying tactical psychology in Afghanistan. To understand how soldiers ended up in the current situation, we need to put the tactics in historical and strategic context.

At the end of the Second World War, the Allies had a sound grasp of tactical psychology. British forces were particularly well set in 1945, with considerable research on battle morale, artillery suppression and psychological warfare. These were all waiting to be combined with hard-won combat experience and boiled down to useful facts. But then, even before the victorious sigh of relief in 1945, tactical psychology was hidden by the nuclear arms race and the expected armour-heavy fight against the Soviet Union.

Despite the efforts of a few good men, tactics and research were dominated by machines and attrition. There was a recurring debate about manoeuvre and psychology, but this, as I am sure you will be bored with reading by now, was hamstrung by wishy-washy concepts like morale or momentum.

Then along came wars of choice and the War on Terror. Eventually everyone started to talk about 'influence operations' (getting people to think like us), 'non-kinetic effects' (not killing the enemy) and even 'courageous restraint' (not blowing everything up). Sadly, most of this talk did not help the fighting soldier do his job. Instead, the main tactical result of these big ideas was to produce reams of procedural control that stifled the low-level initiative essential for applying tactical psychology.

So while generals focused on hearts and minds, the fighting soldier was still taught that the infantry battle is 'essentially one of attrition'. Many characteristics of the Afghan War have served to reinforce this notion.

* * *

At the highest strategic level, invading two countries, killing a few hundred thousand people and spending three trillion dollars is not an efficient way to assassinate two men. Essential planning steps such as picking a fight you can win and working out who the enemy is were simply brushed over. So Western forces were thrown into vague wars; no army is designed for vagueness. The strategic setting created a tragedy of errors right down to the fighting soldiers that this book is about.

Psychologists use the term 'demand characteristics' to describe all the things that go wrong in an experiment when the people being experimented on try to work out what is going on and then adjust their behaviour accordingly. In Afghanistan, the experiment was to see if bombs and bullets could be used to build a nation. The demand characteristics came from people on all sides trying to profit from the experiment.

None of what follows is a criticism of commanders or soldiers. Most were thrown in and told to get on with it, and it is hard to see what they could have done differently given the circumstances. But demand characteristics caused tactics to mutate in the face of a crazy mismatch of agendas, skills and weapons, helping to hide the benefits of tactical psychology.

The British experience in Helmand province illustrates the problem particularly well. The first men in were supposed to protect the reconstruction effort but their intervention was launched in a way that was sure to annoy as many locals as possible. As far as the Pashtun locals were concerned, British troops came to burn the only viable cash crop (poppy), emasculate traditional power structures and promote Western depravity. The British were seen to barge into Helmand at the behest of a corrupt puppet government and an army dominated by Tajiks and Hazaras, traditional enemies of Pashtuns. Half a dozen different groups lined up or joined up to try and kick British forces out of Helmand. Western ignorance called all these enemies Taliban.

British soldiers were soon fighting off waves of attackers who could be forgiven for seeing our men as invaders. Desperate insurgent attacks on heavily defended outposts allowed little room to apply psychology of any sort. Like Corporal Rabuka in his platoon house back in Chapter 6, our young men were killing their young men at long range with little opportunity to send any messages.

Superior training and equipment beat off these attacks and eventually allowed the British task force to build up enough strength to send men out on patrol and 'take the fight to the

Taliban'. The mantra was 'clear, hold, build': winkle out the bad guys, separate them from the people and then make the people's lives better so they would accept the Karzai government. In practice, British troops spent their time clearing and re-clearing the same villages; killing 'Taliban', blowing things up and making people's lives worse, then dashing off to the next hot spot, allowing the real Taliban to fill the vacuum.

For a while there was a chance that some tactical psychology could be applied but, as with Sergeant Spencer's platoon, training and equipment encouraged attrition. As with any long war there was a cycle of adaptation, with each side trying new tricks and new counters. The war's demand characteristics twisted this cycle of adaptation. One such demand was risk-aversion.

British forces were never able to accept a lot of casualties in Afghanistan. Soldiers fought hard but commanders could not expect them to risk their lives too often for a vague objective that rapidly became unattainable. This changed the 'is it worth it?' calculation from the outset: instead of fighting to win, everyone was fighting to not lose. This risk-averse ethos is a direct result of sending soldiers to fight avoidable vague wars. It will likely taint Western armies for many years to come and make them worse at fighting unavoidable wars.

* * *

A specific consequence of risk-aversion is soldier load. Soldiers are now weighed down with protection in the form of body armour, mine detection kit and electronic gadgets. Men walk out of their patrol bases with up to 100 kilos on their backs. Often working in forty- or fifty-degree heat, coalition troops can be close to exhaustion before they make contact. Many small battles have been lost simply through dehydration and fatigue.

Historically, the combat load (all the stuff soldiers cannot throw on the floor when they are in a fight) has stayed close to twenty kilos; now it can be up above sixty. In the words of one young sergeant, soldiers are trying to fight while giving a teenager a piggyback.

Fighting a well-rested enemy who carries an assault rifle and a few magazines, coalition soldiers usually find it impossible to get around or close to enemies who are far lighter on their feet. Most have given up trying. Even if they were taught the psychological effects of speed, proximity or flanking, they would be unable to exploit them. The weight soldiers bear means they cannot manoeuvre and must therefore rely much more on attrition. A platoon can fire 10,000 rounds to try and suppress enemies who are now so agile and so well camouflaged that the fire misses them completely. This fire has very little physical or psychological effect on the enemy.

Many corners of the military are blind to the problem with soldier load. They point to individual incidents when Soldier X was saved by the extra plate in his body armour, or the bomb-jamming gadget in his backpack. But they fail to see that piling more kit onto every soldier makes the whole army slow, so it cannot catch and defeat the enemy. So the enemy usually escape, to take another shot the next day or to make a bomb that the jammer cannot jam.

In some ways Sergeant Spencer's fight was unusual because his platoon managed to corner the enemy. But then his fight came early in the campaign, before much of the load and the caution was piled on.

It is worth considering how other wars would have played

out if the men involved had carried this extra weight. Let us ignore most of the weight soldiers lug around today and consider how past battles would have run with each man carrying only an extra twenty kilos that come with body armour and a little extra ammunition.

At Wireless Ridge it would have been much harder for Sergeant Dawson to get his men back on their feet with that extra weight on their backs. Two nights earlier, 3 Para would have had an even tougher time getting up Mount Longdon. Body amour would have saved some of the men who were hit but more of them would have been hit because they could not dash uphill out of the killing area. They would also have had problems returning fire. Current body armour prevents soldiers from giving accurate fire from a prone position because it pushes a man's helmet down over his eyes. It forces men to spray-and-pray. Or to stay upright, presenting a larger target.

Meanwhile 42 Cdo, fit as they were, would have had no time to do their big right hook carrying that extra twenty kilos. A Longdon-style frontal assault might have been their only option, and Longdon-style casualties the result.

Even this gloomy assessment assumes that these units would have been able to get to the fight in the first place. Most soldiers had to walk the 90 kilometres from the beachhead to the battle and it is far from certain that they would have made it. Most British casualties in the Falklands were due to foot injuries as it was. It is possible that the whole campaign would have ground to a halt with an extra twenty kilos per man.

If we go back further, imagine how the retreats to Dunkirk or through Burma and Korea would have played out with each man burdened by an extra twenty kilos. Would US assault troops have managed to get off Omaha Beach with this extra weight? How much longer would it have taken to capture Iwo Jima or Okinawa?

It is too late to do much of anything about overloaded soldiers in Afghanistan, if indeed anything could have been done in the first place. The demand characteristics that created this situation will endure because no one is going to agree to dumping armour and gadgets when the end of the occupation is in sight.

*   *   *

There are also some fundamental problems with language that are stifling the ability to apply tactical psychology. In this respect, Sergeant Spencer's fight was typical of the patrol engagements in Afghanistan: the platoon had no real option of offering surrender. Those five or six insurgents might have liked to live through the day but they never got the chance. Spencer's platoon had an interpreter but he was a Dari speaker with a weak grasp of the Pashto spoken by the insurgents. He had no loudspeaker that would allow him to be heard over the firing and, in any event, he hated the Taliban and anyone who might be associated with them. He wanted them dead.

The rest of the platoon was talking a different language too. The war had already evolved to a point where most men were intent only on slotting some bad guys and surviving their tour intact. Meanwhile, the air controllers with Spencer were speaking in the language of 'kinetic effects': they had been trained to drop a bomb on anything that got in their way. They expected to drop a bomb on something in their way. Designed for a battle of attrition, the platoon was never likely to apply much tactical psychology. Even talented soldiers like Sergeant Spencer have been able to do little against this.

Things have improved a little in the last few years. Most units on patrol have a competent interpreter, a loudspeaker and the ability to cut into enemy radio nets. But the window of opportunity for tactical psychology has passed. Most loudspeakers are used to ask civilians to stay indoors or, as was the case when fighting Japanese soldiers trapped in bunkers, to shout variations of 'come and have a go if you think you're hard enough'.

The failure to apply any tactical psychology in Helmand has encouraged the war to spiral to a level of barbarity which undermines the willingness to offer or accept quarter. Coalition soldiers see insurgents as cowards for not fighting fair and for using mines and booby traps; insurgents see coalition troops as cowards for relying on drones, bombers and helicopter gunships. Both sides are fairly sure they will be tortured if captured. Both sides shoot on sight.

The combination of load, language and no tactical psychology training means that most units are only half applying the confusing side of tactics, and even then this is usually accidental. Very few units have been able to apply the obvious side of tactical psychology. On the rare occasions when a clear message is sent to the insurgents it is usually to withdraw. The mass of firepower does not say surrender, it says run away and fight another day. An agile insurgency can do this indefinitely.

The number of insurgents captured in battle is far fewer than the historical average. I wish I could give you a killed-to-captured figure, like I did with historical battles. But with the exception of raids by special forces, so few insurgents have surrendered in contact that no one has bothered to count them.

Forget all that nonsense about insurgents being fanatics that never surrender. Most of them are just disaffected boys. They might be worried about being tortured but, as with the Japanese and the SS, even fanatics surrender if they are given a clear choice between life and death.

The war in Helmand has moved on. British forces eventually turned away from 'taking the fight to the Taliban'. Instead they started 'fighting the FOB': protecting Forward Operating Bases with layers of surveillance equipment and firepower in order to dominate a tiny area of operations. Most movement has been limited to short patrols to try and avoid fighting while completely exhausted.

Now the whole show is being dismantled or handed over to the Afghan security forces.

There are still a few deliberate offensive operations, but these rarely happen unless coalition forces have at least thirty times the firepower of the enemy. The enemy usually see these operations coming weeks in advance and simply move on to attack the places that had to be stripped of men and equipment to support the offensive. Tactical psychology had little opportunity to change the outcome of the Afghan War but its absence helped accelerate the decline. The war's demand characteristics stifled the ability of soldiers or scientists to relearn the benefits of tactical psychology. For a while some units were doing the best they could to apply the tricks that their fathers and grandfathers used. Now everybody is just hanging tight and waiting for the plane home.

*   *   *

The specific problems in Afghanistan have helped blind Western armies to the value of tactical psychology, but the main problem is still down to numbers. For decades, psychology has been paid lip service with adages like Napoleon's 'the moral is to the physical as three is to one', but with no guidance on how it might be put into practice.

Tactical psychology has been hidden by the mumbo-jumbo of 'morale' and the obsession with super-soldiers. Defence account-ants and combat soldiers cannot be blamed for leaning towards the numbers that support attrition. But now, in this book and in a few select places in defence departments, we have the numbers that support manoeuvre.

By increasing confusion through common-sense suppression, mixed fire and weapon-push, units can make enemies less than half as effective while they move. Then, by increasing obvious-ness through flanking, proximity, weapon-push and advertising, they can make enemies four times less effective. With luck, the numbers are written down in a way that makes it easier for soldiers and defence accountants to speak the same language. If this happens then maybe our wars can involve more winning and less slaughter.

When our soldiers come home from Afghanistan, there will be a chance to take stock and think about the next war. Assuming there is a decision to fight only wars that are winnable or unavoidable, tactical psychology can be used to make them more winnable and less costly.

ACKNOWLEDGEMENTS

There is no classified information in *War Games* but defence departments are a little touchy at the moment so some false names have been used. The reticence of old soldiers provided added incentive for anonymity. There are also a few false dates in the book, a couple of characters have been condensed and some minor details altered or obscured to hide identities. Some accounts have been pared down to control the word count and some acronyms, slang and archaic words have been replaced for clarity. Please accept my assurance that these changes do not detract from the factual content of the book.

I must also apologise to readers for using some ludicrous pseudonyms while thanking the soldiers who helped me or let me use their stories. Particular thanks go to: Jack Fidler for inspiration; Sydney Jary for loving the infantry; Chunk Johansson for not punching me at BATUS; Eternal Corporal Mac for not punching me at BGTU; Tick-Tock Dawson for kicking my arse when I needed it; Pat Rabuka for the unconvincing Fijian impression; the sloggers at ARRSE and AKX, the Deverell, George Brooks, A. G. & Sons, all the Tank Colonels and Sennelager Clubbers for soldiering on.

On the science side, thanks should go to about forty people from the Defence Operational Analysis Establishment, Army Personnel Research Establishment and their fragmented descendant organisations and related bodies in Australia, Canada, France, Holland and the USA. Special thanks to: David Rowland for reviving battle morale; Painterman for checking my sums; Old-Old Boss for opening doors; Barman, LTC (ret'd) Vaguely-Familiar, Gary L. Hackworth, Franck Klippe and Monkeydad for encouragement and reviewing. Valuable data also came from the UK and US Schools of Infantry, Artillery and National Archives, from the National Army Museum and the remnants of Staff College. Double thanks to Foxy Bookwitch for all that legwork.

A few fully-fledged civilians have helped along the way too, notably Christopher Fricke and Grandpa J. for help with navigation in the publishing world. Drinks and firm handshakes are also owed to my agent Peter Buckman and everyone at Biteback for taking me on and steering a skittish virgin author with calm professionalism.

Anyone keen on understanding tactical psychology through first-hand accounts could not go far wrong with *Soldier's Song* by Ken Lukowiak, *Quartered Safe Out Here* by George MacDonald Fraser, Ken Tout's *By Tank* and, of course, Sydney Jary's *18 Platoon*. The best regimental history of the Second World War, *The First and The Last* by J. D. P. Stirling, is back in print and available from the Royal Dragoon Guards museum. If you prefer compilations by historians, try John Keegan's *Face of Battle* or Richard Holmes's *Acts of War* (formerly *Firing Line*). For a geekier read, there is an English translation of Ardant du Picq's *Battle Studies*, and Marshall's *Men Against Fire* is beautiful despite its quirks.

Steven Pinker describes the evolution of aversion to killing in

Better Angels of Our Nature. But if weapons and tactics are more your fancy, *Firepower* by B. P. Hughes describes how musket and cannon shaped pre-Napoleonic battle, then Rory Muir's *Tactics and the Experience of Battle in the Age of Napoleon* takes over and throws in some psychology. *On Infantry* by John English and Bruce Gudmundsson provides a hearty account of tactical developments from 1900 to Vietnam. Useful extensions of Marshall's work include *Canadians Under Fire* by Robert Engen (anti-Marshall) and Dave Grossman's *On Killing* (pro-Marshall). For a wider view of psychology and war try Jim Storr's *Human Face of War*.

If numbers and graphs are more your thing, David Rowland's *Stress of Battle* describes some of his historical analysis and Terry Copp's *Montgomery's Scientists* covers many of the Second World War field studies, including much of the work on suppression. Other books will pop up if you search for those listed here. To go much beyond this you will have to try national archives, military museums and the dusty boxes dumped in skips outside defence research centres.

If you are a black-belt war geek or a psychologist you will have been frustrated by the corners cut to fit tactical psychology into a compact volume accessible to civilians. Tough. What you have here is a coherent and testable theory based on the best available data. This is not one of those plucked-out-of-your-arse theories that clutter defence research but one which quantifies and explains important real-world phenomena. Your job is to take the data, test the theory and make a better one. Oh, and if you are paid to be a military analyst, don't forget that you work for the Crown (or the people) and for soldiers. You owe no allegiance to your cost centre manager. Crack on.

Finally, grudging thanks have to go to New-Old Boss and Gobby Scouser for goading me when I needed it and for doing most of the difficult stuff. Any mistakes are theirs; I am only responsible for the good stuff.

This book is dedicated to the four mahoomoos for putting up with distracted Dad for so long.

GLOSSARY

Advertising: Presenting the enemy with an obvious or exaggerated problem (e.g. you're going to get cooked by this flame-thrower) and a solution (these cheery Tommies will accept your surrender).

Basra Road: The 'highway(s) of death' between Kuwait and southern Iraq, down which Iraqi forces retreated in 1991 in an effort to escape encirclement.

BAR: The Browning Automatic Rifle, effectively the light machine gun for US infantry squads (see *Fire-team*) in WW2 and Korea.

Bite-and-hold: An attack tactic developed during the Great War, combining an infantry advance with overwhelming artillery support. Bite-and-hold deliberately aimed at modest objectives to ensure that infantry would not move out of range of their supporting artillery or have difficulty directing its fire.

Bren, or Bren gun: The light machine gun used by British and Commonwealth infantry sections in the Second World War and Korea. A version of the Bren was still in service for the 1991 Gulf War. Based on a Czech design, the name is a combination of Brno, where the gun was invented, and Enfield, where it was adapted and many were built.

Buffalo horns: A Zulu double-envelopment tactic or pincer movement, designed to threaten opponents on three sides, leaving
the option of flight to the rear.

Bunker-buster: A catch-all term for any missile used to attack
buildings or field fortifications. Most often refers to infantry
weapons designed to attack tanks.

Chally: A Challenger (or Challenger 2) tank.

Cognitive blink: I made this label up to cover a range of phenomena including the 'attentional blink', 'inattentional blindness'
and subsequent processing errors which prevent people
processing important new information under stress.

Cohesion: The glue that binds a small unit and encourages them
to react in a (fairly) consistent manner rather than as a collection of individuals.

Company: See *Fire-team*.

Direct fire: Shots that travel almost in a straight line from firer
to target. This includes most fire by infantry small-arms and
tanks. (See *Indirect fire*.)

Falaise Pocket: A battle in Normandy in 1944 where German
forces attempted to escape encirclement.

Fear wobble: Generally assumed to reduce effectiveness by 10 per
cent, it is the only measurable effect fear has on human performance in combat, largely as a result of physiological responses
to stress.

Firebase: A designated position from which to direct fire at the
enemy. In infantry close combat this is usually a temporary
position adopted to provide fire in support of an attack.

Fire ratio: The percentage of soldiers in a unit who actively engage
the enemy at any point during the course of a battle.

Fire-team: In the British army this is a sub-unit of four men, led by a lance corporal (the first rank above private soldier). Two fire-teams make a section, which is led by a corporal. A section is roughly equivalent to the US squad, although this tends to be considerably larger. Three sections make a platoon once a small HQ is added. The HQ includes the platoon commander, who is usually a lieutenant, the platoon sergeant, a radio operator and a runner for when the radios break. Three platoons and another small HQ make a company. Three companies make a battalion. However, all of this is a very general rule of thumb. Due to enemy action, administrative interference or personal preference, a fire-team can have two or six men in it, a section can have three or four fire-teams, a platoon can be commanded by a captain or a corporal, a platoon HQ can include a light mortar, a medium anti-tank weapon and a few spare corporals, a battalion can have twenty platoons and every unit can have attached tanks, artillery and engineers. To catch people out, new names are often invented for organisations, including brick, battle group and multiple.

Fire-and-movement: The basic tactic of splitting a unit into two, with one firing to cover the movement of the other, and alternating these roles to step close to, away from or around the enemy.

Friction: The grit in the military machine that makes grand plans fail. In *On War*, Carl von Clausewitz used 'friction' to describe the stacks of errors, disasters and delays that occur in a battle to make war more the province of chance than any other human endeavour.

Gympy: The British General Purpose Machine Gun or GPMG.

Hit rate: The number of rounds fired to hit an enemy soldier. (See *Kill rate*.)

Indirect fire: Any fire lobbed at a target that the firer cannot see. This usually refers to artillery or mortar fire but also includes lob shots from tanks or machine guns and, confusingly, fire from aircraft whose crews can see the target. (See *Direct fire*.)

Kill rate: The number of rounds fired to kill an enemy soldier. (See *Hit rate*.)

Manoeuvre: In this book the original term 'movement to a position of advantage' has been used but the definition was horribly chopped around in a doctrinal spat in the 1990s.

Panzerfaust: The German 'tank fist', a simple anti-tank weapon of the Second World War. ('Panzerfaust' is also a potent war-porn word, like 'Stuka' or 'penetrate'.)

PIAT: The British 'Projector, Infantry, Anti-Tank', a simple anti-tank weapon of the Second World War.

Platoon: See *Fire-team*.

Sangar: A small improvised fortification with walls and sometimes a roof, often used when hard or wet ground make trenches impractical.

Section: See *Fire-team*.

Small arms: Any weapon one soldier can carry and operate on his own.

Storm tactics: Trench-war assault techniques usually associated with German stormtroopers but actually developed and used by both sides. Fire-and-movement was broken down to much smaller units than previously. To help break into strong defensive positions, infantry were provided with new specialist weapons, such as light machine guns, trench mortars and flame-throwers.

Suppression: Any reduction in a soldier's effectiveness by fire which does not injure or kill him, ranging from the rational choice not to return fire to being rendered catatonic.